Bolivia, the Strength of Political Courage
35 years of CIPCA history

Bolivia
the Strength of Political Courage

35 YEARS OF CIPCA HISTORY

Vera Gianotten

KIT Publishers — Amsterdam

Bolivia, the Strength of Political Courage
35 years of CIPCA history

Centro de Investigación y Promoción del Campesinado (CIPCA)
Calle Claudio Peñaranda 2706, Esq. Vincenti, Plaza España (Sopocachi)
La Paz – Bolivia
Tel: + 591-2-291.07.97/98
Fax: + 591-2-291.07.96
cipca@cipca.org.bo
www.cipca.org.bo

KIT Publishers
PO Box 95001
1090 HA Amsterdam
The Netherlands
E: publishers@kit.nl
W: www.kitpublishers.nl

Original Spanish title
CIPCA y poder campesino indígena. 35 años de historia. / Vera Gianotten. – La Paz

© 2006 – Centro de Investigación y Promoción del Campesinado (CIPCA), La Paz, Bolivia
© 2011 – Centre for Research and Promotion of the Peasantry (CIPCA), La Paz, Bolivia /
KIT Publishers, Amsterdam, The Netherlands

Graphic design
Ronald Boiten and Irene Mesu, Amersfoort, The Netherlands
Text
Vera Gianotten, La Paz / Amsterdam
Translation
Keith John Richards, Bolivia
Printing
Bariet, Ruinen, The Netherlands

ISBN 978 94 6022 096 8

This publication was made possible by support from NOVIB

Voor Ton

Activism is a type of commitment that absorbs a person to such an extent that he or she finds neither the time nor the peace of mind to reflect. The prevailing characteristic of activism might be described as a lack of perception, a lack of clarity. Activism is always present in an atmosphere of protest, resistance and change. The very opposite of the notion I call activism is embodied in the concept of reflection. The flesh and blood of reflection is history.

Sjef Theunis in: *Socialism and Participation*, June 1988.[1]

INDEX

10 ABBREVIATIONS
16 PRESENTATION
17 ACKNOWLEDGEMENTS
20 INTRODUCTION

PART I
RECUPERATING DEMOCRACY (1971-1987)

1

30 **CIPCA IS BORN AND EXPANDS (1971-1980)**

30 HISTORICAL OVERVIEW

35 CURRENTS OF THOUGHT
Liberation theology
Liberation education
Critical social science and action-research
Rural development theories

40 BIRTH (1971-1974)
Internal organisation
Activities

44 FIRST CONSOLIDATION (1974-1976)
Internal organisation
Activities
Self-evaluation

52 EXPANSION (1976-1980)
CIPCA – National
CIPCA – La Paz
CIPCA – Cochabamba
CIPCA – Charagua
CIPCA – Santa Cruz

66 CIPCA AND THE POLITICAL DEBATE OVER THE YEARS 1978-1980
The hunger strike
The first elections in twelve years
Independent unionism
Political openness
Monochrome versus multicolour

2
74 **CIPCA CAMOUFLAGED (1980-1982)**

74 HISTORICAL OVERVIEW

78 GOING UNDERGROUND
CIPCA – National
SETECO – La Paz
SATA – Cochabamba
COTEICO – Santa Cruz
SASVAC – Charagua

85 COMING OUT OF HIDING

3
87 **CIPCA RECUPERATES (1982-1987)**

87 HISTORICAL OVERVIEW

92 CURRENTS OF THOUGHT
Popular education and participative research
Integrated rural development

96 RESUMING ACTIONS AND NEW QUESTS
CIPCA – National
CIPCA – La Paz
CIPCA – Cochabamba
CIPCA – Charagua-Camiri
CIPCA – Santa Cruz

105 TOWARDS INSTITUTIONALISATION

PART II
CONSOLIDATING DEMOCRACY (1987-2005)

4
110 **CIPCA INSTITUTIONALISES (1987-1996)**

111 HISTORICAL OVERVIEW

116 CURRENTS OF THOUGHT
NGOs in a democratic context
Environment and sustainable development
Gender

121 THE INTERNAL ORGANISATION OF CIPCA
Objectives and strategy
Work zones
Managerial aspects

124 ACTIVITIES
CDT: the great dream
Adjusting the economic dimension
Micro-regional plans: the organisational motor
Popular Historical Project: the ideological dimension
Radio as educational support
Publications, research and library
New themes: environment and gender

152 CONCLUSION

5
153 cipca consolidated (1996-2005)

154 HISTORICAL OVERVIEW

160 CURRENTS OF THOUGHT
Role of the State and civil society
Local development and popular participation
Peasant economy
Business management

169 INTERNAL ORGANISATION
New legal status
Strategy, mission and challenges
Management model
Financial and human resources
Systematisation and knowledge management

176 WORK ZONES

178 REGIONAL OFFICES
CIPCA – La Paz
CIPCA – Cochabamba
CIPCA – Cordillera
CIPCA – Santa Cruz
CIPCA – Beni
CIPCA – North

193 ACTIVITIES
Democratic peasant and indigenous organisations
Land property rights, territory and natural resources
Sustainable rural economy
Intercultural democracy and efficacy in local and intermediary institutions and governments
Public policies favourable to peasants and indigenous peoples

PART III
DEBATES OF YESTERDAY, TODAY AND TOMORROW

6
210 SOME RECURRENT THEMES

Relations with peasant and indigenous organisations
Democracy and intercultural citizenship
Sustainable rural development
Role of research
Public impact
Relation with co-financing agencies
Final reflection

234 BIBLIOGRAPHY

239 APPENDICES

1 People interviewed
2 Research Notebooks and other significant publications
3 Development cooperation agencies

247 Notes

ABBREVIATIONS

AA	Aid in Action
ACF	Co-Financing Agency
ACLO	Cultural Association Loyola
ACSUR	"Las Segovias" Association for the Cooperation with the South
AND	Nationalist Democratic Action
AIPE	Association of Institutions of Promotion and Education
AIPE	Inter-Institutional Association for Emergency Programmes (until 1986)
ALCA	Free Trade Area for the Americas
AMUPEI	Articulation of Women for Equity and Equality
ANAPO	National Association of Oleaginous Crop Producers
ANDEB	National Association of Evangelists of Bolivia
ANED	National Ecumenical Development Association
AP	Popular Assembly
APARAB	Association of Agroforestry Producers of the Amazonian Region of Northern Bolivia
APCOB	Support for the Peasant-Indigenous of the Bolivian Oriente
APDHB	Bolivian Permanent Assembly of Human Rights
APG	Assembly of the Guaraní People
APP	Association of Potato Producers
APT	Association of Wheat Producers
ATICA	Peasant Land Water Programme
BOCINAB	Block of Peasant and Indigenous Organisations of Amazonian Northern Bolivia
CABI	Captaincy of Upper and Lower Izozog
CAFOD	Catholic Agency for Overseas Development
CAINCO	Santa Cruz Chamber of Industry, Commerce, Services and Tourism
CANOB	Ayorea Native Central of the Bolivian Oriente
CAO	Chamber of Agriculture of the Oriente

CARITAS	Social Pastoral Episcopal Commission
CBDHDD	Bolivian Chapter of Human Rights, Democracy and Development
CCFD	French Catholic Committee against Hunger and for Development
CDT	Work community
CDTAC	Departmental Central of Salaried Agricultural Workers
CEAAL	Council of Adult Education of Latin America
CEBEMO	Netherlands Catholic Co-Financing Agency
CEDIB	Bolivian Centre for Documentation and Information
CEMSE	Multiple Educational Services Centre
CENDA	Andean Communication and Development Centre
CEP	Centre of Studies and Projects srl
CEPAL	United Nations Economic Commission for Latin America
CETHA	Centre for Technical, Humanistic and Agricultural Education
CIAT	Research Centre for Tropical Agriculture
CIDETI	Inter-Institutional Coordination for the Development of Tiraque
CIDOB	Central Indigenous of the Bolivian Oriente
	Confederation of Indigenous Peoples of Bolivia
CIPCA	Centre for Research and Promotion of the Peasantry
CINEP	Centre of Research and Popular Education
CIPYM	Indigenous Council of the Yuracaré People – Moxeño
CNRA	National Council of Agrarian Reform
CNTCB	National Confederation of Agricultural Workers of Bolivia
COB	Bolivian Workers' Central
CODEL	Committee of Organisations of Local Economic Development
CONADE	National Committee of Defence of Democracy
CONAMAQ	National Council of Ayllus and Markas of the Qullasuyu
CONAP	National Planning Council
CONDEPA	Conscience of Patria
COPIM	Central of Indigenous People's Organisations of Moxos
COPNAG	Central of Guarayo Native People's Organisations
COR	Workers' Regional Centre of La Paz
CORACA	Peasant Corporation for Agriculture
CORDAID	Netherlands Consortium of Catholic Co-Financing Agencies
COREP	Regional Planning Council
COSUDE	Swiss Development Cooperation
COTEICO	Technical Commission of Peasant Research in the Oriente
COTESU	Swiss Technical Cooperation
CPEM-B	Central of Ethnic Peoples of Moxos-Beni

CPESC	Coordinator of Santa Cruz Ethnic Peoples
CGNP	Central of Indigenous Peoples of the Beni
CRS	Catholic Relief Services
CSUTCB	Single Union Federation of Peasant Workers of Bolivia
DED	Deutsche Entwicklungsdienst [German Service of Technical Devedlopment Cooperation]
DESEC	Socio-Economic Development Community
ECORA	Community Education and Radio
EED	Evangelische Entwicklungsdienst [German Evangelical Agency for Development]
ENDE	National Electricity Company
ENTEL	National Telecommunications Company
ERBOL	Bolivian Education Radio
EZE	Evangelischen Zentralstelle für Entwicklungshilfe [Evangelic Central of Germany for Development Aid]
FADES	Foundation for Development Alternatives
Fastenopfer	Katholisches Hilfswerk Schweiz [Catholic Swiss Aid Action]
FDC	Peasant Development Fund
FDCSC	Santa Cruz Departmental Federation of Colonisers
FDMCSC-BS	'Bartolina Sisa' Santa Cruz Departmental Federation of Peasant Women
FDMCLP-BS	'Bartolina Sisa' La Paz Departmental Federation of Peasant Women
FDNMCB-BS	'Bartolina Sisa' Bolivian National Federation of Peasant Women
FDUTC-LP	La Paz Single Departmental Federation of Agricultural Workers
FDUTC-P	Pando Single Departmental Federation of Agricultural Workers
FDUTC-SC	Santa Cruz Single Departmental Federation of Agricultural Workers
FEDECOR	Departmental Federation of Irrigators' Committees
FEJUVE	Federation of Neighbourhood Committees
FES	Social Economic Function
FFAA	Armed Forces
FIS	Social Investment Fund
FONDECO	Communal Development Fund
FOS	Fonds voor Ontwikkelingssamenwerking Belgian Development Cooperation Fund
FSE	Social Emergency Fund
FSUTCC	Single Workers' Union Federation of Cochabamba
FSUTCMD	Single Workers' Union Federation of the Madre de Dios Province
FSUTCVD	Single Workers' Union Federation of the Vaca Díez Province
GDT	Work Group
GIS	Geographic Information System
GOM	Gemeenschappelijk Overleg Medefinanciering [Dutch Consortium of Co-Financing Agencies]

GTZ	Gemeinschaft Technische Zusammenarbeit [German Technical Cooperation]
HDI	Human Development Index
HIPC	Heavily Indebted Poor Country
HIVOS	Humanistisch Instituut voor Ontwikkelingssamenwerking [Humanistic Institute for Development Cooperation]
IBTA	Bolivian Institute of Agricultural Technology
ICCO	Interkerkelijke Organisatie voor Ontwikkelingssamenwerking [Dutch Interchurch Organisation for Development Cooperation]
ICT	Information and Communication Technology
IDERCO	Cordillera Institute of Rural Education
IDB	Inter-American Development Bank
IICA	Inter-American Institute of Agricultural Sciences
IICD	International Institute for Communication and Development
ILO	International Labour Office
IMF	International Monitary Fund
INC	National Institute of Colonisation
INRA	National Institute of Agrarian Reform
INTERMON	Spanish Agency of Development Cooperation
IPADE	Institute of Promotion and Support to the Development
IPTK	Tomás Katari Polytechnic Institute
KIT	Koninklijk Instituut voor de Tropen [Royal Tropical Institute]
LAB	Lloyd Bolivian Airlines
LPP	Law of Popular Participation
MACA	Ministry of Peasant and Agricultural Affairs
Manos Unidas	Joined Hands [Spanish Catholic Volunteers]
MAS	Movement to Socialism
MBL	Free Bolivia Movement
MCTH	Netherlands Technical Cooperation Mission
MIP	Pachakuti Indian Movement
MIR	Revolutionary Left Movement
MISEREOR	German Catholic Agency for Development Cooperation
MITK	Tupaj Katari Movement
MNR	Nationalist Revolutionary Movement
MNRI	Independent Nationalist Revolutionary Movement
MR	Micro-region
MRTK	Revolutionary Movement Tupaj Katari
MSM	Movement without Fear
MST	Movement without Land

NFR	New Republican Strength
NGO	Non Governmental Organisation
NOGUB	Support Programme of Swiss Development Cooperation for Non-Governmental Organisations
NOVIB	Nederlandse Organisatie voor Internationale Bijstand [Netherlands Organisation for International Aid]
OC-OI	Peasant Organisation – Indigenous Organisation
OCO	Trading Company of the Oriente
ODA	Official Development Aid
OECA	Economic Peasant Organisation
OI	Indigenous Organisation
OICh	Chiquitana Indigenous Organisation
OTB	Territorial Organisation
OXFAM	Oxford Committee for Famine Relief
PAAC	Agro-Energy Programme for Peasant Support
PADA	Agricultural Products of the Altiplano
PADER	Promotion of Rural Economic Development
GNP	Gross National Product
PCB	Bolivian Communist Party
PDCC	Pesant Development Programme of Cordillera
PDDI	Plan of Development of Distrito Indigenous
PDM	Municipal Development Plan
PHP	Popular Historical Project
PIEB	Programme of Strategic Research in Bolivia
PLUS	Plan for Soil Use
PMC	Military-Peasant Pact
PME	Planning, Monitoring and Evaluation
PMR	Micro-Regional Plan
POA	Annual Operational Plan
PRACA	Peasant Agricultural Recuperation Programme
PROCADE	Peasant Programme for Development Alternatives
PROCAVA	Peasant Products of the Valley
PRODEMO	Trading Company 'Promotion of Moxos'
PRORURAL	Bolivian Association for Rural Development
PRSP	Poverty Reduction Strategy Paper
PS	Socialist Party
REMTE	Network of Women Transforming the Economy
SASVAC	Social Assistance Service of the Apostolic Vicariate of Cuevo

SATA	Service of Agricultural Technical Assistance
SEMTA	Multiple Services for Appropriate Technology
SETECO	Technical Service for Cooperation
SNV	Stichting Nederlandse Vrijwilligers [Foundation of Netherlands Volunteers]
SRL	Society of Limited Responsibility
TCO	Indigenous Communitarian Land
TICh	Chimán Indigenous Territory
TIM	Multiethnic Indigenous Territory
TIMI	Moxos-Ignaciano Indigenous Territory
TIPNIS	Indigenous Territory of the Isiboro Sécure National Park
UAGRM	Gabriel René Moreno Autonomous University
UAM	Municipal Support Unit
UAP	Political Support Unit
UAR	Regional Support Unit
UCS	Civic Solidarity Unit
UDAPE	Unit for Analysis of Social and Economic Policies
UDP	Democratic Popular Unity
UE	European Union
UMSA	Universidad Mayor de San Andrés (La Paz)
UMSS	Universidad Mayor de San Simón (Cochabamba)
UNDP	United Nations Development Programme
UNIBAMBA	Union of Institutions of Cochabamba
UNICRUZ	Union of Institutions of Santa Cruz
UNILAPAZ	Union of Institutions of La Paz
UNITAS	National Union of Institutions for Social Action Work
UNRISD	United Nations Research Institute for Social Development
UPEA	Public University of El Alto
USAID	United States Agency for International Development
VSF	Veterinarians without Frontiers
YPFB	Public Oil Company of Bolivia
WB	World Bank

PRESENTATION

We welcome this publication, commissioned by the CIPCA Assembly two years ago. Its excellence is thanks to Vera Gianotten's enthusiasm and experience, the companionship and assistance offered by Xavier Albó and Lorenzo Soliz, and the commitment and contributions of so many other people who participated at distinct moments and in various ways.

Over 35 years CIPCA has, without any doubt, covered a lot of ground. At the same time there is no particular landmark to be celebrated here; simply the commitment and the will to share from the institution's memory. This is a part of Bolivia's history; of social movements, academic debate, development initiatives and their manifold influences and international cooperation through NGOs. If CIPCA was able to offer something in particular – and for those of us who are part of CIPCA, it is something we wish to be maintained – it is the capacity to be an always contemporary institution in accompanying the changing processes and challenges faced by the country's indigenous peasant organisations.

Those of us who have been involved with CIPCA, from within and from the outside, certainly imagine this provocative challenge resulting in a particular history, possibly one different to the product we have in our hands today. The design of this research, the available antecedents and materials and the initial discussions held, all showed us that this path was not always obvious and the departure not necessarily urgent. For this reason its content does not exhaust our history; rather it provokes challenges and invites.

From CIPCA it betokens us to thank all the people who were involved in this history in one way or another, especially the staff who passed through the institution, but including our counterparts with individual faces.

A very special place is occupied by the indigenous peasants, women and men, who challenge us, understand us and allow us to accompany them in their permanent quest for a worthier country, a more dignified humanity.

Carmen Avila
President of the CIPCA Assembly

Carlos de la Riva
President of the CIPCA Management Committee

Oscar Bazoberry
General Director of CIPCA

ACKNOWLEDGEMENTS

When I had finished the final draft of this book, I still hadn't yet written the acknowledgments. I didn't consider this a difficult assignment, but rather as a small fiesta, as a very welcome task. It is in itself a small history of the year 2006, a year in which I have received so much valuable support from so many people in writing this book. The group of people who have helped me through this odyssey grew day by day.

First of all I would like to mention the kindness of five people, authors of previous documents which I have been able to use without the need to quote them permanently: Denise Parmentier, who made the first attempt to write the history of CIPCA, utilising the methodology of oral history. She provided me with transcriptions of interviews with key people in CIPCA between the years 1970-1986. This material has been extremely important for the first three chapters. The fourth chapter is based on the systematisation made by Xavier Albó, Rafael García Mora and Freddy Salazar of the years 1987-1996.

Faithful to its democratic vocation, the CIPCA directors installed a group of critical readers who have made observations, both in writing and in the course of several meetings and workshops. It was an honour to work with them and receive so many good (and at times tough) criticisms and suggestions. Thanks to Hugo Fernández, Ismael Guzmán, Mauro Hurtado, Eduardo Mendoza, Rafael Puente, Gloria Querejazu, Carmen Beatriz Ruíz and Bernardino Soliz.

I have also had the support of many people who have provided information in writing, especially on the history of the regional offices: Eduardo Acevedo, Marcelo Arandia, Carmiña García, Ismael Guzmán, Germán Huanca, Carlos Laruta, Cristina Lipa, Judith Marca, Eduardo Mendoza, Juan Carlos Rojas and Eufronio Toro. Armengol Caballero very kindly gave me his chronology of the history of Bolivia (in *PowerPoint*) and Kees van Dongen, responsible for Bolivia in NOVIB in the 1980s, provided me with his visitor's reports from those years.

Although this is the history of CIPCA and not of the co-financing agencies, it is clear that without them CIPCA would not have been able to survive and grow. In appendix 3 there is a list of all the cooperating agencies. My thanks also go out to all of them.

This book would never have contained so much first-hand information if I had not had the chance of interviewing more than 100 people. I want to thank all the peasant and indigenous women and men, union and political leaders, and current and previous CIPCA staff, for the frankness with which they responded to so many questions. Proof of the open relationship between CIPCA and the women and men of the countryside, is that they did not only told me success stories, but also offered sometimes tough criticisms of CIPCA's role. I would also like to thank the previous and current staff of numerous co-financing agencies who, with great affection, have spoken about their relations with CIPCA. In Appendix 1 there is a list of all the people who have contributed in some way to this history of CIPCA.

Many thanks to all of them for their sincerity, availability, contributions, criticisms and support. It proves difficult to say exactly who has contributed to which part or supplied which idea, in a text to which so many people have contributed. They are all, to some extent, co-authors – but perhaps not all of them would be prepared to sign their names to what is affirmed and proposed here. For this reason responsibility for the final text, with all its faults and defects, falls entirely upon the author.

Logistic and administrative support has been of great importance in my visits to the regional offices, the interviews, the revision of the archive, the sending of documents, etc. The following people have been indispensable in completing this task: Lola Paredes (librarian), Milton Rivas (messenger), Janet Lifengos (auxiliary accountant), Gabriela Sabat (accountant), Mery Figueroa (secretary of the general directorship) and Teresa Monrroy (previous secretary). Moreover all the administrative staff in the regional offices have always been prepared to solve any logistical and administrative problem. The final edition under Hugo Fernández has undoubtedly enriched the text.

I still have to mention three people: Oscar Bazoberry, Lorenzo Soliz and Xavier Albó. Oscar, as Director General of CIPCA, decided (audaciously) to give me the responsibility of writing the history of CIPCA. He also made another audacious decision in not requesting finance from any cooperation agency, but rather looking for a way to finance it internally. Lorenzo Soliz and Xavier Albó have been much more than colleagues. I would like to call them co-authors. But this they are not, because they have given me complete intellectual independence, for which reason I alone am responsible for the present text. Lorenzo Soliz, so knowledgeable about the history of the Guaranís and Quechuas, has never imposed his version of history. And when Xavier Albó read anything positive about himself, he always wanted to erase it immediately. But later I decided to put it back again.

I wrote this history during 2006, a year full of friendship and intellectual commitment. My thanks to all the people I have already mentioned for having given me an unforgettable year. To conclude, I would like to mention one person in particular who gave me the daily happiness and optimism I needed in order to keep working, and with whom I have been able to have profound discussions on the content of this book. Ton de Wit, my lifelong companion, revised it a million times, each time coming up with new and always accurate observations. In July 2006 this situation of intellectual and personal happiness was brusquely cut short when Ton became very ill. However, it is thanks to his crusading spirit that I was able to resuming the work with an optimism that was his more than mine. He taught me that, despite the malevolent people and creatures one encounters on the way, it's always worth struggling for a noble cause. Ton's life and the history of CIPCA are, without doubt, noble causes.

Amsterdam, December 2010
Vera Gianotten

INTRODUCTION

The Centre for Research and Promotion of the Peasantry (CIPCA)[2] was conceived one afternoon in October 1970 in Jenaro Sanjinés street, in the colonial area of La Paz. Luis Alegre, Xavier Albó and Francisco Javier Santiago, three Jesuits who had just graduated from university, met up in a small room on the third floor of San Calixto School. These men shared the unshakeable conviction that Bolivia's problems should be confronted with a collective effort, through which it would be possible to contribute to social change in the country. They had less than 5,000 dollars. The new institution's objective went something like: "seek out the most efficacious ways for Bolivia's peasants to find their own channels through which to achieve structural development and their integration into the country".

35 years later, in December 2005, there are 110 people working at CIPCA with a budget of 2.5 million dollars to year. Of these 110 workers, there are only two Jesuits and these, moreover, do not have executive duties. As well as the central office in La Paz, there are six regional centres: La Paz departmental office in El Alto, CIPCA Cochabamba, the Cordillera office in Camiri, CIPCA Santa Cruz in the eastern lowlands, CIPCA Beni in San Ignacio de Moxos and CIPCA North in Riberalta. CIPCA also boasts one of the best social science libraries in Bolivia.

It was no surprise that the Jesuits were to place great importance on research, enquiry, reflection and systematisation. Befitting their condition as Jesuits, the founders have always been searching for a kind of social praxis in which action and reflection were conjoined. Another characteristic that the Jesuits impressed upon CIPCA was always to work from an ecumenical perspective. In the words of Albó (2002: 138): "many of the deadlocks and advances in the relationships between churches occur at the level of their own structures, internal legislation and system of authority. At the same time as these efforts at interrelation, dialogue, collective actions and search for unity originate in these very ecclesiastical norms and structures; ecumenism becomes institutional and even official."

For this reason, groups that have worked alongside and demonstrated solidarity with CIPCA include not only Catholic agencies, but also protestant and secular bodies. Two of these non-Catholic agencies have, over many years, provided institutional finance: NOVIB (secular) and EED (evangelical)[3]. It is worth re-telling a story remembered by Herculiano Ramos, a former CIPCA promoter who was, at the same time, an evangelical pastor:

When I applied to be a promoter in 1978 I informed them that I was an evangelical pastor. The reaction from Lucho Alegre, Jesuit and national director at that time, was: 'if you don't mention to anyone that you're a pastor, I won't say I'm a priest; we're working for the peasants, damn it'

Why publish the history of CIPCA?

Between 1970 and 2005, Bolivia lived through military coups, democracy and dictatorship. It suffered discontinuity and erratic political change, experiencing constant meddling from international cooperation. It is in this context that we find the continuity of organisations like CIPCA which contributed to the dawning, in 2006, of a new political era in which people who had been excluded since colonial times reached positions of formal State power.

The primary aim of this book is to present the history of CIPCA as an exemplary non-governmental organisation (NGO) in Bolivia and in Latin America. It is exemplary in the sense that the CIPCA story can be a model for the history of the NGOs that emerged in Latin America during the 70s and 80s. But it can also be seen as an example, in which personal characteristics make the history of CIPCA unique. This is why it must be made known; so that we may learn from it, understand why certain decisions have been taken instead of others, why the historical context has at times obliged CIPCA to make reluctant decisions and why this same context has been influenced by CIPCA's actions. NGOs are always criticised for not systematising their experiences. This book's systematisation of 35 years of CIPCA history offers the reader a frame of reference that might serve as a guide, helping to deepen reflections on themes of rural development that are still matters of debate.

During its 35 years of existence, CIPCA has gone through many changes. Some of these are due to fluctuations in the economic and social context, and CIPCA has been sufficiently flexible to adapt to these changes with innovative proposals. It has reacted to other changes because institutional growth demanded adaptations in organisation and management. Which of all these changes are the most important as landmarks, and should be emphasised for today's reader? There is no doubt: the most crucial changes are those that have bestowed upon CIPCA ever greater institutional authority in Bolivia, as a creative actor in the processes of (rural) development. For this reason the book emphasises key points (as well as unanswered questions) concerning development policies. However, the history of CIPCA has also seen moments in which changes in organisation and management have been of the utmost importance for institutional survival. Both kinds of historical changes will be analysed in the book, with priority given to those that have influenced political development. The organisational changes will only be analysed in those cases that had direct influence on the redefinition of working strategies.

CIPCA as a Non-Governmental Organisation

It is true that the bodies later to become known as NGOs had already emerged in Latin America in the 1950s – basically as a form of Catholic Church social action and social extensions of universities – the main features of their image only began to crystallise during the expansion of their presence in the second half of the 1970s. The socio-political climate of the period 1970-1980 in Latin America, when CIPCA was born, was strongly conditioned by the predominance of dictatorial regimes, which had closed all the democratic spaces in which social actors and political movements found opportunities for action. Under these conditions a variety of NGOs appear, carrying out supplementary functions in relation to actors and democratic institutions whose ability to fulfil these roles have been weakened, or which could no longer carry them out in their entirety.

Towards the end of the 80s there were several efforts to change the name "NGO" so as to be able to identify these organisations by "what they are" rather than "what they are not". Instead of the term NGO there was talk, for example, of "private organisations", "private development institutions", "private organisations with social ends", "private social development institutions" etc. Today the very *non-governmental* nature of the organisations is, once again, considered a strength.

For the aims of this book we will use the following definition when speaking of the kind of NGO that interests us here: "springing from diverse sectors of the ideological spectrum (sectors tied to the Church, to mostly left-leaning political parties, universities or independent groups of professionals) and dedicated to activities of investigation, action and/or training in distinct themes (for example housing, health, education, employment, youth, urban development, agricultural extension), these non profit-making organisations are fundamentally made up of technicians and professionals who, supported by national and international finance, carry out programmes and projects aimed at promoting social and economic development among the population's most vulnerable social sectors" (based on the definition given in Bombarola et al., 1992:15).[4]

This definition is quite applicable to CIPCA which, as an NGO, is externally oriented by nature. Its existence is defined on the basis of the relationship it establishes with social actors. As an NGO, CIPCA does exists not in accordance with its own members (as would be the case, for example, with an association, a union, a federation), but to serve other groups, especially the peasant and indigenous organisations. For this reason, writing the history of CIPCA implies analysing the relationships it has established with other social actors and their ability to exert political influence.

Elements of regulation in the history of CIPCA

The history of CIPCA is one of people and of relations between people. CIPCA began as a small informal group of individuals and gradually turned into an institution, with precise goals and objectives and with formal staff policies according to those objectives. Staff relations are still human, but an institution with more than 100 people cannot function in the same way as a group of three people. This is the first distinction that marks the history of CIPCA: the first phase of its life, personal and informal, is followed by a second phase which is more formal and institutional. This change is also expressed by historic documents and is therefore expressed in this book.

A second element of ordering is the context in which CIPCA moves. In its first decade of existence, the activities responded to the need to re-establish the validity of peasant organisations and democratic institutions in times of military dictatorship. Once this objective was reached in 1982, the institution was able to dedicate itself to working with peasant organisations with a more integral focus. In 1987 a third phase began, one of consolidation. Recognition in the 1994 State Political Constitution of the multiethnic and pluricultural nature of the Republic, the Law of Popular Participation and the subsequent municipalisation (1994-1995), the new Agrarian Law (1996) and other legal reforms, obliged CIPCA to begin a process of internal reflection on its role in the new national context. CIPCA again restructured its focus, its internal organisation and the reach of its work.

The third element of order has to do with content. CIPCA has always worked in three fields: economic, organisational and educative (formation and training). Similarly, CIPCA has always attempted to combine research with action and work at a local level with impact at national level. CIPCA has formed relations with different actors in Bolivian society but its most important counterpart has been, and still is, the peasant-indigenous organisation.

The chronological analysis of the history of CIPCA has been carried out according to CIPCA's own perspective. It is the history of CIPCA and not the history of the actors with which it has always had very close relations. In other words, it is neither the history of social organisations nor that of the cooperating agencies. It is the history of CIPCA and its relationship with those actors.

CIPCA and peasant and indigenous organisations

During the early years CIPCA spoke only of peasant organisations (and not of indigenous organisation) in accordance with the vocabulary in use at that time. During the 1960s and 70s the appearance was noted of new themes in anthropological research: there was a move from culturalism and developmentalism to dependency theory and Marxism. Now no one wanted to see lyrical representations of indigenous, bucolic and idealised elements; instead new themes were emphasised, such as modes of production and the formation of social classes in the countryside (Pajuelo, 2000: 152). Instead of using the generic word 'indigenous', which expressed the ethnic condition of the rural population, the preference was to speak of *'campesino'*, shifting emphasis onto the social and working condition of rural people. This change of concept allowed anthropology to achieve a coherent image of the nature of rural communities, distanced from the cultural mythification given by *indigenismo*. Out of the study of productive organisation, an understanding was reached of the organisational, territorial, institutional and inclusive aspects of communal identity and of the family units that comprise communities (Albó 2005: 160). However, the non-use of the generic word 'indigenous' does not mean that CIPCA is not concerned with the cultural and ethnic element of the rural population. On the contrary, CIPCA's work has always respected people's own culture and has considered, in its research, the indigenous or native fundaments of peasant organisation, preferring to use the specific names of indigenous cultures such as Aymara, Quechua, Guaraní, Guarayo and Moxeña. Only when lowland populations (which have always been deemed indigenous in Bolivia) began to demand a political place in national life, was the concept 'indigenous' retaken, its pejorative connotation removed and a positive nuance returned to it. Thus, in this book different words will be used in accordance with their era, but always referring to the same concept: peasant and /or indigenous organisations (OC-OI, to follow the initials used by CIPCA).

Methodology and limitations of the book

This book was written with the participative and democratic spirit that has always been characteristic of CIPCA. Many people were consulted through personal and group interviews, telephone interviews, etc. There was also a group of critical readers, made up of people who had worked in CIPCA, with whom several workshops have been organised. There were so many consultations that the author at times despaired at having to satisfy thousands and thousands of opinions (subjective and objective). On the other hand, only with the help of all these people were we able to order all the documentary and experiential material (see appendix 1: people interviewed).

It should be made clear that writing history is not only a matter of ordering and selecting, but also of evaluation and interpretation. This evaluation and interpretation is entirely the responsibility of the author. History is more than an account of how, what and why. It is also an effort to capture the context of all these events, to grasp this vague notion that we call the "spirit of the age". When the historian is still an integral part of this same spirit of the times, it becomes even more difficult to present objectively. Historical facts allow themselves to be ordered in a different ways according to the historian's interpretation; historical truth changes colour depending on the magnifying lens with which one looks. To conclude, CIPCA's historical truth is coloured by the history of the author herself, a professional and personal history related to the Latin American NGO, especially those of Peru and Bolivia.

During the process of redaction, many people working or having worked previously in international cooperation, suggested that I should be very critical with CIPCA. Some will certainly be disappointed and consider the author a "*broodschrijver*".[5] However, the author's own history has been influential in the adoption of a critical position, but at the same time constructive and comprehensible in judging CIPCA's achievements.

Entre 1977 and 1983 I worked together with Ton de Wit as coordinator of a programme of peasant research and training at the National University San Cristóbal de Huamanga in Ayacucho (Peru). I learned there that it is easy to criticise and very difficult to put theoretical ideas into practice regarding education, training, outreach and rural development. After 13 years' work in Latin America on rural development projects, I returned to Holland where I perform various duties in advising cooperation agencies. I realised that it was very easy to make criticisms and negative judgements of the workings of NGOs, because of the great distance from everyday life in the countryside. I was bothered by unfounded criticisms from academics who themselves have never had concrete experience of field work. I still have great respect for all those technicians (educators, agronomists, sociologists, veterinarians, communicators, etc.) that work in the countryside with peasants and indigenous families, seeking ways to improve its economic and social situation in a not very favourable context for rural development.

The history of CIPCA serves to show critics of NGOs, as well as new generations, that the work of NGOs does have a positive influence in the lives of poor families. In writing this history I have been guided by the following question: what would have happened without CIPCA? I invite the reader to be guided, too, by this question, because in answering it he/she will realise that CIPCA, together with many other actors, has indeed influenced the economic, social and cultural emancipation of peasant women and indigenous families. These families, totally excluded 35 years ago, now play an important role in Bolivian life.

Each chapter begins with a short historical summary of the most important relevant events. In this way, each chapter can give a brief analysis of the different currents of thought that were prominent in the era under discussion. Both paragraphs serve to show how the social, economic, political and academic context has influenced CIPCA's thought and how CIPCA's contribution, in turn, has served to influence this very context positively and with lasting results.

The first part of the book (los years 1971-1987) is divided into three chapters. This first part is principally based in interviews carried out by Denise Parmentier[6] and then verified by Xavier Albó and Marcos Recolons. It has an experiential and personal nature, for numerous reasons:
• during the first years of its existence, CIPCA was an informal group of people; it only gradually turned into an institution;
• there were still no very elaborate documents being written about mission, objectives, strategies, logical frameworks, indicators, activities, expected results, etc.
• of those documents that actually were drawn up, few have survived;
• during the dictatorship of García Meza (1980-1982) part of the archive has disappeared despite several people risking detention and torture in attempting to save it.

The second part (the years 1987-2005) is divided into two chapters. The fourth chapter is an internal CIPCA document entitled "*An Eight-Year Decennial*", drawn up by Xavier Albó, Rafael García Mora and Freddy Salazar[7]. The fifth chapter (1997-2005) is based on the quinquennial strategic plans that CIPCA has presented to NOVIB and EED, the two cooperation agencies that, from 1997, provided institutional finance. Likewise, the evaluation reports have been an important base for this second part. Interviews carried out with current and former staff, as well as people related to CIPCA, have been extremely useful to in lending a taste of lived experience to formal documents.

The book ends with a chapter that sums up some matters of debate from yesterday, today and tomorrow. It was preferred to avoid using the term "lessons learned" because the process of change that CIPCA has gone through is more than a collection of lessons learned. It is a process of action and reflection, of having and implementing audacious ideas (both correct and mistaken) and of constructing theory, in a world in which there are many more actors (some of which are even more powerful than CIPCA) who define this process of change.

One theme that will not be dealt with is the history of the CIPCA financing. It was impossible to recuperate, in detail, the slow and complex odyssey of financing CIPCA activities, becoming ever broader and more demanding. But it is only correct to make it clear that, without continued support from the co-financing agencies (ACF)[8] and the many thousands of people within its circle, making the CIPCA dream a reality would have been totally unthinkable. CIPCA would be nothing without its main counterparts. Just thinking of what would have happened to CIPCA without the support of these people and institutions would turn into a nightmare (see appendix 3: list of co-financing agencies that have supported CIPCA).

Social, cultural, political and economic exclusion has been CIPCA's ordering theme ever since its creation and, consequently, it is central to this book. The struggle for inclusion has been, and remains, the institution's chief *raison d'être*, as well as that of its staff and, without any doubt, its founders. Today, in the early 21st century it has become more than ever manifest that exclusion is no longer only a problem for the poor in developing countries. Exclusion is a political and cultural theme applying to all countries. With an analysis of the processes of exclusion and the corresponding struggle for inclusion we can understand globalization, its reach, the challenges it sets and the dangers it presents.

The book closes towards the end of 2005, when Bolivia began a new political period marked by the inclusion in the political field with the arrival – by democratic means – of the first indigenous president, with a political party made up of the indigenous peasant organisations themselves and with a voting figure of 54%, exceeding all expectations.

It is certain that CIPCA and many other NGOs have contributed to the advance in the process of political emancipation in Bolivia. CIPCA, with its 35 years of experience in taking on ever newer new political, economic and cultural challenges, will once again have to find responses, ways to confront the challenges of the 21st century and to combat rural poverty, so that campesinos and indigenous people might be full citizens with all their democratic rights and duties and so that Bolivia might be a single pluricultural, intercultural and multiethnic country.
Let us view the history of CIPCA, so as to be able to enrich our own ideas on the process of development and the role of NGOs active in rural environments in Bolivia and in Latin America. I would like to finish this introduction with an invitation to the reader: "Before interrupting the past, we must first of all hear it out".

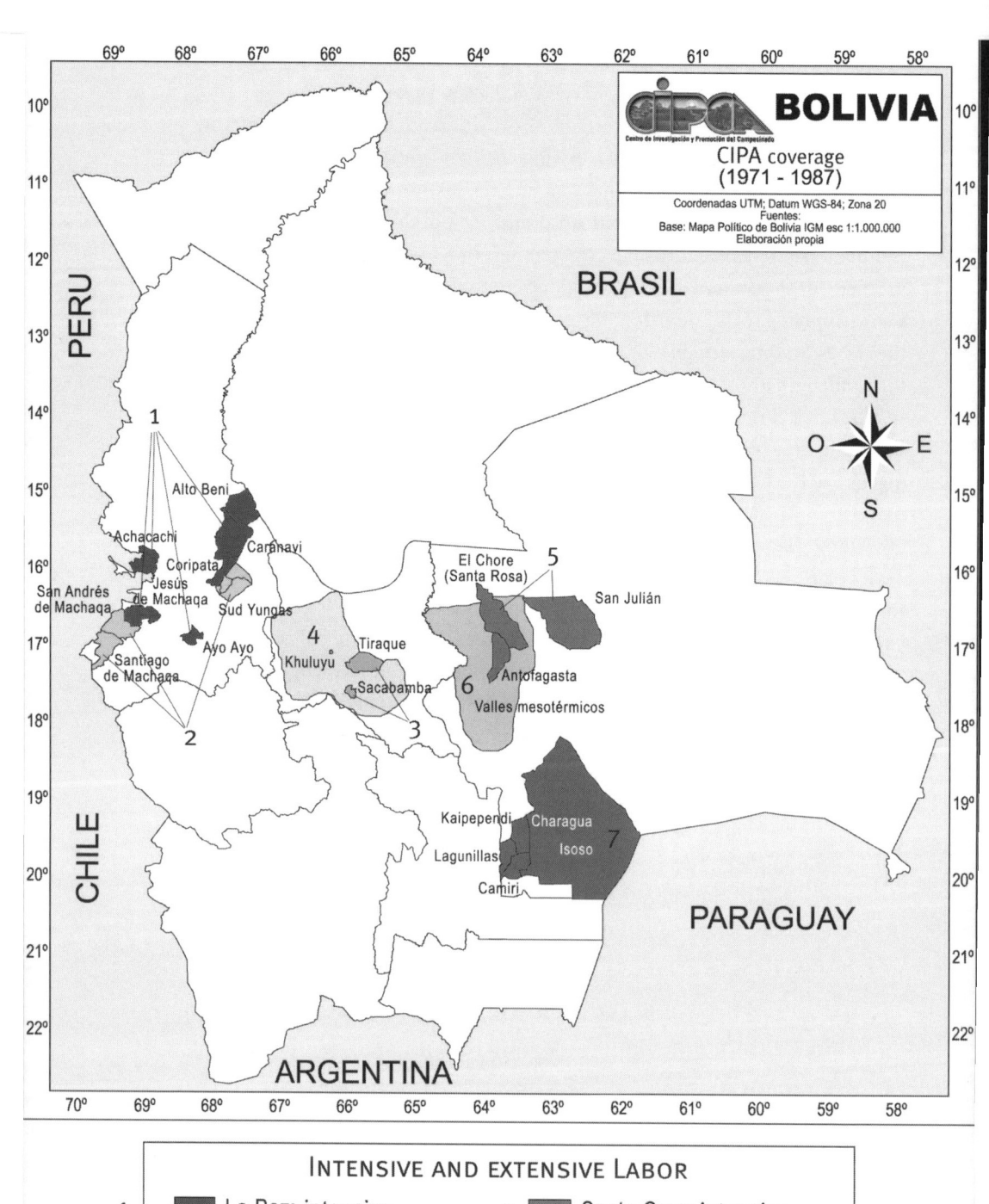

PART I
RECUPERATING DEMOCRACY 1971–1987

The story of CIPCA between 1971 and 1987 is marked by the creativity, charisma and the audacity of an informal group of people who, from different but complementary perspectives, worked to establish an institution at the service of the Bolivian peasantry. Activities during that time were carried out against a background of military dictatorships, with the main objective of restoring the validity of democratic institutions. Once democracy was restored in 1982, CIPCA went through a few years of institutional searching in an attempt to define how best to serve the Bolivian peasantry in this new democratic context.

This first part is divided into three chapters, the first of which tells of CIPCA's birth on the Aymara Altiplano and chronologically narrates its expansion to Cochabamba, Charagua and Santa Cruz (1971-1980). The second chapter deals with the events that stained two of the darkest years in Bolivian history, the military dictatorship of García Meza (1980-1982) whilst the final chapter tells how CIPCA came out of hiding to recuperate an institutional presence in a context of natural disaster and economic crisis (1982-1987).

These first 17 years of life of CIPCA are written as experiential history, being principally based on personal interviews with the protagonists of that time.

CHAPTER 1
CIPCA IS BORN AND EXPANDS
1971-1980

CIPCA was not born in an ideological vacuum. Some historical landmarks previous to the 1970s, such as the Agrarian Reform of 1952 and the Cuban Revolution, had an important influence on political life and on the ideological analysis of Bolivia's structural problems. Below we present a historical overview[9], along with an analysis of the chief currents of thought at that time.

HISTORICAL OVERVIEW

To begin with, it is opportune to mention a momentous international event that had repercussions throughout Latin America at a political level, as well as in the thinking of the youth of that time. The Cuban Revolution of 1959 changed the balance of power in Latin America and opened spaces for Marxist movements that attempted to take power. The response of the then president of the United States, John F. Kennedy, was to create the Alliance for Progress. At that time, the most important doctrine and the one with greatest consequences for Latin America was that of national security, which implied strong backing for Latin American armies, anti-guerrilla preparation and, finally, promotion and support for military dictatorships as part of an anticommunist politics.

Seven years before, Bolivia had experienced the National Revolution of 1952. The new Revolutionary Nationalist Movement (MNR) installed Víctor Paz Estenssoro and Hernán Siles Zuazo in the governmental palace. Their first step was the decree that established universal suffrage. This measure broke with the exclusive and qualified democracy of the past, giving the vote to women and the illiterate, and making adult citizens eligible. On the 2nd of August 1953 a measure was taken that is fundamental to the theme of this book: the Agrarian Reform, which gave the land back to the peasantry in the valleys and on the Altiplano.[10]

The reform managed to give peasant families in the highlands access to property divided into small plots of land. A consequence of this reform was a greater incorporation of the peasant economy into the market. Immediately after the application of the decree, the participation of peasants in the national economy increased significantly; innumerable 'peasant fairs' were created, new villages or communities and informal markets for capital, goods and services (Urioste, 1992:103).

The birth of the agrarian reform also gave rise, above all in the Andean region, to a nationwide "peasant" union organisation: the National Confederation of Peasant Workers of Bolivia (CNTCB). With the recuperation of the haciendas accomplished, communal organisations at more local levels adopted the name of unions with the innovation that they were now also becoming part of a national organisation very much tied to the new government. These 'unions' were not the typical organisation of workers' origin voicing protests and claims; rather they maintained their nature as native communal organisations from pre-existing communities. In this way they coexisted, and in many places these traditional authorities still coexist, with the union authorities.

In a complementary fashion, the MNR gave impetus to several initiatives that allowed greater State presence in the development of the Bolivian lowlands in the Oriente: the road connection between Cochabamba and Santa Cruz, colonisation programmes and, above all, support for the then still incipient agro-industrial and cattle-rearing companies[11].

In 1964, a military coup by René Barrientos Ortuño closed the cycle of twelve years of MNR government, giving way to a series of military regimes framed within the model of Latin American dictatorships. General Barrientos, born in Cochabamba of Quechua origin[12], promised to maintain the achievements of the Agrarian Reform and contributed to expansion of the agricultural frontier in the Oriente, strongly motivating colonisation programmes for small peasant producers initiated by the MNR. With this kind of support to the rural sector, he was able to consolidate a Military-Peasant Pact, initially also dubbed "Anticommunist". The Military-Peasant Pact was the main instrument of political backing for Barrientos' military government; it was also a means of controlling the peasant union movement, until then obedient to the MNR. Smaller groups of former peasant leaders remained at the periphery of the Military-Peasant Pact, closer to the miners and the Bolivian Workers' Central (COB), which formed the "Independent Peasant Block".

Paradoxically, at the same time as it implemented the Agrarian Reform in the west of the country, the MNR aided the development of a new bourgeois landowning class in the east. The Agrarian Reform began to become distorted, particularly from the Barrientos regime onwards, with gifts of great swathes of land to friends of whatever government was in power, many of these being kept only as "fattening lands" for speculation, despite the constitutional prohibition of large estates.

Barrientos died in a helicopter accident on the 27th of April 1969. In October 1970, after other military governments, General Juan José Torres became president. Torres set out to consolidate the inclination of military government towards the left. Towards the end of 1970, President Torres made a proposal of co-government to the COB, with the aim of keeping it on his side. However, on the first of June 1971, when CIPCA was in its first year of operation, a Popular Assembly was installed with Juan Lechín at its head: the COB described itself as the real organ of power. The Popular Assembly sought to replace traditional democracy, constituting popular power with 233 delegates from the mines, factories and universities, as well as teachers and intellectuals. However, the Popular Assembly failed to survive its organisational phase, being riddled with polemics that totally weakened it.

It was during this period of greater tolerance of the left in the late 1970s that three Jesuits, who had completed specialised studies abroad, met up again in Bolivia. These three, some months later in January 1971, would formally inaugurate CIPCA. Some months later, on the 19th of August 1971 came the coup d'état of Hugo Banzer, whose first years in power were marked by his implacable and iron-fisted response to any opposition. He represented the military face of nationalism, with the fiercely anticommunist ingredient of the epoch. Banzer outlawed left-wing parties, cancelled the activities of the COB and of any other union organisation, closed the universities and sent hundreds of Bolivians into exile. That Banzer government lasted longer than any other in the history of the 20th century and coincided with the first years of CIPCA (1971-1978).

Banzer, originally from Santa Cruz, also facilitated the rise to power of the new eastern Bolivian agrarian bourgeoisie, initiated by the MNR. Expansion towards the east was finally consolidated, supported by an improved road network, and with this two forms of land ownership were established in the country. On the Andean side, the Altiplano and the valleys, family production continued on small properties (smallholdings) among members of peasant communities, while in the eastern lowlands the agricultural and cattle-raising companies expanded rapidly. Since then, the two models have competed for the attention of the State without much interaction, except that the Andean indigenous population (Aymara and Quechua), having migrated to the *Oriente*, has been the one which – together with the indigenous peoples of the lowlands – has provided the workforce for the capitalist companies of the *Oriente*.

Banzer also continued the colonisation programmes set up by previous governments, setting up projects in the areas of Alto Beni, Chapare-Chimoré, Yapacaní and San Julián with finance from the USA International Development Agency (USAID) and the Inter-American Development Bank (IDB). The colonisers, mainly of Quechua origin with a minority from other places and cultures, were still small family farmers as they had been in their places of origin, although now more market-oriented.

This cycle of peasant expansion, initiated in 1953 with the Agrarian Reform, reached the limit of its growth in the second half of the 1970s. This was a period in which easy external credit financed decisively the cost of public investment for the productive infrastructure of agribusiness on the eastern plains. The mid-term consequence was a national debt that spiralled from 460 million dollars in 1971 to almost 3,000 million in 1978. By the mid 1970s it was already evident that the Bolivian economy could not sustain this level of external debt. (Mesa et al. 2003: 703).

With Barrientos and Banzer the Military-Peasant Pact was prevalent, but at the same time dissident groups were emerging that were closer to the COB and to the political parties of the left. The most significant innovation was the recuperation of ethnic identity, above all among the Aymaras, after the end of the 1960s. This orientation meant that the nucleus of protest became the questioning of neo-colonialism and indigenous dissatisfaction with approaches merely in favour of the "*campesinos*", which it viewed exclusively as a social class (Calderón 1999: 443-44). In the Andean region, this change of focus occurred at the very heart of peasant organisation. In the Potosí peasant congress of August 1971, the ascent of Katarism[13] culminated in its leader, Jenaro Flores, becoming overall leader of the CNTCB.[14]

In 1977, as a result of international pressures linked to the human rights policies of North American president Jimmy Carter, the Banzer military government agreed to a restricted form of democratic openness. Banzer promised elections, but barred the return of the chief political and union leaders who were exiled or persecuted. This stance provoked a massive hunger strike which forced the government to concede a 'total and unrestricted' amnesty from January 1978. The years 1978, 1979 and 1980 were years of constant change; coups, elections and party conflicts. There were some periods of greater openness and others of renewed repression, but they were part of a process of transition towards democracy during which authoritarian regimes became increasingly discredited.

In 1979 the new Single Union Confederation of Bolivian Peasant Workers (CSUTCB) was created, under Katarist hegemony, which immediately refused to recognise the Military-Peasant Pact and became the matrix organisation of all the peasantry, besides gaining an important position within the COB. This openness was brusquely interrupted by the García Meza military coup in 1980 and the subsequent persecution of Jenaro Flores (who was left paralysed by a bullet) and of the Katarists (see Albó, 1999). After the fall of this regime and the return to democracy in 1982, the CSUTCB was practically the only organisation recognised by peasant unionism and the defunct CNTCB was never heard of again.

Democracy also saw the emergence of the first 'Indian' political parties, among which the most significant were the Tupaj Katari Revolutionary Movement (MRTK) – more amenable to alliances with the COB and with other non-indigenous parties – and the Tupaj Katari Indian Movement (MITKA), whose greater emphasis on ethnic identity foregrounded the persistent contradiction that was the legacy of colonialism. Both stood in the numerous elections held during that time. They still had few votes and suffered various internal divisions, as did other rural and popular organisations, but thanks to them the ethnic thematic began to seep into the public agenda.

During this whole period, as a result of the public activities of some peasant women within so-called 'feminine organisations', such as mothers' clubs, a feminine leadership emerged that actively inspired peasant women to organise themselves independently. The example of the women miners who, in 1977, spearheaded the democratic struggle against dictatorship, may have been the impulse needed for the emergence of the first militant organisations of peasant women. On the 23rd – 24th of April 1978, the historic I Assembly of Peasant Women was held in La Paz and the committee was organised *ad hoc, for* the preparation of the I National Congress.

The mothers' clubs – without realising it – played an important role in the problems of peasant women. They were also an important nexus between women at grassroots level and the feminine leadership that emerged from the Katarist movement. Above all, it was the determined and strategic participation of women in roadblocks on the Altiplano and in the Yungas in 1979 that convinced male leaders of peasant organisations to recognise explicitly the need for peasant women to establish militant organisations. The I National Congress of Peasant Women was held on the 10th of January 1980, which concluded with the creation of the 'Bartolina Sisa' National Federation of Bolivian Peasant Women (FNMCB"BS"), popularly known as the "Bartolinas"[15]. Lucía Mejía (Katarist tendency) was chosen as first Executive Secretary (León, 1990). Due to García Meza's coup, the second congress of the 'Bartolinas' could only be held in November 1983.

This is the background against which CIPCA's trajectory unfolds: its birth in 1971 and its gradual expansion to other regions from 1976 onward. Before writing about the first ten years of CIPCA it is necessary to revise the different currents of thought that nourished it during that time.

CURRENTS OF THOUGHT

One of the founders of CIPCA, Luis Alegre, had studied economics at the Sorbonne in Paris and had personally lived through the student revolution during the historic month of May 1968. During his theology studies he participated actively in the workers' pastoral in Barcelona. Francisco Xavier Santiago had studied economics in the USA and was a teacher at the Catholic University of Bolivia. The third founder, Xavier Albó, had studied anthropology and linguistics at Cornell University, New York, renowned for its Programme of community development in Vicos (Peru), financed by USAID.

In the 1950s the General Superior of the Company of Jesus, Jean-Baptiste Jansens, had already recommended that Jesuits in Latin America should become more engaged in social action and promotion. Thus Centres of Research and Social Action (CIAS) emerged in all Latin American countries. The Provincial Superior for Bolivia, Carlos Palmés, in turn entrusted Alegre, Santiago and Albó with the foundation of a CIAS in Bolivia. However, they considered that a CIAS ran the risk of being too intellectual and theoretical. In order for it to be better integrated into everyday reality, generic action had to be exchanged for concrete promotion, oriented specifically toward the peasantry. For that reason, instead of a CIAS, they founded CIPCA.

Previously, in 1966, the Company of Jesus had founded Cultural Action Loyola (ACLO), a sister institution that worked in the departments of Chuquisaca, Potosí and Tarija. There was also Christian Democracy's ARADO Project, carried out by the Centre for Socio-Economic Development of Communities (DESEC). Over these same years, similar institutions were founded in neighbouring countries like the Ecuadorian Fund *Populorum Progressio* (FEPP) in Ecuador (1970), the Centre for Research and Popular Education (CINEP) in Colombia (1970), CIPCA-Piura in Peru (1971) and the Bartolomé de las Casas Centre for Regional Studies in Cusco, Peru (1974).

Of all the major currents of thought of the 1960s and 70s, here we are interested in those that explicitly set out a political and ideological commitment with the popular sectors. Furthermore, this commitment is expressed not only in theory or theological reflection on the established social order, but also in concrete action. We will give a brief overview of liberation theology, liberation education and action-research to summarise the development theories of that time.

Liberation theology

Some Jesuits adhered to the force-idea of a "poor church, committed to the poor and the marginalised", part of the renovation of the II Vatican Council (1961-1964) and expressed in the encyclicals *Pacem in Terris* by Pope John XXIII (1963) and *Populorum Progressio* by Pope Paul VI (1967). Another source of inspiration was the Document of Medellín, conclusion of the II General Conference of the Latin-American Episcopate (1968), whose wealth consisted in having assumed, from Latin America, the pastoral orientations of the recently-concluded II Vatican Council.

During those years the so-called 'Third-Worldist' priests emerged, such as the legendary Camilo Torres in Colombia. Special mention should be made of the archbishop of El Salvador, Arnulfo Romero, and the heroic Jesuit Luis Espinal – a comrade of the CIPCA founders. Both men were assassinated within the space of one day.

As with the Cuban Revolution and the insurrection movements of that time, dialogue between Marxist theorists and Christian theologians has had certain influence on the political praxis of Christians. We find the first organised expression of a new liberation praxis in Brazil. Literacy and popular education programmes were carried out, mainly through teams from the Base Educational Movement, where Paulo Freire had his formative experiences. The military coup of 1964 put an end to this first attempt to work in ecclesiastic base communities. It is worth emphasising the influence exerted by the bishop of Recife, Dom Helder Camara, on the first generation of 'rebel priests'[16].

In Colombia the sociologist and university chaplain, Camilo Torres, opened a United Front for the socialisation of the means of production, which would finally lead him to opt for the guerrilla of the National Liberation Army (ELN). With the death of Camilo Torres, in an ambush in 1966, groups of theologists and priests were formed with a commitment to work beside the oppressed. One of these groups was ONIS (National Office of Social Information) in Peru. Periodical discussions and everyday political praxis spawned liberation theology, whose main spokesman became Gustavo Gutiérrez.

For Gutiérrez, liberation theology was inscribed in "the revolutionary struggle that radically questions the existing social order and postulates the need for popular power in order to construct a truly egalitarian and free society" (Gutiérrez, 1977: 13). "To opt for the poor is to opt for one social class in opposition to another. To become aware of the fact of confrontation between social classes and take the side of the dispossessed. To opt for the poor is to enter the world of the exploited social class, its values and cultural categories. It is to show solidarity with its interests and with its struggles" (ibid: 19).

Liberation Education

From the end of the 1960s the thought of Paulo Freire on awareness-building education began to gain currency as educational theory. The oppression suffered by a social class, an ethnic group or an entire people, and the means available to the oppressed with which to become conscious of it (consciousness of oppression) constitutes the central theme of *Pedagogy of the Oppressed* (Freire, 1968). In the final chapter, Freire expounds the theory of cultural action, seen as the dialectical unity of action and reflection. The general characteristics of that new educational paradigm rooted in the works of Freire and named "liberation education", are:
• educational activity that departs from the reality of the participants and their concrete historical situation, providing an awakening of consciousness in relation to their economic and social position;
• popular culture is considered a thing of value and deepens a sense of cultural identity;
• a horizontal pedagogical relation is sought; talk is of self-learning, self-evaluation and self-management;
• education is closely related to action: to depart from reality, reflect on it, return to it and transform it;
• it is important to stimulate organisation that permits community participation, and effective community intervention in the process of change.

When later we look over CIPCA's first activities, it may be clearly seen that the founders and the first employees were not only influenced by this new educational paradigm, but also contributed to its content.

Critical social science and action-research

Many young intellectuals rigidly applied the ideological principles of political organisation. To show the ideal nature of the committed intellectual, it was deemed sufficient to adopt historical materialism as a guide for configuring the 'proletarian science' that would oppose and neutralise 'bourgeois science'. But radical intellectuals found no concrete expressions of proletarian knowledge. Impatient with this situation, researcher-activists and their political comrades in leftist (Marxist-Leninist) parties began to inject their own definition of proletarian science into the base groups. In this way, party political education became a recipe-book for historical materialism and Leninist party theory. On the other hand, disappointment at the failure to configure a proletarian science meant that many intellectuals again retreated to their university bastions to continue the search for, and development of, a 'science for the people' (Fals Borda, 1978).

However, from these experiences a more positive current also emerged: critical social science, which considered knowledge as an essentially social product, continually changing in accordance with concrete historical conditions. "The last criterion of scientific knowledge's validity was to be praxis, which was understood as a dialectical unit formed by theory and practice in which practice is cyclically determinant" (ibid: 223).

In the 1960s there were increasing numbers of social scientists who worked with poor peasants or inhabitants of the urban barrios, directly confronting experiences of political repression. "It was no longer possible to see the people we studied or worked with only as an 'interesting object' or a 'client'[17]; rather we came to identify, willy-nilly, with their fate. During the IX Latin American Sociology Congress in 1969, it was officially declared that the social sciences should be placed at the Service of Human Rights and the creation of an economic, social and political democracy. Fals Borda described this congress as 'the culmination of an intellectual attitude, of a commitment to social change, with the necessary action to transform Latin American society, without losing scientific rigour" (Fals Borda, 1978). Stavenhagen has been one of the first scientists to explain that the ideological commitment of the social scientist with the *anti-status quo* can lead to the emergence of his or her role as activist, and not as a "mere participant or observer" (Stavenhagen, 1971:33). This gave rise to what would later be known as action-research and/or participative research. Instead of seeing people as simply an object of research, researchers should situate the people as the subject of research.

Action-research can be considered as the first experience of a critical social science which correctly incorporated the researcher's political commitment and concrete action. It also highlights the active participation of the 'people researched' in scientific work by sociologists, anthropologists and educators. In the first world congress on action-research, held in 1978 in Cartagena (Colombia), Xavier Albó had participated with a paper in which he explained how CIPCA had introduced action-research as one of its core activities. The first experiences with participative diagnostics in Caranavi (1979) were also a clear example of how CIPCA was one of the first institutions to apply participative research[18].

Rural development theories

From the 1960s development cooperation began to spread in European countries. It was justified implicitly and explicitly as a way of 'stemming the advance of international communism, as for example the Alliance for Progress of 1961. But it was also justified from a more humanistic position, seeking changes that improve the situation of the poor in so-called Third World countries.

Initially the problem of underdevelopment was presented as a problem of lack of western modernity. Rostow, advisor of the Alliance for Progress, considered the modernisation of society as indispensable, understanding modernisation as greater industrial development. The peasantry was considered a passive sector which presented various forms of resistance to modernisation, an obstacle to development. Consequently, the theorists of modernisation concentrated on the study of the cultural and psychological factors that might be found in the peasantry, which would explain the peasants as an obstacle to the spontaneous diffusion of modernity. The title of Banfield's book shows this clearly enough: *The Moral Basis of a Backward Society* (Banfield, 1958).

The debate over community development has embraced two broad polemics. The first is circumscribed by the general discussion on social change and the role of education (in its broadest sense). Community development was strongly based on a psychodynamic focus, sustaining that a change in peasant attitudes and values is a precondition for social change[19]. On the other hand, there were theories of development ranging from the need for material incentives to the imperative for social change as a precondition for the change of attitudes in itself (from an attitude of resistance to one of acceptance). Peasant resistance was analysed as a fatalist, individualist and conservative attitude. According to Erasumus (1968), the peasant is timid, mistrustful and apathetic because he lives in a situation of comprehensive material scarcity. One cannot expect initiatives or progress from anyone who has this 'pathological profile'. Equally, Foster (1965) explains the resistance to change by the fact that the peasants only have access to a limited amount of available goods. This scarcity can only be overcome at another's expense. Hence nobody wants to advance individually, since whoever takes possession of an inadequate portion of those 'limited goods', is despised and criticised. Significantly, these culturalist focuses coincided with the orthodox Marxist currents that considered the peasantry as an anachronistic traditional remnant. None of these theories credited the peasantry with the potential to participate decisively in the process of social change.

Such culturalist and Marxist approaches have been broadly refuted by Huizer (1976) who rightly argues that the problem of the peasant is not a purely psychological problem. A large part of the resistance to change is a rational attitude and shows the revolutionary potential of the peasantry: the resistance to change must be interpreted rather as a "resistance to minimal changes, which are basically useless and not structural" (ibid: 123).

The second polemic has to do with the supposed homogeneity of the community. For many years, the community was conceived as a homogeneous social unit, without internal conflicts or contradictions, where everything was developed and organised in total harmony, and where the people had a natural inclination towards cooperation and collective production.[20] Another focus dating from the 1970s and 1980s which also sprang from the notion of collective work was that of cooperativism, perceiving the community as an autonomous cooperative of workers that produced collectively and distributed equally.

The Cornell University experience in Vicos (Peru) began to change the system of land ownership of the hacienda so as to be able to do away with the master-servant relationship involving obligatory and unpaid work. This experience, similar to that of CIPCA in El Espino[21], overcame one basic limitation of community development programmes, because it departs from a recognition of conflicting interests at local level (Holmberg, 1966).

BIRTH (1971-1974)

CIPCA was conceived in October 1970 and its formal history began in January 1971. During the entire gestation period the three Jesuit founders were in intense contact with a pastoral team established in 1969 in the parish of Tiwanaku, some of whose reflexions and practices influenced in the initial focus. Similarly, the Maryknoll fathers and other priests and innovative religious figures were working in Altiplano communities, dedicated to the formation of catechists. The Jesuits wanted to manifest themselves among the people through the promotion and organisation of communities. After a series of meetings that lasted over a month, the conclusion was reached to prioritise attention to the peasantry, the country's most forgotten sector. Once this foundational decision was made, towards the end of November 1970, a name was also agreed upon: Centre of Research and Promotion of the Peasantry: CIPCA.

Catechists were trained in the parishes of Tiwanaku and Jesús de Machaqa on the initiative of the future bishop Monsignor Adhemar Esquivel, supported by a team of Jesuits and university students[22]. The parish of Tiwanaku filled with volunteers from the nascent Faculty of Social Work[23], which visited the communities and undertook activities within a Programme of "University Approach to the Community". The students that went out to the countryside took with them an ideological wave of structural change that was influenced by Marxism at a political level and by historical materialism at a philosophical level. Also emerging at this time was the culturalist current in Katarism that wanted to change pro-government unionism. The youth conducted activities of social promotion, but lacked profundity in their research into the zone's priority needs. In this way, the Tiwanaku group and the CIPCA founders linked up in order to undertake joint work.

Internal organisation

In a report on its first five years (CIPCA 1978) the founders describe how work was initially organised. The only available resources were the enthusiasm and conviction that something worthwhile was being created. The office operated in the house of the founders themselves[24]. The bed would be turned into a sofa to receive visitors during the day[25].

Apart from its tiny office in La Paz, CIPCA also acquired a small borrowed room in the parish of Tiwanaku. It was necessary to climb into trucks in order to make trips into the countryside; timetables were as unpredictable as the degree of safety. The initial fund was made up of 3,000 dollars saved by Xavier Albó from a grant, $5,000 from the Bolivian Jesuits' social fund and $1,500 from a donation by the Vatican's *Propaganda Fide* office (the oficial Vatican bank). In October 1973, thanks to help from *Oxfam*, CIPCA was able to leave the cramped rooms of its founders' residence and establish itself in more spacious and functional premises[26]. Finally, in January 1974, with the arrival of funds from Misereor, CIPCA became a formal institution with internal departments dedicated to specialised activities and increased staff of 16 regular members.

CIPCA's objectives were not defined overnight: this was a relatively long process, based upon some initial intuitions, which were conditioned by the real experience acquired during coexistence in the countryside. In a report dated November 1973 – two and a half years after CIPCA's birth – a certain in-depth consideration of its objectives is noticeable, including a first formulation of the three work dimensions that were later to characterise the CIPCA focus: "put our efforts into training the Aymara peasants, help in the reorganisation of their institutions to make them dynamic and functional, and seek a change in the peasants' socio-economic structures."

The integration of the peasantry into national life was not understood simply as assimilation into the dominant groups; neither was it mere isolationist 'autochthonism'. The aim was the peasantry's full participation as an equal in the country's economic and public life, respect for the peasants' particular mode of being and consideration of Bolivian cultural plurality. This peculiarity, already formulated in the early 1970s, shows that CIPCA has always taken seriously one of the most acute and conflictive problems in the history of Bolivia: pluricultural and intercultural coexistence. 35 years after its birth, CIPCA continues to prioritise this aspect.

As previously mentioned, CIPCA received a formal petition from bishop Esquivel to commence its activities on the Altiplano region, in coordination with the pastoral team of the parish of Tiwanaku. This request was influential above all in the choice of some of the first zones of work more than in the work's focus itself. It was not a matter of repeating something that the parish was already doing. It was a matter of doing something new.

In seeking to be representative of the Aymara peasant problematic of that time, towards 1972 CIPCA came to select three zones on the basis of critical aspects such as the local economy (which might fluctuate between the most traditional and the most market-oriented), local organisation (which might derive from a greater or lesser previous link with the hacienda system and current link with the city), and previous participation in militant political struggles (a necessary condition to ensure reception of the political message). In this way the following three work zones were chosen:

- *Jesús de Machaqa* (Ingavi province), which then contained some 40 communities and 15,000 inhabitants. It is a zone of the Altiplano rooted in its culture, traditional *par excellence*, which had been largely untouched by the haciendas. Its climate and land quality are especially adverse[27].
- *Achacachi* (Omasuyos province), then with some 60 communities and 50,000 inhabitants. It is another Altiplano zone which, due to better climatic conditions next to Lake Titicaca, had long been an area of haciendas and had maintained contacts of all kinds with the city. Since the recuperation of these lands in the 1953 Agrarian Reform, it became one of the most conflictive and politically-involved Aymara regions[28].
- *Coripata* (North Yungas province), then had some 30 communities and 10,000 inhabitants. It is a semi-tropical zone, long famous for its coca-cultivating (ex-) haciendas, coca being a traditional product to which later coffee and citrus were added, all of which was fully market-oriented. Consequently other types of economic, ecological and social problems emerged which, however, served to complete the 'shows' of the Aymara world that CIPCA had chosen as a field of work[29].

Activities

At the beginning the team offered its services to anyone who was interested. The first formal course of 'civic promotion" was held in Coripata, in April 1971, with the participation of some 30 peasants. It was the first formal activity to go beyond mere design and coexistence and set the CIPCA proposal in motion.

In the CIPCA focus, research and direct action activities had been conceived from the start as tasks that should always be developed simultaneously and interrelated to avoid two effects: theorisation and dogmatism on the one hand, and an activism without reflexive knowledge on the other. But, within this complementarity, CIPCA has known different styles of research. In its first years, anthropological studies were the overall focus of CIPCA research. The need was felt for a better understanding of the Aymara people's culture so as to be able to orientate the activities.

CIPCA was also keen to develop a research style that incorporated the peasant, but no longer as an 'object' but as a 'subject' of study, at the same time, making sure that the results of research 'returned' to their original source, and that they would be used, as far as possible, by the peasants themselves. The first work on Jesus de Machaqa, for example, was fruit of the first workshop with the local indigenous authorities, and provided material for later workshops. In this sense, researchers of CIPCA were inscribed in the new currents of social sciences in Latin America and later adhered to the concepts of popular education. However, in the first years, scientific research was still carried out according to traditional research methodologies and on frequent occasions the two activities –research and promotion – were relatively separate one from the other.

Most of the efforts were aimed at direct action in the Aymara peasant communities. A central aspect of the style of work in this first era was in training and awareness-raising among "civic promoters". As we have already seen, the initial idea of creating a network from this new category of promoters was greatly inspired in the methodology that already existed for the creation of networks of catechists, the intention of which was to maintain a complementary relationship. The notion was that the civic promoters, elected by the peasant communities, should be able to analyse their reality and identify the main needs of their communities.

In these first years innumerable communal short courses were given and regional meetings of the network of promoters were organised. Thus, in 1973, the formation of work teams was indentified as the year's principal objective; this would enable various civic promoters to exercise common leadership or at least coordinate within their communities. During this year the number of civic promoters rose to 136 and six short courses a week were given for the formation of promoters.

FIRST CONSOLIDATION (1974-1976)

Financial support from Oxfam and Misereor allowed consolidation of the initial process and facilitated access to other sources. Thus in 1975 CIPCA received a visit from Sjef Theunis, then director of Novib, a contact which has subsequently turned into a lasting relationship of cooperation. Other friends from international solidarity were Belgium's *Entraide et Fraternité*, the French Catholic Committee against Hunger and for Development, Christian Aid from England and Germany's EZE[30].

Internal organisation

On the 7th of January 1974 the internal statute of CIPCA was defined, as an autonomous institution constituted by the Company of Jesus, through a document signed by the Jesuit Father Jorge Trías, as interim Provincial Superior of the Jesuits in Bolivia[31], and the founders of CIPCA, Xavier Albó and Luis Alegre[32]. Armed with this document, CIPCA obtained its legal status on the 12th of February 1974. This was ratified on the 8th of August 1978 through a testimony of written approval of autonomy accorded to CIPCA by the "Society of Jesus".

In 1974 the CIPCA staff was still very limited: 16 on the payroll and various others employed on a casual basis or gradually incorporated as the institution obtained resources. The same people might occupy various positions on the organisation chart. For example, all the members of the management committee were at the same time organic staff of the institution, some with more executive duties, others more technical; researchers also travelled to the countryside and supported courses and other activities.

In response to its own declared commitment towards the countryside and the objectives and goals it had set, CIPCA was refining its focus and activities around three dimensions: economic, organisational and educational:

-Raising the peasant's economic-technical capacity, through an increase in production and productivity in its main crops, better commercialisation, etc;

Organising the peasantry at community, inter-community and even regional levels so that, as a social force, they may pursue and defend their own social interests;

-Overcoming all the ideological, educational and cultural impediments that, on the one hand, impeded the development of their knowledge, and on the other, prevented them from escaping their fate as a culturally oppressed mass.

To sum up, CIPCA's vision was that peasants should acquire greater economic strength, through their own dynamic, functional organisations. They should be armed with a coherent ideological awareness of what is happening to them and what should be done as a result. At that time the English loan word 'empowerment' still had not been introduced, but the theme was already clearly present.

Activities

In this institutional vision, it was assumed that objectives could be reached only when the three dimensions were the subject of a joint focus. These were CIPCA's famous "three legs". If the economic dimension were ignored, there was the risk of falling into simple politicising; if only the economic dimension were insisted upon, the result would be a developmentalism which, even if it made some improvement in living conditions, would leave the peasantry in a just as bad a situation of dependency, or one even worse than before. If the focus was purely educational, it would have no effect upon the structural causes of opresion.

Research

Research still figured as a separate entity from action, which embraced the agricultural training and extension departments. But at the beginning – due to CIPCA's modest size any researcher had also to perform other roles within CIPCA. We can distinguish three types of study that have been carried out in the 1970s:

- Research on social organisation: the first studies were mainly anthropological research. An important theme was that of relations within and between families in various zones on the Altiplano, looking for the underlying system of values and mechanisms that led to alliances or to the formation of certain conflicting groups within communities;

- Research toward non-formal education: the aim was to study non-formal education in a pluricultural context. The first studies were at a diagnostic level, attempting to understand the country's sociolinguistic and sociocultural profile, and the role that schools and communications media play in this context;

- Zonal studies: more comprehensive studies which covered the main social, economic and institutional aspects of a given region. These have been carried out on the Altiplano, in Sud Yungas province and in Coripata[33].

The principal channel of systematisation of these first studies constituted the *Research Notebooks,* whose first number appeared in 1973. The series was intended for a general public, in particular students, researchers, study centres, etc. to provide fresh ideas on the rural problematic. This series, as well as studies undertaken or commissioned by CIPCA, included some works by other scholars, whom CIPCA considered worth making known. Many of these studies were subsequently reedited, almost always with new contributions and formulations. In 2005, after 32 years, CIPCA published Research Notebook number 63[34].

Productive projects

The principal innovation after 1974 was a more complementary rapport between awareness-raising (of central importance until then) and the productive elements that constituted the great peasant demand. This latter was facilitated by the incorporation of new technical staff, under the direction of the engineer Adolfo Aramayo. But the extreme climatic conditions of the Altiplano did not facilitate the task in the slightest and in the process of its execution there was a lot to be learned for the institution itself.

After 1974 what were then called 'pre-projects', 'productive group projects' or 'project-packages' began to be drawn up. The idea was that these would be profitable and satisfactorily combine economic, organisational and awareness-raising dimensions. After a year with this focus, the team had reached the conclusion that the results had to be measured not only by good technical application, but also by their profitability and by the solution of the associated problems such as the supply of consumables, a way of obtaining investment capital and commercialisation of the product.[35]

Suma Wallpa

The first experimental Programme was called *Suma Wallpa* ('Good Hen': also the name of the corresponding support pamphlet). The Programme consisted initially in small units of production of eggs, on a family scale, with the application of modern chicken-rearing techniques, adapted to the peasants' reality and limitations.

The move from individual to associated production – a small group of families, rather than the community as a whole – was made after considerations that were practical as much as theoretical. At the practical level, it was clear that CIPCA's capacity would only allow it to tend to a very limited number of projects. But if these projects were connected, they could reach a greater number of families with less effort. At the theoretical level, it was hoped that with linked work it would be possible to help in strengthening the organisational sphere of the peasantry, which could then advance towards an economy of greater scale, more profitable than the typical small economy in which the families had operated. It was, besides, an era in which opposition to the existing military regime meant that notions of a socialist utopia were very much alive among the country's more progressive sectors.

At the beginning the project was seen as a success. It allowed an improvement in the participant families' diet and provided them with additional income from the sale of eggs, apart from providing a new organisational experience. However, one fine day many thousands of eggs began to appear in La Paz, on sale at lower prices, coming from Japanese farmers on the plains of Santa Cruz who produced on a much greater scale and at a lower price. It was impossible to compete, and the *Suma Wallpa* programme had to be closed.

Associated production of potatoes

The potato has been, since time immemorial, the most widespread product on the entire Altiplano. It is the fundamental staple for communities living at high altitudes. However, potato production and commercialisation was open to a series of technical improvements. It was included, as part of the project, in associated production using combined plots of land, which presupposed an important change in attitude. The project also included direct and coordinated commercialisation.

The results of this potato-growing Programme proved unforeseeable. In some years production was surprisingly good, but in others the frost wiped everything out. Due to the traditional importance of this crop, CIPCA and the villagers persisted for a long time with the potato without achieving stable and defined successes. Several years would go by until, in the 1980s, the difficult decision was taken to withdraw technical and credit support for this item, so central to the Aymara diet.

Other projects

In Coripata, in the subtropical Yungas where the principal crop was coca leaf, other kinds of projects were carried out. Although in those years the international cocaine *boom* had not yet begun, coca had an assured internal market in Bolivia, due to the traditional practice of mastication in the countryside and in the mines. Nor did it need greater technical assistance because the peasants traditionally mastered all the stages in this crop's cycle. For this reason CIPCA opted to seek complementary and diversifying alternatives. This sizing-up process passed through several trial-and-error options that included vegetables, to improve the family diet, strawberries and jam-making. But in the end almost all the efforts were concentrated on the associated commercialisation of coffee, the second local item.

Revolving Fund

Setting these diverse projects in motion implied, in many cases, some small initial credit in modest quantities. In these cases CIPCA served as a channel enabling peasants to obtain credit on favourable terms. Except for the initial experiences with family henhouses, CIPCA decided to facilitate credit only when it favoured groups that were already organised and had demonstrated a capacity for autonomous management.

It should be clarified that in those years only certain small producers had access to the Agricultural Bank of Bolivia (created in 1942) and that savings and credit cooperatives functioned only in urban areas. Since the peasants had no access to credits from the world of formal finance, the NGOs that worked with them began to give informal credits. Rotating funds were set up whose main characteristic was that, once the money was given back (with or without interest), the fund could be utilised for other activities in the same community.

The above-mentioned examples show that CIPCA was sincerely concerned with its contribution to the improvement of the peasant's economic situation. The characteristics of these proposals were typical of the kinds of ideas in vogue at that time: advising associated or communal production took preference over guidance for individual peasant families. Ideas on the economic organisation of peasant family units still did not contemplate the logic of production and organisation of the peasant economy. Not only CIPCA, but many promotion organisations besides, imposed their own notions of ideal forms of organisation, without taking economic logic into account. So, in the 1970s, the peasants were induced to adopt collective forms of economic organisation that did not always help to improve production and productivity.

Support for peasant organisation

After 1974 there was less and less talk of "civic promoters" and much more of "union leaders" and of "productive groups". The previous work of civic promotion, through short courses in innumerable places, permitted CIPCA to know much more about the reality of the peasant community and the role within it played by the so-called 'peasant union', a name that ever since the Agrarian Reform of 1953 had been given, in many parts of the country, to the old communal organisation.

The debate within CIPCA and of other NGOs concerned whether or not it was convenient to support union organisation, which at its highest level maintained the formal structure spread by the MNR with the Agrarian Reform, and which continued to support the government under the influence of the Military-Peasant Pact. In the countryside around La Paz, however, the unions were not so prone to pro-government stances. The Tupaj Katari Revolutionary Movement had opted for support from the union organisations at community level, without accepting the aforementioned pact[36]. The Independent Peasant Block, on the other hand, rejected that pro-government unionism and, along with it, the union organisation at community level.

Little by little, emphasis was passing from the network of civic promoters to that of communal authorities, which appeared with the title of "union" leaders. The main expression of this process was the decision taken by CIPCA not to create any kind of new organisation within the peasantry. The organisation was already there, and it was called peasant union. CIPCA reached the conclusion that, despite the deferential pro-government character of the peasant union organisation at its higher levels, at the base level it was the ancestral matrix organisation of the community, called *ayllu*. The main difference was that since 1953 it had this new name, apparently more "modern". On the other hand, "union" discourse was opening the door to broader organisational applications, militant in nature. Instead of creating something new, CIPCA dedicated itself to strengthening that organisation, making it independent of the strong governmental guardianship that it still had.

In 1974 Jenaro Flores himself, who had returned to the country after his exile from the Banzer coup, proposed to CIPCA the organisation of a first short course with leaders from Aroma province, his native region. Accompanied by one of his followers, representatives of CIPCA were making clandestine visits from house to house, inviting the community leaders. It was enough to tell them: "Jenaro needs you" to pledge their commitment to attend the meeting. One of the key activities in that course was the presentation of various sociodramas on military repression, followed by prolonged plenary reflection. This historic short course in Patacamaya was the starting point for the restructuring of the Katarist movement underground. Similarly, the work of organisationally strengthening CIPCA began to have a referent, both ideological and organisational, that went far beyond each community. In the future, CIPCA was to have the task of escorting and advising peasant (then also indigenous) organisations not only at communal level, but also at provincial, departmental and national levels.

Education and training

With its greater institutionalisation, after 1974 CIPCA also redefined its style of work. Unlike research, promotion required division into various 'departments' depending on the specificity of the work to be developed. Besides, each one of the three working zones required a person to act as a nexus between the office staff and the different communities, so that the programmed activities would have certain coherence. The activities in each zone were mostly short courses, but their content might be technical, organisational or educational. They required, besides, appropriate didactic materials and differentiated teaching methodologies. Given the responsibility for organising this tangle in some way, after 1974 Hugo Fernández was hired to preside over the recently-created Training Department.

In order to put this new strategy into practice, the training department had to adopt two different styles: intensive and extensive work. The former consisted of direct and continuous action in the three selected zones after 1972. There were short courses, each better delineated than the last, under those responsible for the zone or for training itself. Another group of activities was added, which were of greater overall impact but less intense, which constituted "extensive work". These extensive activities were centralised in the new Broadcasting Department under Néstor Hugo Quiroga, and basically included two lines of work: radio programmes and the drawing-up of popular pamphlets.

Radio and written broadcasting

In 1973 the first attempts had been made to incorporate a scriptwriter and an operator for the making of radio programmes. The work began with a campaign of backing for the CIPCA action team's efforts in the work zones, through short, repetitive and permanent messages, and with the Programme *CIPCA Informs*, which went out every day.

From 1974, thanks to the contribution of *Misereor* and *Oxfam*, CIPCA was able to install a complete recording studio in which three hours' programming a day were made and then broadcasted through Radio San Gabriel, property of the Maryknoll fathers. Apart from its informative functions, the central activity was a radio serial in Aymara, under the name *Panqar Marka* (People of the Flowers). Its central theme was the joy, sorrows and problems of the peasants in their Aymara communities. New complementary programmes were also created, all of them in Aymara, intended for an exclusively peasant audience. They had titles in Spanish such as *The peasant thinks and opines, Technology and the countryside, CIPCA in the peasant's heart, Let's all think together* and *CIPCA informs*. One of the commentaries collected during those years summed up the type of impact produced by this focus: "…CIPCA programmes entertain and amuse – and, in the process, they also make us think."

From 1975, with an already fully assured audience, *Panqar Marka* ceased to be an entertaining radio soap-opera, to be transformed into the centre of an entire distance-learning programme that focused, from various viewpoints, on the problems and feelings of the Aymara people. Apart from all this, a system of peasant participation was organised. Within this framework, for example, a competition was held for stories in the oral tradition told by the peasants themselves. 78 popular narrators participated, eight groups carrying out the edition and illustration of the stories. Equally fundamental was the creation and broadcasting of the radio serial *Julián Apaza* (= Tupaj Katari), with similar characteristics.

Juan Pando, who worked in those years as technical operator in the Broadcasting department had the following commentary on the radio programmes' function:

"*Before 1980, during the Banzer dictatorship, programmes went out camouflaged. In other words they were codified; programmes like, for example, 'Tales of the Achachila' had stories with animal characters in situations that peasants were living through at that time. In the short courses it was perfectly clear that people understood it all. A letter sent from the countryside, about 'Tales of the Achachila', put it literally: 'The lion is Banzer, the dogs are his military, the sheep are us...' Naturally, we couldn't reproduce it like that over the radio."*

Inocencio Cáceres, who worked between 1974 and 1984 as an Aymara presenter and scriptwriter, told us:

"More than presenters we worked as historians. Panqar Marka captured much of the peasants' reality. Panqar Marka means 'People of the Flowers'. There were other opposed communities, in this serial, such as Wila Marka, which means 'Red People'. The communities did not want to join the Reds, but eventually did so. The serial was a huge success. I remember they wanted to call one of their communities Panqar Marka. Through these serials CIPCA became very well-known and for CIPCA it was a way into the countryside. So as not to lose our audience we developed another radio serial, 'Willka Marka'[37] and a Programme about Unionism and the Chaco War. Again, visits to the office doubled. For example, in 1975 450 peasants came; in 1976: 971; in 1977: 879 and in 1978: 1278. What interests people is their own history. CIPCA played an important role in awakening the peasantry through their own history and giving value to their own personality".

After 1975, CIPCA's other form of extensive work was written diffusion. In the first short courses and trips to the communities, the participants always asked for something written so as not to forget the things they had learned and discussed. In this way a series of small duplications was born. Some of them reflected group discussions, others recorded more formal talks. In several cases they dealt with the same themes as the radio serials or the contributions of the peasants to the whole *Panqar Marka* system, such as the one called *Jiwasan Arusawa*, an anthology from a radio competition for Aymara poetry, which was published in 1975.

Some of these duplications were later turned into pamphlets, redrawn up by the Broadcasting Department. Some examples are: *Suma Wallpa, Our History,* the *Peasant and the Law, Rural Accounting, Potato cultivation, History and cultivation of cacao*, etc. This latter example was the first attempt at a publication that combined technical elements with others aimed more at raising awareness, with a text that incorporated both the history of this autochthonous crop – chocolate – and the problems involved in its commercialisation.

Self-evaluation

Various evaluation and self-evaluation reports reflect certain doubts about the work. Firstly, there were still many misgivings with respect to productive proposals.

There were people who supported communal forms of organisation, others who preferred technical advice and directed those individual peasants who wanted innovation. In synthesis, the opinions expressed within CIPCA mirrored the general debate on the process of change: idealists seeking a socialist society versus theorists of modernisation.

One strong criticism was aimed at the limited coordination between promotional activities and research. The relation between research activities and the immediate demands of action was not always fluid. Action teams sometimes complained that it was a waste of time carrying out studies that would only later produce results. Researchers, in turn, criticised the activist insistence on excessively immediate results and defended their own focus, arguing that the results of their studies would be of medium-term help in the global focus of CIPCA and in anticipating problems before they occurred.

This dichotomy between doers and thinkers, activists and researchers, those who worked more in the countryside and others who were office-based, has existed ever since CIPCA was born and has continued to exist until the decision was made not to have separate offices for researchers.

Another debate revolved around the theme of whether the peasants are resistant to change, whether they have revolutionary potential and what should be CIPCA's role: vanguard or accompany. It was noticeable that, in this debate, there was no clarity over the role of CIPCA. Questions included whether CIPCA wanted to impose a change not wanted by the peasants, whether the process of change would be too rapid for the peasants and whether CIPCA also wanted to act in the name of the peasant organisations. These are still valid questions today, because discussion continues over whether the peasants oppose change and whether they want to modernise. We will also see developments in the debate over whether the institution would be simply a facilitator, accompanying the peasants in their process of organisational strengthening, or if CIPCA could and should be an actor *sui generis*. This discussion has continued throughout the history of CIPCA and is still a matter of constant debate without any single, clear reply.

EXPANSION (1976-1980)

CIPCA was born with a national vocation and wanted to contribute to structural change across the country. It had begun its work in La Paz for what were then unavoidable strategic reasons. But now, as it consolidated this first headquarters, opportunities seemed to open up for expansion to other cities which, ever since its foundation, CIPCA had characterised as the *socio-economic axis of the country*: namely

La Paz – Cochabamba – Santa Cruz.

In 1976 came the inauguration of the new CIPCA offices, opened in Cochabamba and Charagua (in the Chaco) and finally, in 1978, a fourth office was created in the city of Santa Cruz. After assuming an Aymara face for the first years of its life, CIPCA was acquiring a Quechua, Guaraní and coloniser face, thus increasing its range of experience so as to reach conclusions that were ever more representative of the national rural problematic.

A detailed analysis of how each office was set in motion shows the way in which a single foundational idea was shared, but also shows the broad margins of creativity and adaptation that each new office enjoyed in the process of finding its own strategy and way of functioning. Firstly we will see how CIPCA adapted in terms of organisational development to the new situation of four offices, before pausing on the history of each one of them. The chapter ends with some reflections on how the political-organisational dimension was very present in those years in the daily debates in CIPCA.

CIPCA National

Internal organisation

Growth meant change across CIPCA's entire organisation chart. At the beginning, in 1976, the new Cochabamba and Charagua offices liaised with La Paz without major restructuration. But in 1977 a Management Committee had already begun to function regularly as the main decision-making organ, and a National Directorship oversaw the La Paz, Cochabamba and Charagua offices. Within the management committee Xavier Albó and Luis Alegre, independently of their posts, maintained their roles as legal representatives and links with the Company of Jesus, from whose legal status that of CIPCA was derived. The other members of the management committee were Carlos Quiroga in Cochabamba, Marcos Recolons in Charagua and Rafael Puente in Santa Cruz. Four of these five men were Jesuits. After 1978 the directorship of CIPCA La Paz passed into the hands of Hugo Fernández, who was thus incorporated into the management committee. Xavier Albó stayed in the department of research, where he is still working today. In the first meeting of the management committee Luis Alegre, until then general manager, was nominated first National Director of CIPCA

A fundamental debate about the general structure of this new CIPCA was then inevitable. CIPCA had already expanded to four regions with distinct problems, handled by people who all had their own ideas and, at times, different political commitments. It was common to hear discussions described as the *Unitarians versus the Federalists*. The Unitarians were in favour of a single national institution with four subordinate 'departmental' offices, and the Federalists wanted four departmental institutions, independent but associated in a federation with the aim of coordinating policies and actions. Also influential were considerations of a party political nature. Cochabamba had a focus more explicitly tied to MIR (at that time more clearly leftwing than in subsequent years) and wanted their staff to be of the same political persuasion. Because of this it was said that it had a 'monochrome' option, seeking greater autonomy from the rest of CIPCA. The other three offices, in contrast, had a 'polychrome' focus, with distinct policy tendencies. The La Paz office and the national office were closer to Katarism and emphasised that CIPCA should not identify, as such, with any party. Santa Cruz was closer to radical Trotskyite groups. For the people in Charagua not only political interests, but also pragmatic reasoning, entered the debate. The Charagua office had begun life as much more of a natural expansion of work in the parish and, as such, its everyday reference was still the parish rather than the rest of CIPCA. Its administrative relations with the central office were also encumbered by distance and poor communication.

Throughout its history the CIPCA management committee has maintained the original principle of unity, befitting a single institution with its own mission, objectives and goals. However, the organisational and administrative format has known different eras, some with more centralised administration and others more decentralised. During the 1970s the arguments in this debate were political in nature, as opposed to the prevalence of managerial arguments during the 90s.

With the expansion to new regions, the quantity of cooperation agencies was also on the increase. In the second half of the 1970s, CIPCA already had financial and technical support from Oxfam, Misereor, EZE (today EED), Novib, SNV, DED and Christian Aid.

Besides its more specific work, CIPCA has been actively involved in forming networks and working within them. By 1976, under the military dictatorship, CIPCA already participated in the creation of the National Union of Institutions for Social Action Work (UNITAS). UNITAS was founded on the 23rd of March 1976, constituting a defence mechanism with which to confront the threat posed by military dictatorships inimical to institutions dedicated to popular promotion in a context of systematic repression. UNITAS was founded by 5 organisations[38]; today there are 29 associated institutions.

Library
Before moving on to the history of the four CIPCA offices, it is opportune to pause briefly on the history of an activity that, despite being secondary, is

nonetheless of great importance. There are few NGOs that have taken so much care in archiving, not only their own publications and internal documents, but also books, leaflets and documents from other persons and institutions.

The small La Paz office was stocked with archives, didactic materials and most of CIPCA's specialised library, initially made up of the founders' personal books, particularly Xavier Albó's and a valuable donation from Sra. Blanca Muñoz Vda. de Ormachea. One librarian worked part-time in both the cataloguing of books and in attending to university students. Towards the end of 1975 the CIPCA Library already contained some 7,000 volumes. Thanks to a book review service, the exchange of publications, a small regular budget and occasional donations, this was constantly increasing. For example, in 1976 the British Council donated a set of British publications in socioeconomic and agricultural sciences. After 1976 a close collaboration began with the recently-created Centre of Information and Documentation of Bolivia (CEDIB). Unfortunately this centre's materials, including those that CIPCA provided, were destroyed by the military during General García Meza's coup in 1980.

CIPCA La Paz

Within the research team, even when an interdisciplinary focus was seen as important, agreement did not always turn out to be easy. Economists and agronomists often had more pragmatic ideas, whilst sociologists and anthropologists emphasised political analysis. The same dichotomy was visible in the field; the educators' focus was more ideological, and that of field technicians more pragmatic. One of the technicians said in an interview:

CIPCA had no real interest in doing agricultural work. There were sufficient requests for technical assistance, but CIPCA did not attend to them. It only wanted to do things through a group. There was always an exaggeration of the political and organisational issues.

In principle, the same three work zones were viable as in the previous period: Jesús de Machaqa and Achacachi (Altiplano), and Coripata (Yungas).

The presence in Jesús de Machaqa was concentrated in the few communities that had managed to fit in associated productive projects. The greater emphasis on Achacachi was due to two factors: there were more visible productive possibilities, and the people showed greater union and political muscle, precisely at moments in which democratic openness was beginning in the country and in which the Katarist Movement was in its first fervour. Katarist leader Víctor Hugo Cárdenas was, at that time, responsible for CIPCA's organisational and educational work in this region.

In the course of 1977 CIPCA decided to work systematically in the zones of colonisation: the region of Alto Beni and the neighbouring area of Caranavi. In 1979, it decided to abandon its work in Coripata.

The experience in Caranavi is an example of how action-research was understood in these years. The Caranavi leaders presented a proposal: they were interested in a census, but one done by them and for them. CIPCA pondered the pros and cons and agreed to work with them on both the census and a complementary in-depth survey. At the beginning of 1980 a broad multidisciplinary team was mobilised that practically transformed one of the hotels in the town of Caranavi into an office. The team spent several months alongside local leaders and people conducting the surveys, travelling around the 160 communities contained by this vast region. The questionnaires were discussed, together with the leaders, during numerous short courses and meetings. Both Alto Beni and Caranavi, with almost 100,000 inhabitants, were becoming a new field of action for CIPCA. But just as this work was under way, so new and participative, García Meza's military coup arrived, and everything was brusquely cut short.

What was causing a bottleneck on the frigid Altiplano was still the technical aspect. CIPCA still had not drawn up a productive proposal and its efforts were based on the sound initiatives of the technicians through a process of trial and error. Worthwhile to mention are crop rotation proposals, improvements in pasture, animal health such as cattle vaccination, control of foot-and-mouth disease and carbuncles, and the use of salt and mineral complements.

The economy of the colonisation zone was distinct from that of the Altiplano: it was a marked oriented economy, based on the produce of coffee, bananas, cacao and, to a lesser degree, citrus. In Alto Beni the chief product, and the one considered as having most potential, was cacao.

1978, the year of the first elections after many years of dictatorship, was for CIPCA a difficult year because of the need to refocus its programmes and adapt them to various changes in Bolivia's political situation, particularly in the peasant sector. CIPCA decided to give support to peasant reorganisation, which felt an increasing need for independence from the Military-Peasant Pact[39]. Xavier Albó remembers:

Soon after the triumph of the hunger strike, the first provincial congress with a focus on reorganisation was held in Umanata. The leaders, fearing military reprisals, asked for support from CIPCA. Víctor Hugo Cárdenas, who attended Congress, was authorised to make the journey in the CIPCA jeep. I also went, the following day, but in the bishop's jeep, as a member of the Episcopal Human Rights Commission. Indeed, a Katarist candidate won the leadership of the congress. The pro-government leaders, and the military who were advising them as coordinators of the Military-Peasant Pact, were highly irritated. The CIPCA jeep was stolen and they made an attempt to ambush the newly-appointed leaders.

Luckily we appeared in time with the bishop's jeep, quickly called the parish priest and the nuns and were able to rescue those under threat, hidden under a lorry. Those were hard but challenging times.

In 1979 a difficulty arose for the broadcasting department, which had been one of the stars of recent years. Radio San Gabriel interrupted the collaboration with CIPCA. Various factors contributed to this setback. The first was that ownership of the radio station passed from the Maryknoll fathers to the sisters of La Salle. The second was that a recently-created institution, Community Education and Radio (ECORA), offered Radio San Gabriel to pay more for broadcasting space than what CIPCA could afford. Finally, something that also caused further estrangement was the openness with which some Aymara presenters disseminated their *Katarist* and *indigenista* ideas. They were taking advantage of the new democratic openness and the fact that the director of CIPCA's broadcasting department had only a limited knowledge of Aymara. This was first-hand experience of the vulnerability that came from not owning the medium of diffusion, even though this freed the institution from a series of administrative worries[40].

The young filmmaker Alfonso Gumucio entered CIPCA, who not only obtained better films but also began shooting another film, which was in super 8 format (video was still unknown at this time). Using this dual path he began to set up a small "rural film institute" which, from March 1980, was called *Luis Espinal*, in honour of the Jesuit and filmmaker, very close to CIPCA, who was later assassinated by the 'narco-military' which soon truncated the incipient democratic process. Previous to this experience of cinematographic production with educational ends, CIPCA had made other similar ventures with the production of two films on its areas of work as part of promotional efforts by support agencies Oxfam (England) and Novib (Holland) with the aim of raising funds in their own countries[41].

CIPCA Cochabamba

The valleys of Cochabamba have been known since time immemorial as Bolivia's breadbasket and they support the country's highest demographic concentrations. These valleys were the cradle of the first peasant unions and their hard-won Agrarian Reform. They are also the heart of the Quechua nation, Bolivia's most numerous native group.

In 1975 a small sign saying 'CIPCA' appeared in Augusto Jordán's office window, in Calle San Martín, Cochabamba. As yet it was more symbolic than real. Jordán, a solicitor, was merely an *ad honorem* representative who knew the CIPCA mystique well. At that time he worked mainly in providing legal assistance to the peasantry. Jordán had previously written a brief document entitled *The peasant and the law* together with Néstor Hugo Quiroga[42]. The aim of this document was to make the peasants aware of their human rights. In these difficult times of dictatorship it was an additional risk to speak of rights, but CIPCA offered ways of doing so.

The use of the pamphlet in short courses had much greater resonance than expected. With such stimulating results it was considered opportune to establish, in the La Paz office, a more institutionalised service of peasant legal consultancy. Its function was to inform the peasants and explain their rights to them, since they were frequently submitted to mockery, deceit and abuse. Modest financing was requested and obtained from Entraide et Fraternité, from Belgium, and two young solicitors were contracted on a part-time basis. One of these, Juan del Granado, would become famous years later, firstly as the main prosecutor in the trial of the dictator García Meza, then as leader of the Without Fear movement and mayor of La Paz. Unfortunately after its first year the consultancy had to close as it was unable to find new and more stable financing.

The CIPCA office in Cochabamba was really set in motion, with its own premises, in 1976. Its first director was Carlos Quiroga, a sociologist from Cochabamba who had recently returned from the University of Louvain (Belgium) full of new ideas on how to energise the peasantry. Like many Bolivian ex-Louvain students, he was also an active militant of the Revolutionary Left Movement (MIR). Previously, in the late 1960s, he had been a Jesuit student and in this capacity he had founded ACLO in Chuquisaca. Before long a secretary and a research assistant were added to the team.

Ideologically, CIPCA Cochabamba sought a form of peasant production that allowed productive forces to transform the production relations. It wanted to reinforce the collective activities of production as the peasants' response to traders and buyers-up. Supposedly, due to the individual nature of their production, the peasants were unfamiliar with the macro economic system. Besides, they lacked organisation for economic purposes.

CIPCA Cochabamba's proposal was inscribed in the development paradigm that considered collective production as superior to individual production. Influenced by Marxism and Dependency Theory, it held that at local level the smallholding would have to be replaced by collective forms of production and commercialisation. CIPCA Cochabamba attempted to reinforce collective activities of production as the only viable way that the economies of small producers could emerge from their stagnation. Later we will see that these ideas were ideologically biased and did not take into consideration the economic logic of peasant families.

Paradoxically, the CIPCA office in Cochabamba was the first to accept the validity of the rules of the capitalist game. It sold consultancy services to the National Electricity Company (ENDE), which asked it to carry out a study. With the earnings from this, it was the first to buy a spacious office of its own, barely three years after its foundation.

CIPCA Cochabamba implemented a style of work very much its own, much more extensive and wider-ranging than that developed in La Paz, tending toward the structuring of an association that would embrace all the producers of the department. The Association of Potato Producers (APP) began to develop in the province of Tiraque, after which CIPCA Cochabamba provided advice in extending its coverage and influence at departmental level.

The hope was that, through the APP, the surplus extracted by the traders would be recuperated by the producers themselves, consequently seeking to set up a commercialising mechanism. As a result the work concentrated on supporting commercialisation.

In 1976, the APP was formally constituted, with participation of the peasants of the department as a whole, as an instrument of union renovation. The APP needed a headquarters: CIPCA provided space in its own office, an administrative team and a legal advisor, who worked at the service of the APP. CIPCA also played a leading role in the purchase of consumables, in commercialisation, the keeping of accounts, etc. All this was done under the assumption that the peasant organisation still lacked the knowledge and capacity to do so independently.

Martha García, a history professor who worked first in administration, later in education and, finally, became director shortly before the García Meza military coup[43], remembers:

We started in two small, dark rooms with two desks. I was secretary, messenger and porter. The peasants saw me as a mother figure because I used to wear black clothes (I had been widowed) and I slept in the countryside with the nuns. We started in Tiraque at the Jesuits' request in 1977. We had the help of three Dutch volunteers. We had a great deal of mobilisation and motivation; we gave all the members an inscription book and membership credentials. There were also short courses on production costs and market analysis. We had not expected so much enthusiasm. We used to do everything: purchase of consumables, importation of fertilisers, storage and sale of the potatoes, etc. In order to know the logic of the intermediaries, Domingo Mendoza, a Peruvian economist, used to do the market analysis while travelling to Santa Cruz by truck with the potatoes.

Mónica Méndez (ex-secretary of CIPCA Cochabamba) remembers that the APP remained in the CIPCA offices until 1983:

At times it was impossible to get into the office because the stairs and corridors were full of sacks of potatoes, peasants with their children, etc.

Martha García remembers also how they opened the first bank account in the name of the APP:

I didn't even know how to open a bank account. The leaders arrived with a backpack full of jumbled cash. We had to sort out the money on our knees on the floor of the bank. After having counted it, we realised that it came to a million Bolivian pesos.

The intimate relationship between CIPCA and the APP, in which the role of support institution was confused with that of a peasant organisation, was typical not only of CIPCA. At that time there were various private organisations that acted simultaneously as grassroots organisations. In Cochabamba, for example, the Institute of Education and Rural development (INEDER) – also financed by Novib – acted 'in the name of' the Association of Wheat Producers (APT). The enthusiasm of the young intellectuals and the faith in being able to effect short-term structural change meant the roles and responsibilities of each one were confused.

On the other hand, it is just to mention that the APP was a success at all levels. In the first year it managed to affiliate 500 members. It had begun to make its presence felt in the Cochabamba agricultural world. In the middle of 1978, it had already amassed 6,500 members spread over 59 local associations and seven provinces. Its growth was truly spectacular.

Each local association, in each community, implied new forms of grassroots organisation. New economic approaches and demands were emerging: fair prices, credits, cheap consumables, direct access to transport and to markets. To some extent, the peasantry and their communities were developing the new organisation *at the margins* of pro-government unionism, at that time still under the tutelage of the Military-Peasant Pact.

The CIPCA team considered, from the beginning, that these associations could be the ones charged with "returning economic content to the union struggles and to the union itself", and, stemming from this proposition, sought also to strengthen a new unity of peasant organisation in which, on the one hand, the union would also make claims of an economic nature and, on the other, the associations would come to transcend their primarily economic level.

The APP had more success in the joint purchase of consumables than in the complex scenario surrounding the sale of its products, in which many more factors came into play, such as the varieties of potato, the seasons for sowing and harvest, and distances to market. An activity that ended in failure, showing that CIPCA had gone too far in its support for the APP, and that the two were becoming confused in their roles, was the purchase of several lorries for the work of some associations. CIPCA obtained twelve of these vehicles, which turned out to be inappropriate and their maintenance too expensive. It was impossible to salvage the products and, consequently, to stock up and pay the peasants.

A final reflection on the first five years of CIPCA-Cochabamba comes from Martha García:

In the workshops we reflected on the role of the union and the role of the peasant movement throughout history. We were also active in the organisation of the APP itself and one could perceive a certain unfamiliarity with reality: in fact, we had theoretical proposals, that did not fit to reality. Besides, we made the error of concentrating on the leaders who, at times, created distortions and felt like gods.

The perception grew that there was an excessive identification of the APP with CIPCA, which was not convenient for either of the two institutions. The decision was made to seek greater independence for both, without losing contacts or mutual relations and without interrupting the educational and organisational work that CIPCA was doing with the APP.

CIPCA Charagua

Cordillera province was the traditional territory of the Guaraní. Until the 1960s, this region was remote and isolated, but in the 1970s the Santa Cruz boom had already begun to be felt. The Agrarian Reform of 1953 did no favour the Guaraní indigenous population; on the contrary, it served to legalise the usurpation of communitarian lands by the hacienda-owners. The landowners were able to legitimise and consolidate the usurpation of communal lands and, in several cases, obtained land grants for public land. Thus, the Agrarian Reform was consolidating and legalising a hacienda concept in which both the captive communities (on the hacienda lands) and the free ones (on lands bordering the hacienda)[44], served it as providers of permanent and almost free manpower (Soliz, 1995).

Cordillera was considered a cattle-raising province, with little agricultural tradition. In the 1970s the Guaraní villagers of the region used to go en masse to the sugar cane harvest, where they might spend as long as half the year. With such an outlook dominated by temporary migration they became tied indefinitely to the landlords for the years to come, by means of the classic system of advance payment and permanent debt[45].

The new CIPCA office in Charagua had its historical roots in the pastoral work of the Jesuits, who had arrived in January 1964. The efforts of the parish priest, father Gabriel Siquier, a Jesuit of Spanish origin, were always characterised by a profound preoccupation by the socio-economic situation of the Guaraní people. The parish priest used to go to the harvest every year with the Guaraní. He would even stay to cut cane, trying of offer them support with his personal presence to help them through those months of gruelling, badly-paid work.

In the 1970s two young Jesuits arrived, Francisco Pifarré – nicknamed Pifa – and

Marcos Recolons, establishing themselves as rural professors in two communities of the Isoso captaincy[46]. A few years previously, Marcos Recolons had participated in a survey conducted by ACLO in the zone. Years later he would become National Director of CIPCA.

The Charagua Jesuits sought contact with the Jesuits of CIPCA in La Paz, among other reasons because the Head Captain of the Guaraní, Bonifacio Barrientos -the leader and founder of the Indigenous Central of the Bolivian Oriente (CIDOB)- had suggested to them that, apart from the education of their children, the defence of the land and production were also important matters. They then began to be concerned with improving the agricultural performance of the Guaraní people, trying thus to stem the annual exodus towards the sugar harvest and, at the same time, consolidating their ownership over the land.

Marcos Recolons relates:

We saw the situation of the cane-cutters and of the Guaraní people, whose very existence was threatened the plunder of their land by the stockbreeders, and by the migration of many of them. This situation was analysed to fund with the mburuvichaguasu, Bonifacio Barrientos, monarch and patriarch of the Isoso, and with his second captains. We were faced with a dilemma: continue as rural teachers, or firmly support this new productive project. Resolving this was a long struggle and with moments of profound crisis and desolation, but we finally decided that the explicit demands of the Guaraní people were more important than our approaches to personal spirituality.

A land dispute in El Espino[47] provided an opportunity to establish relations with CIPCA. Marcos Recolons and Pifa travelled to La Paz, seeking and finally obtaining legal support for the villagers. Besides this they secured the commitment of CIPCA to initiate a productive communal project in those same lands that they had just saved[48].

Out of the struggle for the land the idea of the *Work Community*[49] was also born. Before embarking on the El Espino experience, which lasted all of 1975, there was some very serious and studious reflection over which technical and organisational modality to adopt. Work began, not with all the community, but with a group that decided to sever links with the sugar harvest and stay the whole year round in the community, which entailed a radical change. It should be pointed out that several Guaraní captains were also employers of sugarcane cutters, and they did not like the intromission of CIPCA in this sphere.

The Jesuits of Charagua presented a formal request for stable association to CIPCA, despite the distance that separated them from La Paz. The fundamental reason was that they felt the need for the support of a specialised institution to complement educational work with economic and organisational dimensions.

On the part of CIPCA, the acceptance of this proposal took several months of reflection and reconnaissance trips to the zone. From CIPCA's perspective, arguments against this move were the lack of resources, the strategically marginal character of that rural sector, the lack of communications (there was not even a telephone) and the dire conditions of travel from La Paz – an hour by plane to Santa Cruz, then many more uncertain hours by train to Charagua (between 8-10 hours). CIPCA's decision, however, was not unanimous.

While the political focus was stronger in CIPCA La Paz and CIPCA Cochabamba, in Charagua thought focused more on the technical-productive, supporting a new model of economic organisation: the work community or CDT. In these first years the political focus and, even more so, party political variants, were almost absent from the Charagua office.

In January 1976 the decision was finally made to create the new regional CIPCA office. At that moment there was finance to the tune of 5,000 dollars, coming from a donation to the parish by *Mission and Development*[50] in Spain.

To begin with, the work community model had to free those who wanted to initiate the experiment from their debts in the sugar-cane harvest. A 'lightning operation' was carried out.

Marcos Recolons recalls:

In Isoso we worked with two communities, but the peasants were tied by debt to the sugarcane landlords. For that reason, they had to go to the harvest against their will, and had no possibility of starting the land preparation work that the CDT required. In order to free the sugarcane-cutting peasants wanted by the CDT from their debts, we obtained a credit fund. Thanks to short courses in accounting we had done, we were able to calculate precisely the exact amount each of them owed. In a lightning operation, which took the sugar landlords by surprise, we gave them back the money that each cutter from the two CDTs owed them, and off we went with them before the landlords could even react.

From the beginning, the principal line of CIPCA's work in Charagua was the formation of CDTs, first in El Espino, then in communities of the Isoso region and, little by little, also in other places. It wasn't easy; the process meant the team and of the local people had to feel their way along and learn as they went. One difficulty was convincing people who had always worked under orders from a landlord that they were now capable of working independently as small farmers. They saw the CIPCA people as bosses.

Hugo Arias, a villager from El Espino in the Pifarré and Albó book (1986:132):

Everyone works together. So, at the same time, you are owner and worker, the same. There's no single person giving orders, we're all owners. There is no longer that person who makes us suffer in the work.

At the technical level, the learning process was almost the same on both sides: CIPCA members and villagers. The CIPCA director in Charagua admitted that "in those days one of our mistakes was that we had no idea about agriculture". And a peasant from El Espino said:

We didn't know, we didn't understand how to produce, nobody taught us and since the priests didn't know anything, either, about agriculture... both groups had to learn as we went along: the fathers have learned from us, and we have also learned from them. That's how we cultivated that plot that we took from Señor Santa Cruz (ibid: 126-127).

Within CIPCA there was considerable debate over the characteristics of the CDT. The model could be considered as a cooperative adapted to local conditions. The CIPCA members studied the *kibbutz* model in Israel, the Chinese commune and the Soviet production cooperatives (*kolchoze*). Another ideological discussion revolved around the question of whether it was correct that only a small group of the community participate as member of the CDT. There were people in CIPCA who thought all the members of the community should be partners, because the CDT could divide the community.

CIPCA Santa Cruz

The opening of this office served as a point of closure for CIPCA's initial design, which sought to cover the country's socio-economic axis: La Paz-Cochabamba-Santa Cruz. Luis Alegre had asked Rafael Puente, then a Jesuit and very committed in the political effervescence of the moment, to set up CIPCA in Santa Cruz. During these first months work was done in close coordination with two peasant leaders: Jenaro Flores, head of the CSUTCB, and Demetrio Barrientos, then combative leader of the National Confederation of Colonisers of Bolivia (CNCB), to begin a joint work of union recuperation of important areas of Santa Cruz.

Rafael Puente and Gloria Querejazu, both Workers' Vanguard militants, were the two key people in the foundation of CIPCA Santa Cruz. They soon had the support of the Jesuits José Magriñá and Miguel Esquirol, who had been established for some time in the San Julián colonisation zone. Both had come to Santa Cruz from the Potosí region, accompanying a group of peasant migrants constituted in base Christian community.

San Julián was an area with greater agricultural potential than other previous colonies. With the conjoined effort of the Government (through the National Institute of Colonisation) USAID and the Committee of United Churches (CIU) an original colonisation plan[51] had been designed in San Julián which provided alimentation for the new settlers and organised them towards the creation of a first sense of community through communal labour.

As in all beginnings, apart from severe limitations in economy and staff, in those early days there was no profound analysis of the regional situation, nor a medium-term or long-term working plan. Neither had CIPCA's previous experiences in other regions served in this new context of Santa Cruz. There was little coordination of works. Basically, the distant San Julián team was forming almost a clique apart and the rest were constantly travelling around different regions of the department, from short course to short course, covering hundreds of kilometres.

During the coup of Natusch Busch (November 1979) Rafael Puente was in Europe and Gloria Querejazu, administrator and educator, had stayed behind as interim director. On his return from Europe the incompatibility of party militancy with institutional responsibility became clear. Rafael Puente left the direction of CIPCA Santa Cruz. It must be mentioned in his defence that, despite having used the infrastructure of the office for some party activities, the peasants never identified CIPCA or its employees with Workers' Vanguard.

The initial option of the new office did not allow concentration in determined areas, because its labour was oriented towards union formation. Inevitably it was essential to cover the most populated areas of the department and those that had greatest union impact. During this first era no clear zonal definition existed. Instead, work revolved around leaders and communities with which there were better contacts, or which requested the presence of CIPCA, seeking to give a serious and lasting impulse to union organisation. Present was the Confederation of Colonisers' Unions of Bolivia (CSCB), tied to the COB, and with which CIPCA enjoyed very good relations from the beginning. Besides, the CIPCA team was fundamental for the consolidation of the recently-formed subsidiary of the CSUTCB in Santa Cruz.

Short courses were offered on unionism and the history of the peasant movement. A good group of leading figures was formed, which over many years has continued to exert influence on the organisations of colonisers and peasants, and on the country as a whole. Just as in CIPCA La Paz, it was normal for peasant leaders to work at the same time as CIPCA promoters. The relation between CIPCA and that of the grassroots organisations was, at times, diffuse.

There was a fever of short courses: the peasants were hungry for knowledge. CIPCA was the referent, a place where the peasants could meet. CIPCA, against its wishes, turned into a branch of the union organisations. People went out to give courses in the countryside on foot, on horseback, at night, during fiesta days. There were no timetables or working conditions of work. It was mystical work, political work.

CIPCA AND THE POLITICAL DEBATE OVER THE YEARS 1978-1980

The years 1978, 1979 and 1980 saw interminable changes, coups, elections, party squabbles, periods of greater openness and others of renewed repression, which conditioned all CIPCA's work, both positively and negatively. The new political panorama had a bearing, in various ways, on the mechanisms of each office, which occasionally meant intense and heated debates between offices and their members. Let's begin with a fact that may be considered emblematic: the participation of CIPCA in a hunger strike, which marked a symbolic sea-change in the political juncture.

The hunger strike

The immediate motive for the hunger strike was the result of the pressure placed by US President Carter on Banzer to hold elections. Banzer complied, but without allowing the return or the participation of hundreds of people that were still in hiding or in exile. For this reason, when Banzer was clearly unwilling to grant a general and unrestricted amnesty, four women miners, along with their 13 children, began a historic hunger strike on the 28th of December 1977, in the middle of the Christmas period. This was seen at first as somewhat inopportune because it was the festive season, but it was soon proved prophetic. Initially, the four women were merely demanding the release of their husbands. One of them was Domitila Barrios de Chungara, a miner's wife, mother of seven children and leader of the housewives' organisation of the Siglo XX mine[52].

It began in La Paz and, within a few days after the holiday period, it spread throughout the country, with the participation of as many as 1,200 strikers in numerous pickets, supported by a growing number of civic and religious institutions. At the end, on the 18th of January 1978, after an attempt to repress the movement which was publicly repudiated by the archbishopric of La Paz, the government was forced to revise its position and concede the total and unrestricted amnesty the strikers demanded. With this, unions and political parties were newly legalised, the doors were opened to the exiles and it was possible to hold the first democratic elections after twelve years of military regimes.

Various members of CIPCA La Paz, then in its Christmas break, decided to support the actions led by the women miners, under the coordination of the Permanent Assembly of Human Rights. Here are the memories of Xavier Albó and Hugo Fernández:

Xavier Albó:

In an emergency Human Rights meeting, we saw that the women miners' strike, in the Archbishopric, was in danger of failing, since it was a public holiday, and we decided to support it with a new strike picket. It was at when we started to look for volunteers that the difficulties began. Lucho Espinal, from my own Jesuit community, was the first to volunteer. Others did so, but there were not enough people to make up a significant group. I also offered my collaboration. CIPCA was in Christmas recess and there was hardly anybody to consult. I could only find Hugo Fernández and we both agreed that it had to be done. It was one of the most intense and enriching experiences that I have lived through, during 19 days, with other 10 people, plus the growing wave of support and links throughout the country. Almost immediately Hugo himself was named a member of the mediating commission before the government, along with father Tumiri, of Human Rights, and doctor Luis Adolfo Siles, ex-president. Various other CIPCA people – I remember Sonia Dávila, Eulogia Mejía, Javier Hurtado – were active in other support groups.

Hugo Fernández:

A meeting was organised of the Assembly of Human Rights, of which Xavier Albó and I were members. At this meeting the decision was made to support the strike, thereby substituting the four women's 13 children, who were at that moment still part of the strike. Among those who offered themselves as volunteers were Xavier Albó and Luis Espinal. Also the decision was made to give more substance to the strike, with a sheet of four very concrete points intended to force the government to end the repression and achieve a real transition to democracy.

I was part of a committee that had to negotiate with the government. Within a short time (around the 9th of January 1978) there were already 1,000 strikers in the country. The government rejected all the demands and refused to enter into direct dialogue with the strikers. We managed to obtain an intermediary. But the discussions stagnated and the meeting was suspended until eleven at night. When I was passing San Calixto school, shortly before rejoining the negotiations, they told me that the government had broken off discussions and it was necessary to go into hiding. As a committee we were prepared for this eventuality: we began with a lot of propaganda (photos, telex to foreign press media, etc.). The next day there was a lot of military in the streets. They wanted to arrest the chairman of the negotiating committee, father Julio Tumiri, but could not break the hard nucleus of the strike and surprisingly, on the night of the 17th, the government changed position and authorised a complete and unrestricted amnesty in a message transmitted by television. We had triumphed.

This experience provoked broad reflection and controversy within CIPCA. The national director, Luis Alegre, did not agree with the participation of CIPCA people in the hunger strike. He mostly feared for the institution. He wanted to ensure that there would be no reprisals. For other reasons, Carlos Quiroga, Cochabamba director, also took a dim view of CIPCA's participation. He thought, as did his MIR party, that it was necessary to resign oneself to the feeble democratic openness offered by the government. He feared that, if more demands were made, the democratic process would be put at risk. In February, at the first annual meeting of the management committee, these diverse perspectives showed through. CIPCA realised that, even if everyone shared the same utopian ideals and basic commitment, there were people with diverse perspectives and strategies. It also realised that these divergences were normal, and that it would be necessary to work on them, mostly to maintain internal cohesion and achieve the unity of criterion that a well-organised institution required.

The first elections in twelve years

Having secured the principle that it was necessary to free prisoners, the clandestine and the exiled to return, the first elections in twelve years were held. These were notable for a scandalous level of interference on the part of the government. But the recent triumph of the hunger strike had given wings and creativity to the people. Initiatives unfolded and the contacts with national and international public opinion were used to demonstrate adequately that the pro-government candidate, Pereda Asbún, had won by fraudulent means. Seeking to save face, Banzer was inclined towards annulment of the elections, an attitude that provoked Pereda, who had been his Interior Minister, into opting for a coup d'état against his own boss.

CIPCA made a systematic compilation of all that had occurred in the countryside during those elections of 1978, after so many years of dictatorship. It was a fundamental historic moment. Together with the Assembly of Human Rights, CIPCA collected qualitative information from a large part of the country, through individuals, grassroots organisations, institutions or parishes, and published a book by Carmen Alcoreza and Xavier Albó entitled 1978: *the new peasantry faced with fraud* (1979)[53], full of spicy anecdotes and testimonies[54].

Independent unionism

In the countryside, one of the first consequences of the incipient democratic openness was the generalised discredit of the military peasant pact and the quest for an independent unionism. We have already seen examples of this, above all in the La Paz and Santa Cruz offices. In Cochabamba, the alternative route gave a more important role to the Association of Potato Producers. In Charagua, the Guaraní communities were still very much at the margin of all this problematic.

CIPCA has been lucky enough to have worked with distinguished leaders such as

Bonifacio Barrientos, Jenaro Flores, Demetrio Barrientos and Víctor Hugo Cárdenas – this latter being also a member of CIPCA – who defended the interests of the peasant and indigenous communities. On the other hand, short courses on union formation and the radio programmes, nourished by three editions of the text *Peasant unionism: yesterday, today and tomorrow* (CIPCA 1974, 1976 and 1979), have shown support for the organised emancipation of the peasantry. CIPCA's organisational work during these years increased overwhelmingly. Around 1980 the common line (which nobody opposed) was organisational work: strengthening independent peasant unionism.

At the same time as it supported independent peasant organisation, CIPCA had to walk a tightrope between firm support for the democratic process and its declared institutional impartiality. This wasn't easy, given that in its own ranks there were many militants, from one party or another, who were not easily convinced that it was better not to use the infrastructure and influence of CIPCA for party ends. Despite sound institutional politics, this inevitable tension between supporting peasant–indigenous organisation and preserving party independence as an institution, was repeated every so often in the life of CIPCA, especially during electoral periods.

With its decisive and active support for the peasant organisations, CIPCA was inscribed in a tendency present everywhere in Latin America during those years. An important number of grassroots organisations developed in close collaboration with NGOs. Many NGOs have supported grassroots organisations financially, provided services free of charge in the fields of social and technical training, offered legal and economic assistance, or given administrative and commercial assistance. Moreover many NGOs have, in the past, played the role of protectors against the political repression suffered by these organisations. It is also true that many promoters of NGOs were at the same time leaders of their grassroots organisations and/or political parties.[55]

The functions that organisations such as CIPCA performed with regard to the peasant organisations were often indispensable in the constitution of these organisations. Former leaders remember that CIPCA acted often as secretary of the grassroots organisation. Also in periods of crisis and other difficult moments, grassroots organisations sought out the NGOs. One debate that was never resolved concerned the extent to which an NGO like CIPCA could also act as a grassroots organisation.

There were those who sustained that the peasants did not have the knowledge or skills to perform tasks such as writing claim sheets, or carrying out internal administration. So as to avoid internal conflicts between members of the organisation or problems in the handling of administrative resources, NGO staff was allowed to assume the management functions of grassroots organisations, instead of being limited to supporting and advising them. On the other hand, some people were over-anxious and considered that the process of change was developing too slowly. For them, there was no problem in acting in the name of the peasant organisations and taking on responsibilities that corresponded to their members. There were also those who defended a total separation between the functions of the NGO and those of the peasant organisation. They also sustained that this type of assistance was only momentary and that the NGO should have a working strategy that aimed towards autonomy and the total independence from the grassroots organisations. This strategy meant that, ultimately, the point would be reached at which there was no longer any *raison d'être* for an NGO such as CIPCA.

One final problem was that many people had huge expectations regarding the positions that members of grassroots organisations could adopt. These expectations were ideologically-tinged and based on the notion that the popular sectors, in quite a short space of time, would create an alternative society – a society characterised by principles of solidarity and self-government. Too much trust was placed in the leaders; it was frowned upon to criticise them for authoritarianism, nepotism or corruption, even when there were motives or reasons for doing so. One argument often used was that it was better to cover up those errors, because the enemy might take advantage of them. This attitude of self-censorship was common among NGO intellectuals. CIPCA has not been absent from these debates and preoccupations.

Political openness

The national situation generated in 1978 could at the same time be described as an intense struggle to implant a democratic system on ground the military was unwilling to concede, and as a liberalisation of the interests and internal conflicts between those parties that were finally entering the public arena. For several of these parties, above all those on the left, the taking of power was still seen as a very distant objective. For this reason the political struggle frequently passed into the realm of minor entities, including CIPCA itself. As Xavier Albó recalls:

The parties of the left were struggling, of course, to wrest democracy from the military. But, at the same time, they were struggling for something easier and closer. They could not yet think seriously about taking power in government, and as yet they were still struggling, with the same passion, to 'take' the directorships of the popular movement and even to 'take' some institutions that were attempting to support them. CIPCA, like several other institutions, suddenly found itself in the sights of those party snipers.

CIPCA's official posture was clear on this point, aiming to:

- foment the strengthening of a democratic system and support social change but, as an institution, maintain independence from any party; and,
- respect the party political options and activities of its members, in their private life, but demand that they not use the institution for party ends.

One of the first moments in which it managed to define this posture with clarity was in 1976, when Carlos Quiroga and Franz Barrios, recently returned from Louvain, applied to work at CIPCA. Both had worked before in ACLO, were sociologists, and had an impeccable work record. They were honest enough, from the outset, to declare their militancy in the Revolutionary Left Movement (MIR), which at that time was seen as a party that actually corresponded to its name. They were accepted; Carlos as director and catalyst of the new office in Cochabamba, Franz as sociologist in La Paz.[56]

The rules of the political game within CIPCA were set in the terms indicated above, ratified time and again in the management committees, and repeatedly clarified to the members whenever necessary. But, for the reasons explained, the parties did not always share these criteria, much less still at this moment of political aperture at which some considered the party as the universal panacea.

Some parties criticised CIPCA's posture of not wanting to align itself officially with any party, dubbing it 'clerical'. Nor was it unusual to hear in some politicised circles, such as the University, that CIPCA had already been taken by some party or other. Years later the debate was reopened about CIPCA's posture vis-à-vis the political parties and about the CIPCA support for peasants and indigenous peoples with political aspirations, but by that time there were already more reflective postures and less intransigent debates.

Monochrome versus multicolour

The political debate was not only about the relation between CIPCA, as a body, and the political parties. Above all, between 1978 and 1980, the years of democratic openness, there were many internal political discussions. Nobody doubted the inevitability of people effectively having some party preference. Except in the remote region of Charagua, it was almost unthinkable at that time to find people who were prepared to do committed work in the countryside but were not tied to any party.

At the directorial level, debate was mainly polarised. There were those who thought it convenient, in order to ensure independence from any party, to diversify political preferences within each office. Others proposed, rather, that as long as it was made clear that the office was not to be used for party ends, the work would gain coherence if people from the same party were preferred. This latter posture, known as *monochrome*, was that of the more politicised offices of Cochabamba and, though expressed less openly, of Santa Cruz. The *polychrome* position was prevalent in La Paz and Charagua, although this latter was also seen by some as simply *colourless*.

As we have already related above, the Cochabamba office had other political orientations than just towards the MIR. CIPCA La Paz had MIR people, and some others with Trotskyite links, but above all Katarists. Santa Cruz was Trotskyite. In March 1980 the discussions culminated in a management committee meeting in which Lucho Alegre hoped to oblige Santa Cruz and Cochabamba to contract people of other tendencies.

Rafael Puente, ex-director of CIPCA Santa Cruz remembers:

Our national CIPCA meetings could almost be described as 'folkloric'. On one side was Carlos Quiroga, Cochabamba director, who was then MIR: I was on the other side, as director in Santa Cruz and a Trotskyite. Both of use were very passionate and politicised, albeit from distinct angles. We entered prolonged controversies concerning the 'juncture'; which were enjoyed by the others. But it is important to stress that the institution not only tolerated the presence of militants at its heart, but had even valued it, despite the inevitable dangers that this involved. The impact of these different militancies projected towards the exterior was different. The CIPCA office in Cochabamba could not cease to appear identified with the MIR, since that party belonged to Democratic Popular Unity (UDP), the front that won the elections each year and with the biggest majority. In Santa Cruz, with an incipient party, small and unknown, it was easier for us to maintain our 'clandestine' nature without the peasants ever coming to identify either CIPCA or its employees with that of Workers' Vanguard. CIPCA Charagua seemed not to have defined militancies. On the other hand, in La Paz the situation was more complicated due to the presence in which office of MIR militants, Trotskyites and Katarists, whose discrepancies at times became perceptible in the very same communities with which they worked.

The case of that 'multicoloured' La Paz office also merits a brief commentary. At the beginning MIR predominated, but among the Aymara personnel, rather diverse currents of Katarism predominated: some were close to Jenaro Flores' Revolutionary Movement Tupaj Katari; others were closer to the Tupaj Katari Indian Movement (MITKA), the 'Indian' branch. In this 'Indian' branch were Jaime Apaza, broadcaster in CIPCA, who was later to play a role in the National Council of Ayllus and Markas of the Qullasuyu[57] (CONAMAQ) and, outside CIPCA, Felipe Quispe, the future Mallku of the Pachacuti Indigenous Movement (MIP).

Although it did not break out into open conflict, tension occurred above all between Katarists and MIR, the latter being the principal leftist party that sought supporters in the countryside. The former reacted above all against the attempts at

MIR penetration in the province of Aroma, cradle of Katarism. The tension, inside that office, reached such a point that there were Katarists who accused some MIR people of using the short courses to make party propaganda. The MIR defended itself by complaining of not receiving equal treatment to the Katarists who, being of peasant descent, were more tolerated by CIPCA.

Not only the leftist parties were interested in CIPCA; the right was also drawn to it. When, once again, the whole democratic process was brutally interrupted on the 17th of July 1980 by the García Meza coup, CIPCA temporarily had to close its doors. A new phase was beginning.

CHAPTER II
CIPCA CAMOUFLAGED
1980-1982

The period between 1978 and 1982 was the most unstable and chaotic of the entire republican history of Bolivia, with nine Presidents in four and a half years, seven of them *de facto* and only two constitutional[58]. As a preamble to the coup d'état of 1980 came the resurgence of relatively independent political parties and unions, and the country experienced a flurry of coups and countercoups. This chapter does not analyse the different currents of thought from that period, because CIPCA could not even work normally. From it clandestine position, it did everything possible to survive and to help those who were under threat.

HISTORICAL OVERVIEW

1978 saw renewed tensions, with military power and the conservative sectors opposed to the democratising currents, but inimical above all to the parties of the left. The political force that drew civil society together was Popular Democratic Unity (UDP), a front formed by the Revolutionary Nationalist Movement of the Left (MNRI), MIR, the Communist Party of Bolivia (PCB) and some lesser parties. The other important forces were the MNR, Hugo Banzer's recently-created party National Democratic Action (ADN), and the Socialist Party Uno, directed by Marcelo Quiroga Santa Cruz.

In 1979, in the midst of this political upheaval, the Chamber of Representatives elected Lidia Gueiler Tejada (then president of the Chamber of Representatives) as interim constitutional President of Bolivia. A few days after taking office she had to face to the toughest group from the Armed Forces headed by Luis García Meza Tejada, a cousin of hers. During the constitutional government, García Meza had publicly threatened the old political leaders of the left and the most prestigious figureheads such as Marcelo Quiroga Santa Cruz. During the first half of 1980 groups and individuals close to the military involved in the coup had unleashed a wave of violence that claimed many victims. On the 22nd of March came the brutal torture and assassination of the Jesuit priest, journalist and film critic Luis Espinal, who lived in the same house as Lucho Alegre and Xavier Albó. Almost 70,000 people attended his funeral to register their revulsion for this crime (Mesa et al., 2003: 723).

Despite everything, the 1980 elections were held in an atmosphere of absolute calm. The President managed to realise one of her aspirations, presiding over peaceful and transparent elections. These were won by a narrow margin by the UDP, led by Hernán Siles Suazo of the MNRI, and Jaime Paz Zamora of the MIR. Once again Congress had to decide the winner, no candidate having obtained an overall majority. The reality, however, was more dramatic. The whole country knew that the coup d'état would arrive: it was only a question of when. Indeed, on the 17th of July 1980, 18 days after the elections and 15 before the new democratic government was due to take power, came the bloody coup that put General Luis García Meza in power along with his interior minister Colonel Luis Arce Gómez.

It all began with a military putsch in Trinidad, but just a few hours later the streets of La Paz were already full of troops and assault vehicles. Irregular forces and paramilitaries coordinated by the Argentinian army began their repressive operations concealed in ambulances. The most notorious was the raid on an emergency meeting of the National Committee of Defence of democracy (CONADE). Scores of political and union leaders were detained, among them Juan Lechín. Marcelo Quiroga Santa Cruz, wounded immediately, was callously tortured and assassinated. Radio Fides, from where CIPCA broadcast its programmes, was raided eight times; several of its members were detained, the others went into hiding and its equipment was destroyed. A rigorous early curfew was set; no information was available other than that of the national channel, which became the mouthpiece of those responsible for the coup. A living hell began of assassination, torture, imprisonment and exile, though there were also clandestine networks of resistance and solidarity[59].

The military dictatorship of García Meza was been, without a doubt, one of the most appalling governments in the country's entire history. Marked by violence and

1979 golpe de Natusch

1980 golpe de GM

intolerance, it was an example of irresponsible abuse of power. In January 1981 a massacre occurred with the murder of eight MIR leaders in a house on Calle Harrington in La Paz. The clandestine leadership of the MIR had met to analyse an economic package that the government had launched. The group was betrayed and the minister of the interior, Luis Arce Gómez, organised a campaign of elimination that culminated with the murder of eight of the nine leaders present at the meeting. The exception was Gloria Ardaya, miraculously saved but later tortured and sent into exile. She was a distinguished MIR leader, who at that time lived in the same house as Luis Alegre and Xavier Albó.

The 1980s were marked by another dramatic social and economic reality, of historic transcendence for Bolivia. The spectacular growth of drug trafficking was a phenomenon that started at the beginning of the 1970s but it was during the government of García Meza that it found real expansion as a business. Various international organisms and members of the United States Congress formally accused Luis Arce Gómez of involvement in drug trafficking. (Langer, 1999: 84-85).

In October 1982, General Guido Vildoso recognised the legitimacy of the 1980 elections and a new democratic cycle began which has continued uninterrupted up to the present day. The Congress elected in 1980 ratified that year's election result and permitted the presidency to be handed to the UDP, with Hernán Siles Zuazo as President and Jaime Paz Zamora as vice-President.

The trial of Luis García Meza and his government began in 1986; in 1993 he was found guilty and condemned to 30 years of prison without right to reprieve. In March 1994 he was arrested in Brazil, where he had been living under an assumed name. One year later he was extradited to Bolivia and entered Chonchocoro prison (La Paz) where he is currently serving his sentence (Mesa et al., 2003: 726). After the capture of Colonel Luis Arce Gómez in 1989, President Jaime Paz Zamora decided simply to skip some regulations by sending him to the United States, where he had been accused of drug-trafficking. By the time he was condemned in Bolivia (in 1993) to 30 years of prison without right to reprieve, Arce Gómez was already serving a 30 years prison sentence as a drug-trafficker in the penitentiary of Memphis (United States).

GOING UNDERGROUND

CIPCA National

Everyone was surprised at the violence and the savagery with which the García Meza coup was unleashed. As in similar cases, during the first days work was automatically suspended due to the risk of walking down the street and coming up against control points. As it happened, on the 17th of July, the day of the coup, CIPCA was initiating a meeting of its management committee in La Paz. That is to say, its chief executives were concentrated there and there were no directors in the regional offices.

The gravity of the situation was obvious. It was necessary immediately to empty offices of archives and more sensitive materials. The decision was taken to give collective vacations to all the staff until the panorama was clarified. Luis Alegre and Xavier Albó were not even able to return to their own homes. Taking due caution, over the subsequent days these adopted decisions were implemented and meetings arranged in the most unthought-of places, with the necessary camouflage. Moustaches and spectacles appeared or disappeared: there were even wigs and changes of name.

In August a first evaluation was made. The situation was considered too critical to restart work immediately and it was decided that staff would remain on holiday. The decision was made to keep paying everyone who could be contacted and had not made arrangements for their own survival. So as to facilitate payment and the coverage of social benefits, father Víctor Blajot, then director of the jesuit education institution Fe y Alegría (Faith and Happiness), made the supportive gesture of accepting CIPCA staff within the payrolls of his institution. In any case, not even payment was easy. It was precisely during payment of wages that Hugo Fernández was detained and the accountant Cristina Cossio interrogated[60]. As for the staff, all kinds of things happened. Some, the most distinguished, went underground or even into exile. Several people were arrested, but many were waiting in their homes. Still others, faced with the uncertainty of the situation, were looking for new jobs in other places.

Important decisions were made. José Magriñá (familiarly Jose) less eminent than others and a member of the management committee for Santa Cruz, would simultaneously assume the functions of director of CIPCA Santa Cruz and of visible national coordinator. He would maintain constant contact with Luis Alegre, who remained clandestine in the house of some North American priests where he had sought refuge immediately after the coup. The Magriñá–Alegre duo would have full powers until the management committee which, due to the situation, was renamed consultative council, could function regularly. Finally, CIPCA would not be talked about… until further notice.

Not only CIPCA suffered the military repression. This even reached some international organisms that also worked in the countryside. For example, Swiss Technical Cooperation (COTESU) was initiating an innovative Programme of support to rural education in Alto Beni. But its offices were raided, its Swiss head detained and the Programme cut short. It was, then, no surprise that several foreign countries suspended all aid services while the government of Bolivia remained in the hands of arrogant and irresponsible military thugs. On the other hand, there were also many signs of solidarity; for instance, a few days after the coup CIPCA received the agreeable surprise of a visit from *Sjef Theunis*, director general of Novib who was making a quick solidarity visit to Bolivia.

Towards November 1980, when everything began to calm down, it was decided to reopen publicly all the offices, but with new names and, with the exception of Charagua, with new directors. In this way, at the beginning of 1981, CIPCA La Paz was Technical Cooperation Service (SETECO); CIPCA Cochabamba was of Technical Agricultural Assistance Service (SATA); CIPCA Santa Cruz was Technical Commission of Peasant Research in the Oriente (COTEICO); and CIPCA Charagua had the most exotic of the names: Service of Social Assistance of the Apostolic Vicariate of Cuevo (SASVAC). In all these offices it adopted a markedly technical profile, of support for agricultural production.

Each place had its own story, of which more will be said below. But firstly, to complete the human flavour of what was the country's greatest crisis, we will briefly tell some of the personal adventures lived through during these months.

Luis Alegre and **Xavier Albó** had been living for years in the same house. In their own rooms CIPCA had begun to function, and part of the library -for lack of more adequate premises- functioned there too. From the day of the coup onward, they could no longer go back home. Luis Espinal, who had been watched for months, was captured in the immediate vicinity of the house to be assassinated by the paramilitary. Gloria Ardaya also lived in the same house. The house had to be abandoned for months. Only *Doña Julia*, the faithful and much-loved cook, remained to look after the house. Little by little the work was undertaken of packing the books from the CIPCA Library, which were still in the house, and transferring them to another place. Similarly, the books and documents that were in the CIPCA office were packed away and hidden by *Sra. Berna Mayta*, who helped in the maintenance of that office.

Luis Alegre hid in a convent. There he dyed his hair (a startling reddish colour) and grew a moustache. He lived in several houses until, at the end of 1980, he moved to the San Calixto School. In order to the tensions to dissipate he travelled for a few months to Europe, leaving José Magriñá in full charge of the national directorship. Alegre had to move house every 15 days. It was never necessary for him to look for a roof, because there were always people who offered their homes as refuge.

Xavier Albó initially stayed in the San Ignacio School. But a few days after the coup the only civil minister of the military dictatorship appeared suddenly in the house 'to ask for advice' from a former teacher and, possibly, to see if there were people hidden there. He recognised Xavier, as a friend and companion of Espinal. News also came that they had arrested another priest, who they mistook for Xavier[61]. Xavier shaved off his beard and went to another place. It so happened that Xavier and Lucho went to take refuge in the same convent, but as they were moving their car was followed by paramilitaries. After some tense and eventful escapades, it was finally decided that Xavier would stay in the San Calixto School. Another Jesuit companion had been arrested at the end of mass and Xavier inherited his wig, transforming himself into a young man called father Alberto Blanco.

Hugo Fernández was entrusted with the operation aimed at totally dismantling the national office and the CIPCA La Paz office, and of taking all their contents to a safe place. He carried this out, with the help of the office's staff, in the weeks immediately after the coup. He also acted as visible head of the institution and was in discreet contact with those who were in hiding. But at the beginning of August, when he had practically completed his main task and was busy contacting the staff to thank them for the work by paying their wages, he was intercepted and arrested by paramilitaries who also kept the jeep that was in his charge. As a result of the torture and interrogation to which he was subjected during the night, they obliged him in the early hours of the following day to go to the house of the accountant

Cristina Cossio, in which they found part of the money, for which she was also briefly detained and interrogated. They were mainly interested in the question of the money. Cristina was freed within a few hours, but the cash and the jeep were never returned. Appeals for Hugo fell on deaf ears; they simply said that there were *grave accusations* against him. He was detained for about four months, of which two were spent in residence in Cobija, Pando, after which he was exiled to Mexico. He shared with numerous Bolivians one of the hotels that the Ministry of the Interior of that country reserved in order to house political refugees from different countries. After three months he was sent to Nicaragua, where the Sandinista popular revolution was taking its first steps.

Martha García, relatively new director in Cochabamba, saw how almost all the people from her were dispersed. It was impossible to do any institutional work. The archives had already been hidden in the house of the Augustine fathers. One fine day she was also detained, when she was travelling in her own vehicle. Luckily she saw her uncle as he was crossing the road and he was able to secure her freedom within a few days.

Alfonso Gumucio was a journalist and director of the new rural Luis Espinal film institute, within CIPCA. A while before the coup he had published an ironic article in the press entitled "La Mesa de García".[62] When the coup came, he had to disappear totally from the scene. He finally managed to obtain a false passport and left the country.

Víctor Hugo Cárdenas first holed up in various relatives' houses, in communities around Lake Titicaca. For a few months he helped out a relative as a lorry driver, travelling to different parts of the country. In 1981 he managed to return to his old office, now called SETECO.

If this occurred with the Jesuits and the CIPCA staff, who after all had greater institutional and international protection, the peasants had a far worse time. Their organisations and leaders were forced to vanish. To give one example, we can tell the fate of three peasants then very close to CIPCA:

Pedro Condori, deacon of the region of Jesús de Machaqa, who in the past had been invited by CIPCA to follow various short courses, was detained and tortured so that he would give away the hiding-place of Hernán Siles. **Jenaro Flores**, founder of Katarism and leader of the CSUTCB, had also to become leader of the COB, because those who occupied higher positions were either in jail or in exile. It befell him to organise the clandestine resistance of this most important of workers' organisations. However, one day while walking to a meeting he was intercepted by a paramilitary vehicle. When he tried to escape he was shot. After immediate international pressure he received belated medical treatment in France as a guest of the Mitterand government, but from then on he has been confined to a wheelchair.

Gregorio Andrade, ex-leader of the colonisers, had helped CIPCA become established in Alto Beni and even acted for several years as a CIPCA supervisor in Jesús de Machaqa. Once he left the institution he became one of the main peasant leaders in the MIR. Betrayed by an informer in January 1981, he was followed and detained when on his way to a party meeting; this was the incident in which the senior staffs of MIR were massacred. After months of detention and torture, he was finally exiled to Sweden.

By then, CIPCA was already functioning again in the four regions, under brand-new and exotic names. Below are some characteristics of its new focus.

SETECO – La Paz

On the day of the coup, one of the three CIPCA La Paz field teams was in Alto Beni. According to the testimony of the CIPCA La Paz driver and messenger Germán Mamani, they were obliged to stay for a whole week, without provisions and ultimately quite bored. They escaped disguised as colonisers, avoiding checkpoints. When they reached the house of Luis Alegre and Xavier Albó, in which normally the jeep was kept, they found nobody.

A few days after the coup, still on the orders of Hugo Fernández, various members of the team participated in a salvage operation, recuperating all the material and documentation from that office and distributing it in the safest possible places. Indeed, it was known that a paramilitary group had raided the CIPCA office. But these people had mistakenly gone to the previous address, one that CIPCA had already left some years previously.

After the detention of Hugo Fernández, José Magriñá also took over the direction of CIPCA La Paz. But in November, once the initial storm had passed, Sonia Dávila (until then a member of the training team) was named director. The decision, however, was not welcomed by some members of the team who considered that they had more right to the position, for reasons of seniority. Neither did they like the idea of having a woman as boss. The technical team, in particular, had serious reservations in this matter. José Magriñá, the National Director, ratified Sonia Dávila as director and decided to dismiss the reticent technicians, citing abandonment of their work, because they had stopped going to the office in protest.

Besides, so as to work clandestinely, a team of 35 people was too big and vulnerable. It was necessary to dismiss half of them, according to criteria of seniority, rank and competence. SETECO's activities were, inevitably, greatly reduced in comparison with previous years. The research team and the technical team were fused, as were those of education and agricultural extension. So as to avert the problem of the little work in the field, it was decided to capitalise on the occasion for courses of internal formation and preparation of feasibility studies.

As regards the work zones, all activity in Achacachi and in the zone of colonisation had to be closed. There were barracks in both zones and the peasant leaders had been subject to greater persecution. There were no such problems in Machaqa, despite incidents like the already mentioned capture of Pedro Condori. On the other hand, SETECO opened a new front in Aroma province. These were the first steps towards the structuring of a more stable work future in the micro-region of Ayo Ayo. in all this work, almost all the emphasis was then placed on technical projects of agricultural production. Some staff involved in agricultural extension had to go out to the countryside in disguise, because their names were on the military's lists.

Local radios were no longer able to broadcast any programmes. However, they still transmitted programmes in Aymara through the Peruvian station *Onda Azul* in Puno, owned by the Maryknoll fathers, which then had a broad audience on the Bolivian Altiplano. A member of the team travelled every week in public transport, crossed the border with or without safe-conduct and exchanged the magnetic tapes for the recorded programmes. Some very worried peasants came to SETECO to warn that "the Peruvians are stealing your programmes".

SATA – Cochabamba

This was the office most affected by the coup precisely because of its identification with the MIR, a party that, having won the elections, was now the target of all kinds of persecution. One could almost talk of a re-foundation of that office. There was great dispersion and only a small number of staff managed to return to the office, when it was able to reopen. 80% of those employed when it reopened were new people.

We have already mentioned the detention suffered by the director, Martha García, soon after the coup. When that office was restructured with its new name, José Magriñá decided to give the job of formal director to the Dutch cooperator Peter Goossens, who had been transferred from La Paz. In which turbulent zone, the presence of a foreigner unknown to the head of the new office would eliminate all suspicions. The initial idea was that he could work in coordination with the former director, Martha García, who was very familiar with the previous work. But this proved impossible. It was a very difficult period. Two heads and, perhaps worse still, a man and a woman. Martha García decided to resign and, shortly afterward, founded the new institution CEDEAGRO, to which were also incorporated other members of the former CIPCA. This institution still provides service in the Cochabamba countryside and maintains good relations with CIPCA.

Nor was it possible to think, at that moment, about the restructuration of the Association of Potato Producers, which had been the articulating axis of the old CIPCA work in the valleys. The hot seats in peasant organisation had again been occupied by old leaders of the Military-Peasant Pact. This, in many areas, meant opposition to the presence of CIPCA, which they identified with the persecuted MIR.

It was only possible to maintain contact with certain well-known communities that continued their friendly relations as always. It was in them, and in some other new ones from the area, in which the attempt was made to forge ahead with some productive projects. The emphasis was not now on commercialisation, as before, but on support for production. The action was concentrating more in the regions of Tiraque and Mizque. Technical as well as credit support was given. But on more than one occasion some leaders took advantage of the political juncture to say that they no longer had to pay back the credit, because "it was the peasants' money".

COTEICO – Santa Cruz

Being a new and still little-known office, CIPCA Santa Cruz was not in the sights of the new local authorities. During the coup it was semi-closed. When José Magriñá returned from La Paz, it was as director both at national level and of Santa Cruz.

All of CIPCA, and the Santa Cruz branch in particular, suffered a grave misfortune in October 1981, with the sudden death of its young director José Magriñá after a motorbike accident. Secundino Peláez, the economist who had had greatest continuity in which office, returned as acting director and Gloria Querejazu came back from Sucre to offer temporary support.

Due to the particular circumstances of the sensitive Santa Cruz society, it was considered that for the moment, in which office, as long as ideal staff of *camba*[63] origin was not found, it was preferable to have a director who was a Jesuit, as previous ones had been. Both Gloria and Secundino, the two acting directors, were *collas* and, as such, their relations with certain institutions and bodies in Santa Cruz seemed more difficult, even though they had full acceptance in the *colla* colonies. A Jesuit priest, despite being an outsider, in any case had certain advantages in being accepted. Finally, in March 1982, the national direction of Faith and Happiness acceded to a reiterated request from CIPCA and ceded to José Oriol Gelpí, Jesuit educator and until then director of the departmental office of that institution.

SASVAC – Charagua

Charagua was a region that was distant from the centres of power. As such, the effects of the coup made themselves felt much less there, apart from some pressure and threats from the local military garrison. What also helped was that CIPCA was still seen as an organisation related to the church.

At the very beginning Gabriel Siquier, the universally loved and respected parish priest of Charagua, was arrested by military from that population's frontier barracks and was transferred to Camiri. But immediately the local bishop (Monsignor Pellegrini, a Franciscan above all suspicion) intervened and freed him. With this Episcopal protection, the CIPCA office was able to return to its normal functions in September, under the new guise of Social Assistance Service of the Apostolic Vicariate of Cuevo. The staff underwent practically no change. They could still go out to the countryside, in response to the by now growing demand for the work communities, but by prudence they temporally suspended the short courses.

COMING OUT OF HIDING

Throughout 1981 the situation was gradually returning to normal. In March 1982, in the first directors' meeting that year, the decision was made to restore the name of CIPCA everywhere. In this same meeting, decisions were also made on the positions of regional directors: José Oriol Gelpí was ratified in his position as director in Santa Cruz. In Cochabamba Enrique Gómez, an agrarian economist, was nominated as permanent director. In La Paz, Luis Alegre temporally assumed directorship of that office due to the problems that had occurred with Sonia Dávila. The removal of Sonia Dávila, who had saved CIPCA La Paz at the most critical moment, was painful[64]. Towards October 1982, an internal change in the order of the Jesuits presented the opportunity finally to consolidate the situation. Marcos Recolons was named superior of the community of Jesuits in La Paz; under these circumstances, CIPCA also offered him the directorship of its regional office. In Charagua the inevitable removal of Marcos Recolons left a gap that was filled by Francisco Pifarré, as new director[65].

Political survival during the dictatorship had brought CIPCA to a more central and vertical governmental style, in the hands of the National Director, advised by the four regional directors, three of whom were, besides, Jesuits. The fact that most of the directors were Jesuits undoubtedly helped CIPCA survive the dictatorship. The principal positive outcome of the underground period was, perhaps, the greater institutional consciousness of how important the technical-productive dimension was. However, there was also a negative outcome; work had inevitably decreased in the other two *legs* – in other words, the organisational and educational-ideological dimensions. At the same time, the scale of work had also become notably reduced. Now the work was almost exclusively done in communities that were remote from one another. Only in Charagua could an inter-communal vision still be maintained.

On the country's political landscape, 1982 was a decisive year in the restoration of democracy. On the 10th of October 1982 an increasingly weakened military returned power to those to whom it legitimately corresponded; the President elected in 1980, Hernán Siles Suazo. Only then could it be said that CIPCA had fully returned to normality.

CHAPTER III
CIPCA RECUPERATES
1982-1987

Despite the re-establishment of democracy, Bolivia did not find a way out of its problems. The years 1982-1986 were very difficult for Bolivia and for CIPCA. Firstly, because it was no easy task to begin afresh after two years of torture, exile and assassinations in the country. Secondly, because the UDP government did not manage to consolidate, or to respond to the explosion of demands from the population and the expectations that were repressed during years of dictatorship. Thirdly, because it was unable to control the hyperinflation that obliged it to cut short its mandate and had, as a consequence the implementation of the Programme of Structural Adjustment of the International Monetary Fund and the World Bank. These measures, implemented by the succeeding government, meant the definitive crisis of the mining sector, the dismantling of the by now so devaluated state entities in support of rural development and the massive migration of miners and peasants to the tropic of Cochabamba and to the cities, especially to El Alto. If these events were not sufficient, in 1985 there was a crisis within CIPCA that forced it to re-think and reorder its work.

HISTORICAL OVERVIEW

The government of Hernán Siles and his Democratic Popular Union (UDP) had a democratic vocation, but at the same time was not capable of administering the grave economic crisis that previous governments – both MNR and military – had left as inheritance. With a minority in Congress, faced by tough opposition from MNR and ADN and insufferable pressure from the parties of the left and the COB under the leadership of Juan Lechín, the executive found itself abandoned. In addition the MIR, in a show of political immaturity, deserted the government a few months after having imposed a 'de-dollarisation' that brought disaster to thousands of small savers.

With the euphoria of democracy, the peasant movements began to have a great activity in all the country. Roadblocks, initiated in the Banzer years, were adopted as a habitual method of struggle, equivalent to some extent to workers' strikes. The occupations of institutions also proliferated (for example, the National Institute of Colonisation), in the hope that in sympathetic hands they would function better. This did not happen, either because resources were frozen from above or because, rather than goodwill, what were needed were technical skills.

The government found itself in the position of having to respond to a package of demands from a population that had been silent during almost 11 years of dictatorships. This explosion of requests and demands also hampered successful government. All the social sectors had placed enormous expectations in democracy, thinking that it was going to resolve everything: from full employment and just salaries to boundary conflicts between peasant communities, via the euphoria of free expression and exuberant social mobilisations (Toranzo, 1999). The CSUTCB reached its maximum level of representation, organisation and command of audience capacity to mobilise in 1984, to such a point that there was prolonged debate over the possibility and convenience of being an organic part of the UDP government.

With the return to democracy new peasant and indigenous organisations were also consolidated. In 1982 the Indigenous Central of the Bolivian Oriente (CIDOB)[66] was founded. CIDOB had been supported since 1980 by the NGO APCOB which facilitated encounters between the ethnic peoples of the lowlands such as the Isoseño-Guaraní, Ayoreo, Chiquitano, Guarayo and, over the years, between the rest of the lowland indigenous peoples.

At the heart of the CSCB, and partly also of the CSUTCB, a specific group of small coca leaf producers was taking shape in the tropical region of the Chapare (Cochabamba). The great majority of these producers were impoverished immigrants, whose number markedly increased due to the growing commercial demand for this product, the raw material for cocaine.

All this occurred in the context of a generalised economic crisis, which had dragged on since the late 1970s and also had a bearing on the fall of the military regimes. In less than two years the economic situation hit bottom. Production fell by 40%, exports by 1,030 to 670 million dollars, the GNP decreased to a limit of −4.5% in 1983. Inflation, already high in 1982, ended up degenerating into hyperinflation. The immediate cause was the crisis of the external debt, the gravity and duration of which were underestimated by the Siles Zuazo government. In 1982 the external debt had reached 106% of GNP and 362% of exports (Morales and Pacheco, 1999: 182). The annual rate of inflation reached the following percentages: 123% in 1982, 276% in 1983, 281% in 1984 and 11,750% in 1985 (ibid).

To top it all, in the zones of the Altiplano and the Valleys, the population had to face a natural disaster of great magnitude: the most severe droughts in their history, in the agricultural year 1982-83, brought famine and the loss of all harvests.

The economic crisis of previous years had put the question of access to the land firmly back on the national agenda. Being still clandestine, the CSUTCB drew up and finally presented a new law to replace the 1953 Law of Agrarian Reform. This proposal, known as the Fundamental Agrarian Law, reflected a high level of conceptual and theoretical thought in the peasant-indigenous movement[67]. The government of Hernán Siles Suazo received the proposal in a massive peasant-indigenous concentration in 1985, but it never came to be considered by the National Congress. Some aspects were later included in the Law of the National Institute of Agrarian Reform, known as the INRA Law of 1996 (Kay and Urioste 2005: 16). In line with the Fundamental Agrarian Law, in July 1983, the CSUTCB had created the Peasant Farmers Corporation (CORACA), whose legal status was approved by the government of Hernán Siles Suazo on the 23rd of April 1984.

The crisis, with hyperinflation and general shortages, caused a workers' mobilisation that had been unparalleled since the 1950s. Strikes, roadblocks and marches reached paroxysm; the Central Bank was at a standstill for 51 days. Water and electricity supplies to the Governmental Palace and the presidential residence were cut. Demands for pay rises were taking the country to the brink of disintegration and putting democracy at great risk. In March 1984, 12,000 miners took over and paralysed the city of La Paz. In June the President was kidnapped for ten hours in a frustrated coup attempt. Such was the deterioration that Siles Zuazo was obliged to cut short his mandate and call early elections.

In 1985 Hugo Banzer won the election by a relative majority, with Víctor Paz Estenssoro in second place. But congress did not ratify Banzer, instead electing Paz Estenssoro. Paz began his government of the MNR with a dramatic but real phrase: *Bolivia is dying on us.* An economic team, under the leadership of Gonzalo Sánchez de Lozada (President of the Senate, Chancellor and then Minister of Planning), designed a decree with economic measures which is identified historically by its number, 21060. It was the beginning of a new economic politics in the country, one of structural adjustment imposed by the World Bank and the International Monetary Fund. The COB rejected decree 21060 and went on strike. The government responded with a state of siege and the confinement of leaders.

The decree sought the reduction of the fiscal deficit through wage freezing and a radical increase in the price of petrol, the real and flexible exchange rate of the dollar, the reduction of state employees, total liberalisation of the market and tax reform. The Bolivian peso, which had reached as high as 1,800,000 to the dollar, was replaced by the Boliviano, with six zeros less.

The measures were successful thanks to an alliance between Paz Zamorra and Banzer in the so-called *Pact for democracy* which gave the government a majority in parliament and allowed it to approve the laws it required. In 1986 a brutal fall in the price of tin forced even more drastic measures, among others the so-called 'relocation', a euphemism for the dismissal of 21,000 of the 27,000 miners then working for the Mining Corporation of Bolivia (COMIBOL).

With the new focus, a policy was adopted of complete liberation of the internal prices of agricultural products. Until that moment, state policy had been to impose ceiling prices on food produced in the country so as to protect urban consumers, loading the weight of the inflationary crisis onto rural areas (Urioste, 2002: 35). Ever since the 1970s, the tendency had been to diminish the percentage of public expenditure assigned to the peasant sector, within the total of agricultural public spending. The percentage of total central government spending for peasant families varied, in the 1980s, between only 5.1 and 10.2% (Niekerk, 1994: 25). During the period 1981–1987, there was a negative growth rate in agricultural production of –0.2%, partly caused by natural disasters. But the deterioration was greater still over the period 1986-1989 in which the agricultural GNP per capita decreased by -17.8% (ibid: 19).

In 1985, with decree 21060, the World Bank returned to Bolivia after six years' absence. The United States also increased its support, due to which it could be said that after 1987 Bolivia entered a stage in which it received large offers of aid or cooperation, whether multilateral, bilateral or private. Little by little, the investment in rural development projects began to depend mostly on the resources from international cooperation and, in lesser proportion, on genuinely national funds. During the final years, *Official Development Aid* (ODA) reached little more than 12% of GNP (Urioste, 2002: 119).

The government also adopted measures that seriously affected the farming sector and, above all, small agricultural producers: all support activities were suspended, such as credit, research and agricultural extension. The Agricultural

Bank, until then the most important source of public finance for farmers, was closed in 1985. Technological research and extension practically disappeared from the countryside. The Bolivian Institute of Agricultural Technology (IBTA) entered a long process of dissolution without receiving a proposal for any alternative option.[68]

Another factor that influenced in the shrinking of the State was the inefficiency and corruption of public institutions: agrarian funds bankrupted by embezzlement and agricultural funds lost in irrecoverable portfolios. But in closing these institutions the producers were left without public referents. At the same time, direct and indirect subsidies were established – at the height of the neoliberal boom – not to the small impoverished producers but to the exporters of monocrops (Urioste, 2002: 118). The Chamber of Agriculture of the Oriente (CAO) turned into a dynamic hub, articulating the grievances of the great majority of agricultural producers in the department of Santa Cruz. It represented the modern sector of national agriculture and stockbreeding, offering technical and productive services to thousands of affiliates. It also had very important links with financial sectors and parliamentary politicians (ibid: 33).

One controversial form of assistance was food aid. Through the called PL 480 (Public Law 480) of the United States, which had begun to operate back in 1955, Bolivia received 30 million dollars annually during the late 1980s. According to World Bank estimates, around 21% of the population received food donations during those years. Donations of wheat were seriously questioned because of the negative impact that they supposedly had on national production (ibid: 27).

To finish with this panorama it is necessary to emphasise the leading role that began to be played in the Bolivian economy by coca leaf cultivation and the drug-trafficking. As is well-known, coca is an ancestral element of Andean culture, with all type of medicinal, dietetic, comforting and ritual uses, both among indigenous peoples and in the rest of the population. Its association with cocaine is an alien phenomenon, but has implied all types of problems for small producers.

It is estimated that in Bolivia in 1985 more than 135 thousand metric tonnes of coca leaf were produced in approximately 70,000 hectares. It was calculated that almost 10% of the population was, directly or indirectly, linked to the coca economy. The gross value of coca leaf production represented around 300 million dollars, equivalent to 45% of the total value of the country's agricultural production. In 1950 there were in Bolivia less than 3,000 producers of coca leaf for traditional consumption. In 1987 that number had increased to around 70,000 producers (Van Niekerk, 1994: 21). This expansion was due not so much to greater internal consumption of the coca leaf, but rather to the increase in external demand for cocaine.

In practice, the role of *chief enemy* in this *war* was to be passed to the small coca leaf producer, whose activity was not in itself criminal, but who represented the weakest link in the chain. It must be underlined that both before and after the *boom* in this drug, coca leaf production has always been in the hands of small peasant producers, emigrants from the Andean regions in search of better opportunities.

In this war context, the coca-producers began to organise themselves in response to the permanent struggle between the need to save their economy, based on the production of coca leaf, and the constant threat of forced eradication of this plant as the raw material for cocaine. Thus they became, over the years, one of the most active social groups in the country. In their constant marches and mobilisations there have been scores of deaths, mostly of coca-producers, but also of soldiers and policemen.

Within this national context, CIPCA managed to give some interesting responses to the problematic of the countryside: firstly, with a coordinated emergency action during the drought of 1982-83 and, then, with the elaboration and execution of the proposal of work communities (CDT) as an economic alternative to rural development. But before writing of these and other aspects, firstly we will deal with two currents of thought that had their heyday in the first half of the 1980s and that have also influenced CIPCA's everyday activity: popular education and integrated rural development.

CURRENTS OF THOUGHT

Popular education and participative research

In the 1980s a specific type of non-formal adult education gained in strength among NGOs dedicated to social promotion. The theoretical discourses of liberation education, liberation theology and action-research – currents dealt with in the first chapter – have several key principles in common, the same ones that have influenced the theory and practice of popular education and participative research.

Criticisms of traditional research might be summed up as belonging to three tendencies:
- researchers who emphasised the need for new relations between researcher and researched, between subject and object of research (Fals Borda, 1978);
- researchers who championed the need for qualitative research, rejecting quantitative research techniques (Hall, 1982);
- researchers who rejected structural functionalism and proposed a basis of historical materialism, utilising the dialectical method as a method of analysis (Molano, 1978).

There was consensus in the following point; in studying the problems of the popular sectors in contributing to alternatives of structural change, researchers could not simply continue in a role of 'expert in knowledge', but had to become involved in the process of social change. Fals Borda (1978) described the researcher as "an intellectual who, on becoming conscious of belonging to society and to the world at a given time, renounces a position of pure spectator and places his or her thought or art at the service of the cause".

This 'placing knowledge at the service of a cause' could be expressed in different and very varied ways. Among these, we could mention the participant observation of anthropology, the participative survey, auto-diagnostic, research-action, research from below and from within, and participative research. All these forms of social research have been present in the 1980s and their fundamental characteristic was the relation between research and action.

Among committed researchers and educators there was consensus in which they were dealing with a continuous process of reflection and action. However, in practice there were different interpretations of action:

• an educational interpretation: action referred to the educational process, implemented after the investigative phase;

• a developmentalist interpretation: research results constituted the basis for the satisfaction of some basic need;

• a party political interpretation: action could be reduced to a party political action, in which researcher, as political agitator, could only end up as a proselytising activist.

Popular education was considered as a process of social transformation, since it questioned the authoritarian tendencies of society, relations of economic exploitation and cultural imposition. As such, the objectives of popular education were defined as an alternative historical project (Gianotten and de Wit, 1985:84):

• the development of popular knowledge and of control over popular and scientific knowledge; in other words, the socialisation of existing knowledge and the generation of new knowledge;

• the critical development of popular culture, as a historical alternative to cultural hegemony;

• the development of forms of popular organisation, from the popular sectors' own historical interests.

CIPCA subscribed to this new educational focus and has made important contributions, such as the *Popular Historical Project*, which will be dealt with in the following chapter. There was also a change in the methodology of educational activities in CIPCA. There was no desire to continue giving short training courses, people having accepted that the short course could not be the panacea to cure all ills. Internally, talk was of *shortcourseitis*. In order to overcome these limitations, CIPCA opted for a method of teaching-learning based on praxis: action-reflection-action; theory-practice-theory (Jara, 1981: 29). It was reaffirmed that educational action started from the productive, as a point from which to discover social, economic and political implications. This process implied the provision of instruments to create a critical consciousness. Education, then, grew out of the everyday, the concrete, reality itself, and was oriented toward change. Popular education stimulated awareness, brought knowledge, motivated the will to change and encouraged transformative action in the learner (Arias, s.f.).

The concept of participation was debated at length during those years, because everyone had their own proposal of how to ensure the participation of the popular sectors in educational projects or research. Up to today we can find the following forms of participation:
- participation in the collection of data, but not in data analysis;
- participation in the devolution of information;
- participation in the whole process, but on a theme defined by the institution.

We will end this paragraph by summing up some of the limitations of popular education that were already criticised in its peak years (Gianotten and de Wit, 1985: 99-103): at times popular educators idolised the knowledge of the people and popular education was conceived as an immediate, emotive action without theoretical reflection. Similarly, educational activities were alien to the reality of the popular sectors and the peasants were obliged to memorise Marxist manuals. There was also widespread proselytism, utilising educational action for party political ends. However, popular education and action-research have given rise to a whole generation of rural promoters and researchers who took seriously the voice of the peasantry in its approaches to educational, productive and organisational matters. Peasant families were no longer considered as people with a 'backward mentality', but as critical thinkers, capable of transforming reality.

Integrated rural development

In response to the limitations of community development[69], the early 1980s saw proposals for integrated rural development that gave more consideration to the social structure in which the rural population is immersed. Recognising the complexity of social change and the fact that no isolated intervention could be effective if applied at the periphery of other equally important elements, it proposed integral action. Many integrated rural development programmes have been drawn up within the framework of new concepts of 'planned change'. Local or regional planning was seen as an adequate instrument for achieving social change that was ordered, controlled and in concordance with national development plans. This new approach also considered the community as a homogeneous entity, whose members would be prepared to work associatively or collectively. We will see below that CIPCA also utilised technical and ideological arguments to propose a form of collective production through the CDT.

While 1970s modernisation theory set out the problem of development as a mere technical and psychological problem, the development theories emerged in the 1980s that posited a change in economic structures and policies as a *sine qua non* condition for development. The problem of poverty was analysed as a political problem. The relationship of dependency appeared as a central axis of analysis. Dependency theory developed by André Gunder Frank in 1976 and with many followers in the early 1980s, understood underdevelopment as a product of the expansion of world capitalism. Underdevelopment was produced through a chain structure of metropolis-satellite or centre-periphery of the capitalist system. Exploitative relationships occurred between classes and regions.

During these years, under the influence of dependency theory, there was a search for a way to define this situation and the small peasantry's future in relation to capitalist development. On the one hand there were the traditional Marxists who, following Lenin and Kautsky, posited the inevitable disappearance of the peasant's modes of production, to be replaced by the contradiction between an agrarian bourgeoisie and a rural proletariat (De Janvry, 1981:102).

On the other hand there were those who based themselves on the theory of Chayanov, defending the peasant economy as a mode of production different from the capitalist, with its own logic and dynamic (Archetti et al., 1979). In Peru, Caballero (1981:314) argued also that capitalism could not replace the peasant economy due to various factors:

- the resistance of the peasantry to forced proletarianisation;
- physical and ecological characteristics that made capital investment unprofitable for the rural bourgeoisie;
- the limitations of the rest of the national economy in quickly absorbing the peasant workforce into urban-industrial occupations.

In most Bolivian academic circles until shortly before decree 21060 in 1985 Marxist analysis, still at its zenith, attributed the role of vanguard in the class struggle to mining workers. The Marxist position conceptualised the peasants as a transitory class. At a moment in which both political groups and progressive groups within the church put all their faith in the mining sector, supposedly the vanguard of class struggle, the founders of CIPCA had committed to the peasantry from the very beginning. In the words of Luis Alegre, founder of CIPCA: "the future of Bolivia is decided in the countryside and not in the mines."

To conclude this section on rural development, it is necessary also to mention that in the 1980s the green revolution was still seen by many as a good example of technological modernisation, despite studies showing that the green revolution had contributed to the concentration of wealth and to greater inequality in income distribution[70].

One response to the green revolution was the focus on appropriate technology. The publication of the *A Report to the Club of Rome* (Meadows, 1972) marked the beginning of a profound reflection on the reach of technological innovation. *A Report to the Club of Rome* pointed out the limitations of economic growth at world level, sustaining that technological innovation would not be able to confront the central problem: exponential growth. At the same time, criticisms to technological development emerged, setting out the need to create cheap appropriate technologies, within everybody's reach and usable on a small scale. Schumacher's 1982 work *Small is beautiful* had a great influence on thinking about rural development. However, it was soon abandoned as a romantic focus and an apology for everything supposedly natural and non-western. Both books have had great influence on what later became the agro-ecological focus and then sustainable (rural) development.

RESUMING ACTIONS AND NEW QUESTS

CIPCA National

After having come out of hiding, CIPCA resumed its work as before. However, it still had to draw up a detailed work plan with objectives, goals, zones of intervention, activities and expected results. As in its foundation years, CIPCA was again looking for adequate extension methodologies. A principle it never abandoned were the three *legs*: educational, productive and organisational. The emphasis on productive activities, initiated during the final stages of the dictatorship, continued after ward and resulted in various proposals of peasant organisation for production such as the CDT in the Guaraní zone and the association of small producers on the Altiplano. This gave rise to the first experiences of the peasant economy's openness to the market.

The research themes in these years changed in accordance with the new emphasis on productive activities. Anthropological research decreased while technical investigation and zonal and regional diagnostics began to have more importance.

In 1984 CIPCA had drawn up some general policies at national level:
- CIPCA's work seeks to benefit the totality of the community and not mere groups or individuals;
- the entire Programme must be conducted and executed by the grassroots organisation.

CIPCA La Paz

In 1982-83 came the serious drought mentioned above, which particularly affected the Altiplano. In 1983 potato production decreased by approximately 70% across the whole country. At some point in the same year, in the La Paz market, a single normal-sized potato reached the price of 60 pesos – in other words, more than a litre of common petrol, which cost 50 pesos at that time.

CIPCA felt the need to respond to this general emergency. In 1983 a Drought Plan was executed which in 1984 and 1985 became the Programme of Peasant Agricultural Recuperation (PRACA). Not only CIPCA participated in this emergency plan, which constituted the most serious effort towards inter-institutional action ever made in Bolivia. Other participants included Caritas, the Methodist Church, UNITAS, the 'Qhana' Centre for Popular Education, IPTK, ACLO, Radio Pío XII, Multiple Services of Appropriate Technology (SEMTA) and the Centre of Promotion and Cooperation 'Yunta'. The CSUTCB also played an active coordinating role with the grassroots unions. Both for the 1983 Drought Plan and for the PRACA programmes the work was based on a rotating fund, with 10% for administrative costs. CIPCA La Paz assumed the administration of this fund in its work zones, putting in its entire infrastructure for the purpose.[71] The rapid implementation of the Drought Plan and, later, of PRACA, also implied a great mobilisation for international solidarity, which responded in an exemplary manner to this emergency.

The Drought Plan had two objectives: to recuperate the potato seed and to guarantee food supplies for people and animals. This meant a great leap for CIPCA because in the first year it came to work with 500 communities, a total which decreased to 300 in 1984. At the beginning it was chaotic and complicated because it was necessary, without previous experience, to organise the work of many people and build up stocks of a variety of consumables. In a week the plan was drawn up for what was an extremely big operation. Its execution meant the mobilisation of all staff, which was stretched in order to attend to 500 communities. There was a desperate situation in the countryside. This great mobilisation was one of the positive results of the plan.

The parish priest of Jesús de Machaqa commented that such was the quantity of potatoes that had farmers had managed to store in order to replace the seed lost in the drought, that it was necessary to turn the immense colonial temple into a temporary silo. At the end of the mobilisation there were four storage centres in Jesús de Machaqa for 22 subcentrals and 76 unions. Before the construction of the storage centres there was no had infrastructure for this purpose. The CIPCA staff distributed seeds, participated in the recuperation of funds, ran an animal health campaign and organised training courses.

There was also a credit system that was called *waki* contract, whose fundamental use was to make possible the recuperation of potato seeds, both bitter and sweet. In the *waki* system, the villagers and CIPCA were counterparts; one had land, the other had seed. Traditionally in this type of share-cropping contracts, very common among the Aymara, both groups get together for the agricultural work, and once the harvest arrives the produce is shared equally, for example an alternate furrow harvested for each one. Obviously in this case CIPCA could not reach so many places at the same time to the agricultural work, but the clause of distributing production in equal parts was maintained. However, in practice this was not always kept up: when harvesting without CIPCA's presence, many concealed the quantity that was really produced. From the institutional perspective it seemed a failure, but not from the villagers' viewpoint; they recuperated their productive capacity much more rapidly.

Remember that it was in the very years of the return to democracy that Bolivia suffered the worst monetary devaluation in its history. Banknotes were worth less than their weight as used paper, which meant that before going out in search of the few places that still sold potato seed, the van had to journey filled with sacks of ... banknotes!

Altogether, this experience also made the strengthening of local organisations redundant, since the regular counterpart of the Drought Plan was the community, with its authorities and even its higher level entities. But, on the other hand, once the initial euphoria had passed, all attempts at reproducing this intense communal productive dimension in regular communal projects failed.

The great mobilisation involved in the execution of the Drought Plan also made it clear that CIPCA had no technical response for such large investments. Besides, the CIPCA staff was used to intensive work, but the Drought Plan was an emergency plan with work that was, by contrast, extensive.

These changes produced the following fundamental problems:
• little clarity over the type of organisation that CIPCA supported;
• tensions with peasant organisations which claimed intensive attention when faced with the extensive strategy implemented during the era of emergency.

The experiences with credit were not all positive. There was the loss of the rotating fund; the technicians had to spend a lot of time recuperating money while the peasants preferred the aid to be non-repayable. When the technicians began to apply the rules of the credit game, many peasants no longer wanted to work with CIPCA.

A positive point of PRACA, although only recognised after many years, was the innovative proposal of greenhouses.[72] The agricultural experimentation Programme also had important successes. But unfortunately, the other face of these successes on the productive side was the error of trying to create parallel organisations in the community. This produced a conflict with the traditional peasant organisation (union) because there was no clarity over whether the CDT or the associations had to be groups of people that worked with CIPCA or if they were (part of) each union organisation.

The effects of the drought on the Altiplano obliged CIPCA to redefine its geographical area and mode of action: the Ingavi and Aroma provinces would constitute its geographical sphere during these years. It was impossible to continue working in the other zones, Caranavi and Alto Beni, mainly because of budgetary limitations. Confronting the complex problematic of the zones of colonisation, that besides were affected by the drug-traffickers, meant concentrating a great quantity of resources on them for a long time and, probably, creating a new regional office, something that was not within the institution's reach.

CIPCA Cochabamba

When Enrique Gómez assumed the directorship in 1982, he found an office that sought to leave politics aside and in which work had recommenced with a new team. Almost all the staff from before the García Meza coup had left. The period 1982-1986 was unstable for CIPCA Cochabamba, among other things because various different directors were in charge over relatively short periods. When in 1986 Carlos de la Riva (after 1982 Head of the Department of Education) became director, that office was coming out of its disorientation and beginning to function better.

CIPCA Cochabamba had passed from a community-centred focus to one based on larger territories then known as 'zones'. The zone was considered a potentially integrated work unit. With this measure the intention was to achieve greater efficiency, efficacy and profundity in the work, as well as broadening coverage, thus optimising the use of available resources. The decision was made to concentrate on three zones: Sacaba, Sacabamba and Tiraque, within which CIPCA attended principally to 16 communities, considerably fewer than the total sum of the communities in these zones.

The main objective was to avoid the peasants feeling obliged to migrate, either permanently or temporarily, away from the zone – principally to the Chapare, which was the new zone of coca production. This objective was in accordance with the approaches of that time on migration. In academic circles and the development cooperation, the theory was to invest in rural areas to avoid urban migration. There was the hope of being able to detain the exodus, above all of the youth, concentrating on rural development. Another expectation was that this would help country people to have a better rural life.

It is noteworthy that the socialist mystique still existed in productive proposals. There was the objection, for example, to the individual credits on the grounds that these would create social differentiation within the community. The community was seen as a homogeneous entity that had to remain homogeneous. Despite the peasant communities never having been homogeneous entities either economically or socially, the implementation of economic proposals that proved successful only for a small group within the community was interpreted as a desire to introduce capitalism[73].

Contrary to what happened in other regional offices, the working strategy of CIPCA Cochabamba still had educational action as its central pivot, the starting-point for developed organisational work and, finally, productive work. In the educational area the decision was made not to concentrate on contact with leaders, but rather to orientate educational activities toward the bases; this decision was adopted after considering the few results of the work that focused attention on leaders. This was a very well-known dilemma to NGOs, one which they have never been able adequately to resolve: attention to leaders versus attention to bases. Both groups are necessary: the leaders have to orientate organisations in making political and economic demands, without falling into privileged attitudes, nepotism, or acts of corruption; conversely, the bases must have sufficient knowledge to exert democratic control over the actions of their leaders.

In the educational area, audiovisual materials were prepared such as pamphlets, slides, photos, and workshops and seminars were given. Another important gain was the recuperation of the radio equipment, which was still hidden in San Agustín School, which permitted recommencing the creation of radio programmes broadcast half an hour a day.

As far as union work was concerned, the complexity of the peasant movement in the zone meant that actions were only carried out at grassroots level, in the peasant communities, refraining from work at departmental level.

CIPCA Charagua – Camiri

In 1983 the main headquarters moved from Charagua to Camiri, changing its name to CIPCA Camiri. The change was due to the city of Camiri having become a more important and strategic centre for CIPCA, with better road facilities and communications and a higher concentration of communities around it, which facilitated the work of the team. The local civic movement had managed to have the Santa Cruz Development Corporation (CORDECRUZ) open an office in Camiri. CIPCA ceased to work in the zone of Isoso, so as not to interfere in the work that APCOB was undertaking there, and concentrated its work in the zone of *Ava*, the most populated of the entire Guaraní region, in the foothills of the Andes.

From 1982 to 1986 Francisco Pifarré was director of the regional office with Francisco Matzusaki as sub-director, based in the Charagua office, until he was made director of CIPCA Santa Cruz.

CIPCA Camiri-Charagua was the office most deeply involved in developing CDTs. In 1982 the office presented a detailed comparative study of a CDT from its very beginnings, the CDT at El Espino (1976). One of the general conclusions was: "a CDT is a real alternative to seasonal migration, a stabilising factor for the peasant on the land. It is an important factor in organisation and peasant awareness-raising. It offers coverage, stability and continuity in peasant organisations at times of repression". After the experience of El Espino, CDTs in the Guaraní region multiplied and in 1983 the popular pamphlet "*The 10 commandments of the CDT*" was published.

The objective of CIPCA was to produce a change in the production model through a better combination of productive factors: land, manpower and capital-technology. The CDT sought to be an economic model, whose distinctive features were its community element, its quality of self-management and its experimental nature.

There is no doubting the success of CIPCA's justified intervention to stop temporary migration to the sugar harvest and put an end to the subhuman conditions of near-slavery suffered by the Guaraní people. The CDT model was certainly, at that time, an adequate model for structural change to the situation of economic exploitation in which the indigenous Guaraní were steeped. In the following chapter we will deal in more detail with the development of the model: how it served to change the original situation and how it disappeared again once it had fulfilled that objective.

Eliberto Carpio of the Kuruyuki community remembered in 1991:

During 1980-1981 the idea emerged of forming a group with 15 members. But when we presented ourselves as a group we only had 5 members. The others thought that CIPCA was a communist organisation [74] *out to destroy our unity. In 1984 we recuperated the group of*

15 members and began a two-year trial period on the land. Today we number 35 families. For crops we have maize, soya and beans.

Another theme whose importance was recognised for the first time by CIPCA Camiri-Charagua was the participation of women. Until 1988, and the publication of a document on policies of women's participation at national level, CIPCA Camiri-Charagua reports display little consideration of work with women. Their few reflections show the state of thought at that time about the participation of women in development, as can be seen in the following quote from a 1984 report:

"It must be stressed that work with women emerged through the demand by women themselves to be incorporated into the process. Women's cooperatives were born and grew almost under their own steam and only once they were organised did they asked CIPCA for supervision. This work had two aims: a) to incorporate the women into productive agricultural activity, training them in the handling of vegetable crops and b) better utilisation of the agricultural and cattle products in the creation of more balanced diets, and the diversification of the use of products such as soya in family consumption."

In 1983 the *Eity Peasant Women's Organisation* was created, with 17 cooperatives in 5 subcentrales. The women would walk 20-25 kilometres with their children on their backs to attend the meetings. A 1984 report mentions that:

"... unfortunately, faced with the great development of women's organisational groups, CIPCA still had not adopted a clear position as to the response and advice it could give. Comparing these small women's cooperatives with the CDT formed by men one can see how numerous are the entities in which the two meet work together, and it would not too fanciful to think that the future might gradually give us mixed groups, constituted by men and women, in units of associated joint production ".

In these quotes it is possible to observe some evaluations on (the organisation of) women that show the debate at that time in CIPCA, but also in the world of development in general. Three opinions stand out in the 1980s:
• the support for women's productive work was restricted to the handling of vegetables and activities of lesser stockbreeding, whose products are intended not for the market, but for family consumption and that had to be women's responsibility;
• women were not taken into account in activities of agricultural outreach aimed at crops for market;
• from the beginning there was a debate over the legitimacy of a separate organisation, exclusively of women, in contraposition to the mixed, communal organisations.

The year 1985 marked an important landmark of the Camiri-Charagua office. With the support of the Development Corporation of Santa Cruz (CORDECRUZ) a base-line study of all the Guaraní communities of Cordillera province was carried out, and published in 7 volumes in 1986.[75]

It was the first time that CIPCA was undertaking an alliance of such magnitude with a State entity. Although the greater part of the work corresponded to CIPCA, resources came mainly from CORDECRUZ, which also provided logistical support. The diagnostic, carried out between 1985 and 1986, involved a good part of the CIPCA staff as well as authorities and other people from all the communities. The task of returning results to massive assemblies of communities, or groups of communities, was fundamental and very revealing. From this, a little later, the Assembly of the Guaraní People (APG, Ñemboati Guasu, in Guaraní), was born on the 7th of February 1987. Its four thematic portfolios also reflect the main axes for development: Production, Infrastructure, Health and Education (PISE). A fifth portfolio was later added, that of Land and Territory (PISET).

Out of this diagnostic a detailed Programme of Peasant Development of Cordillera (PDCC)[76], was also drawn up. Its implementation meant finding a total investment of 65 million dollars. For the execution of the PDCC a coordinating body was formed with the main institutions of the region, as well as the recently-created APG.[77]

CIPCA Santa Cruz

CIPCA was one of the few NGOs that managed to establish a good working relationship with CORDECRUZ, which was then a totally *camba* governmental entity without a specific development policy for the colonisers. CIPCA has had a positive influence in the openness towards the problematic of the colonisers.

One of the first tasks of the new director, José Oriol Gelpí, was to finish defining the priorities of work that were still too dispersed, with a problematic that was too variegated. It was finally decided that the basic objective had to be that of strengthening the colonisers' organisation in their new settlements, many of whom had come from impoverished regions of the Andes. After some reflection and self-criticism, the '*New Focus*' was formulated. The work of New Focus, due to begin in January 1984, was based fundamentally on attention to the whole community and not to any group within it.

For this purpose four zones were selected, in some of which work had been going on since the creation of the regional office: San Julián, el Chore, Antofagasta and Santa Fe. Such a concentration facilitated closer relations with the communities and their organisations, and greater understanding of a key problematic, very specific to the small producers of this department.

Also influential were the painful events during the Roadblock of San Julián in 1984, which placed at the forefront of public opinion the theme – always latent in

Santa Cruz – of racism in the local population (*cambas*) towards the colonisers and other immigrants of Andean origin (*collas*) and, at the same time, the political and economic power relations concealed behind this mask.[78]

The particular difficulties of the zones of colonisation were identified by CIPCA as people's instability, very diverse origins and lack of a new communal sense. One might read in the reports that a fundamental problem was the incapacity to carry forward a collective project, due to factors such as lack of knowledge of the medium, lack of cohesion, diversity of origin, nomadic tendencies, very adverse conditions (lack of infrastructure), and difficulty in coordinating community work in the collective plot with individual work in an individual plot. Besides, the traditional system of cultivation in the Oriente ('slash and burn') was turning into a system that destroyed the land, due to the great number of colonisers.[79]

The strategy employed was to attend to the economic, having a bearing on the technical capability to exploit the areas of colonisation. Each community needed attention in its entirety along with strengthening of individual economies, as a step leading to the phase of collective commercial exploitation. In organisational terms, this meant working through family relations rather than through the union leadership so as to reach the base. Looking back at these years today, the criticism could be made that there was an attempt to impose a mode of collective production without taking the world of the colonisers into account, meaning an inability to respond to their needs or set out any valid alternatives for them.

With the entry of Francisco Matzusaki, the productive dimension began to have more content. CIPCA Santa Cruz radically changed the activities oriented towards production: it introduced significant credits, mechanisation, technical packages, stockbreeding, permanent crops such as coffee, cacao and citrus. It was also a phase of motivation for creating work groups. The first objective was to increase family production because income was very low. There was distrust and rejection of communal work. For example, the San Julián union boycotted the collective plots, saying that CIPCA had a socialist orientation and wanted to dominate the peasant structures.

As in all NGOs in Bolivia and all the CIPCA offices, the establishment of demonstrative plots began to gain strength as an adequate outreach method. It is necessary to clarify that in those years the State was practically absent from the countryside. There was very little agricultural extension and after 1985 the services of research and agricultural outreach were totally dismantled. It was, besides, quite difficult to find an economic and technically adequate response for the small producers in the zone of Santa Cruz, where agro-export was turning more and more into a powerful economic sector.

TOWARDS INSTITUTIONALISATION

Not only CIPCA but many NGOs in Latin America were faced with a new challenge. These had begun in the 1970s as a group of enthusiastic friends, committed to the fight against rural poverty and having managed to establish relatively formal organisation with stable financing. Now they had to consolidate their organisation and take the qualitative step that would allow the transition from informal organisation to consolidated institution. In other words, they had to depersonalise the directorship and institutionalise the management.

The agencies were now prepared to finance CIPCA for periods longer than a year. The first triennial plan, financed by EZE and Novib, was that of 1982-1985. In 1982 experimentation had already begun with the first management instruments such as logical framework and planning by objectives. Finally, in 1987, an Planning, Monitoring and Evaluation (PME) system was implemented. However, reality was more complicated for CIPCA and the process of 'depersonalisation' was no easy matter. We will mention some factors that have played a role in this process.

First of all, it was necessary to change the activism, a principal characteristic of an institution in conditions of survival due to political repression. In 1985 the conclusion was reached that there was a rupture between the thinkers and the doers, between theory and practice. Secondly, the regional offices felt that they did not have sufficient support from the national office. Thirdly, the external evaluation undertaken by Novib was quite critical and caused discrepancy between two members of the evaluating commission and some members of the national direction. It annoyed the directors that the evaluators assessed only the work of the regional offices and did not take sufficiently into account the totality that was CIPCA. A consequence of this flawed evaluation was that the new 1986-1989 triennial plan was rejected by Novib which, together with *EZE*, was then CIPCA's main financer. This decision was a worry for the directors and caused anguish among the staff.

Another important problem had to do with the organisational structure. Over the years, the constitution of the management committee had gone through several trial periods. Due to the type of legal status, then dependent on the Company of Jesus, the two legal representatives of the Company were original members of the board committee. The rest of the board was constituted, in 1985, by various external members and by delegates of the CIPCA staff, elected in the four regional offices from those who did not perform any directive duties. In these years of democratisation it was normal that the staff of an institution might also be a member of its board, thus combining executive and directive functions. Thus the

CIPCA staff who participated in the board, there had authority over their own Regional Director, inverting the hierarchy of their everyday business.

Between April and August 1985 a proposal for the restructuration of CIPCA was drawn up along with a working manual for each person and a type of rulebook. At national level the National Council of Planning (CONAP) was set up. CONAP's main tasks would be to draw up a national system of planning and evaluation, formulating objectives, goals, institutional policies and working strategy, as well as a model for monitoring and controlled execution.

In October 1985, CIPCA organised an internal seminar to discuss the new organisational structure. Some conclusions from this analysis were:

CIPCA was designed in different political conditions and in relation to a unorganised peasant mass. CIPCA has travelled a long way alongside the peasantry, but joint action now requires greater reflection and planning. CIPCA cannot continue with the same activism. It is essential to question whether CIPCA should maintain its role of leadership in the construction of a political project or whether it should rather change to a supporting role. Besides, CIPCA must cease to impose capitalist or socialist 'revolutions' from the outside.

Despite these debates and analysis meetings, the problems of defining relationships still existed, especially between the regional directors and the National Director. The impact of the crisis among the staff was notable. There were meetings of the management committee, between staff or just groups of friends. There were also several resignations, which were not accepted. Ultimately, they were looking in one way or another for a sensible alternative in order to get out of the crisis. Finally, after numerous conversations with the Company of Jesus, Lucho Alegre decided to resign after having worked for 15 years as CIPCA director. The board appointed Marcos Recolons as new national director.

This first foundation period ended in 1987 and was marked by the creative, charismatic and audacious leadership of Luis Alegre. This leadership helped CIPCA's birth and its survival in an era of severe political repression. Apparently, the intuitions were more important than the strategies, the management was perhaps personalised, but it was capable of enthusing many young people and establishing a solid base of alliances. It is clear that without Lucho Alegre CIPCA would not exist.

BOLIVIA
Centro de Investigación y Promoción del Campesinado
CIPA coverage
(1987 - 2005)
Coordenadas UTM; Datum WGS-84; Zona 20
Fuentes:
Base: Mapa Político de Bolivia IGM esc 1:1.000.000
Elaboración propia
BRASIL
PERU
CHILE
PARAGUAY
ARGENTINA
N
O
E
S
Ingavi
Villa Nueva
Gonzalo Moreno
San Pedro
El Sena
San Lorenzo
Riberalta
Guayaramerín
10
Pelechuco
Curva
Charazani
Ancoraimes
Jesús de Machaca
Guaqui
Viacha
Ayo Ayo
Santiago de Machaca
1
2
San Ana de Yacuma
Cercado Río Mamore
San Ignacio de Moxos
9
Ascensión de Guarayos
Urubichá
El Chore (Santa Rosa)
7
San Julián
Antofagasta
8
OC-OI Regionales y departamentales de tierras bajas
4
Khuluyu
Tiraque
3
Arbieto
Tarata
Sacabamba
Anzaldo
Arampampa
Acasio
Torotoro
Gutiérrez
Lagunillas
Monteagudo
Charagua
5
Camiri
Boyuibe
Cuevo
Huacareta
6
INTENSIVE AND EXTENSIVE LABOR
1 La Paz: intensive
2 La Paz: extensive
3 Cochabamba: intensive
4 Cochabamba: extensive
5 Cordillera: intensive
6 Cordillera: extensive
7 Santa Cruz: intensive
8 Santa Cruz: extensive
9 Beni: intensive
10 Norte: intensive
+ More than 5 years
- Less than 5 years

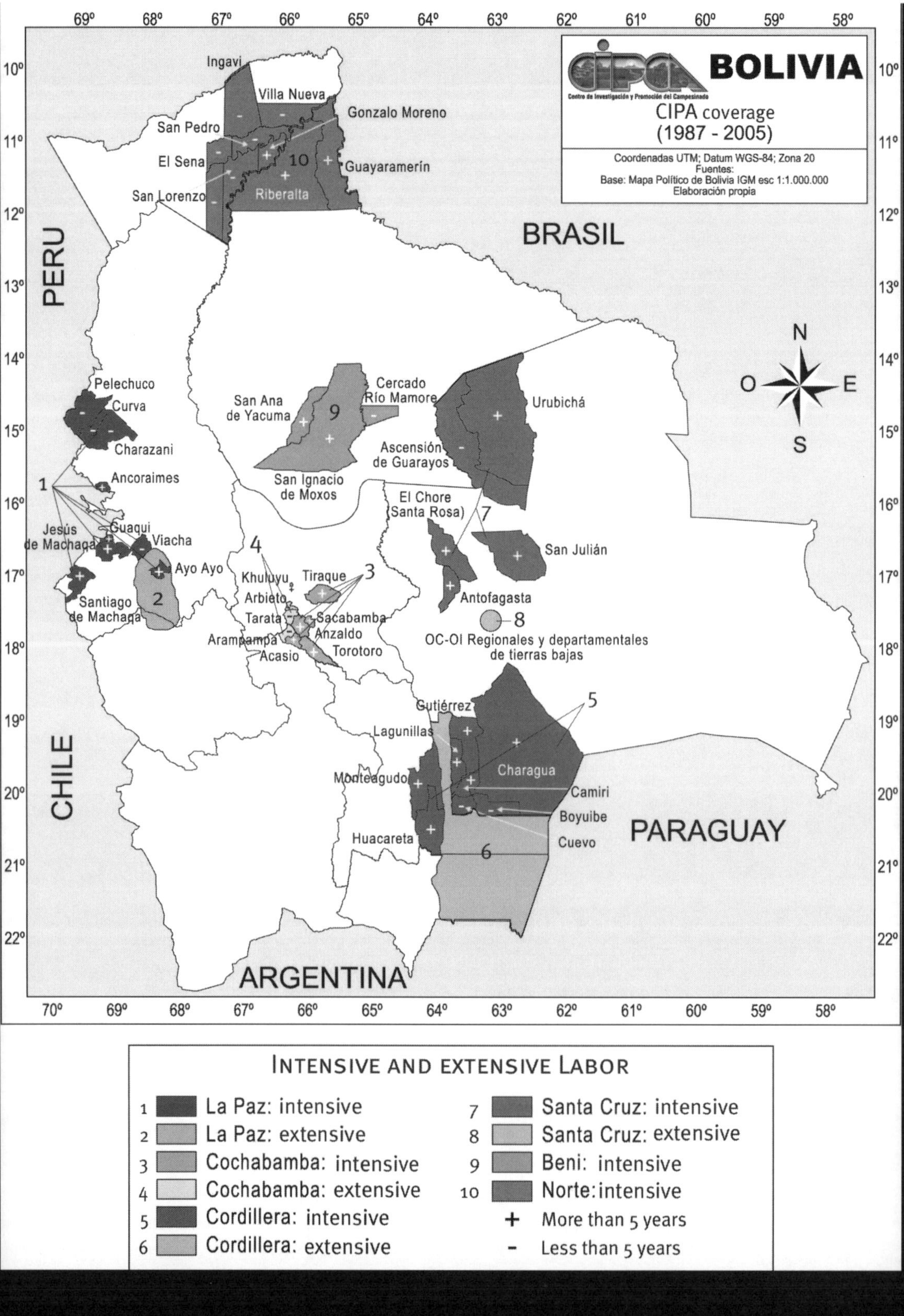

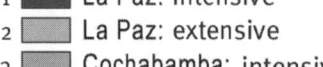

PART II
CONSOLIDATING DEMOCRACY 1987–2005

This second part recounts the history of CIPCA between the years 1987-2005, a period notable for the institutionalisation of CIPCA as a stable organisation with more formal relations. Activities during this period were carried out in an atmosphere of political democracy, in which the economic exclusion of the peasant and indigenous population was nonetheless still applied. CIPCA continued working, as an NGO, with the political commitment of having the peasant and indigenous population of Bolivia occupy its rightful place within the country's economic and political structure. The economic and cultural context was characterized by globalisation and the digital revolution.

This part is divided into two further chapters: chapter four tells of the years 1987-1996 in which CIPCA played a fundamental role in the elaboration of economic proposals for impoverished peasants, as well as advising peasant and indigenous organisations. The fifth chapter deals with the history of CIPCA in the years 1997-2005, in which the triennial plans were substituted by strategic quinquennial plans. Institutional finance was available, and CIPCA began to act with greater emphasis on its political impact at national level.

CHAPTER IV
CIPCA INSTITUTIONALISES
1987-1996

Eva Morales, current president of Bolivia

One the institutional crisis was over, one of the first tasks was to resume relations with the financing agencies, particularly with NOVIB, which had rejected the triennial plan of 1986-1989. It should be stressed that the NOVIB representatives had adopted a very constructive attitude toward the problems springing from the external evaluation of 1985. Kees van Dongen and John Schlanger had promised to do everything possible so that the evaluation report should not have negative consequences in EZE and Bread for the World, German agencies that also financed CIPCA and that had agreed to share the conclusions of the evaluation with NOVIB.

NOVIB provided a financial bridge for 1987, thus opening up the possibility of presenting a reformulated triennial plan. During this bridge year, CIPCA received two visits from representatives of NOVIB, among other reasons to establish an instrument of planning, monitoring and evaluation (PME). As a fruit of these interchanges, CIPCA began to draw up a plan that was no longer triennial but decennial, subdivided into three triennial plans plus a final year of adjustment[80]. Neither did EZE, Bread for the World and other agencies such as OXFAM, Christian Aid and Misereor stop financing CIPCA. Moreover, each one of these agencies understood that CIPCA had to continue to exist because, in turn, it was also functional to these agencies to formulate their development policies and put them into practice.

HISTORICAL OVERVIEW

Recuperating a tradition broken by the 1952 Revolution, in 1987 municipal elections were held. The strengthening of municipal democracy was key to giving greater direct power to the citizen. Since then municipal electoral processes have been regular.

Paz Estenssoro ended his government having performed a task that seemed impossible at the beginning of his term, defeating hyperinflation and stabilising the economy. However the social cost, expressed in high unemployment and under-acquisitive salary levels, was very high. The 1989 elections were held with a new candidate, Gonzalo Sánchez de Lozada of the MNR, who won the elections with a small majority over Hugo Banzer of ADN, followed some way behind by Jaime Paz Zamora of the MIR. Since nobody achieved an absolute majority, Congress assumed the task of choosing a president among those who won most votes. The election gave rise to a surprising alliance between Hugo Banzer and Jaime Paz Zamora, once apparently irreconcilable ideological foes. Through this pact, dubbed Patriotic Accord, Jaime Paz rose to the presidency of Bolivia despite having come third with barely 19% of the popular vote. The government of Paz Zamora was tainted with a high degree of corruption and the reappearance of drug-trafficking links.

A good many of the public-social initiatives, financed with resources from international cooperation, was concentrated in an office directly dependent on the Presidency of the Republic. In 1986, with the support of the World Bank and then President Víctor Paz Estenssoro, the Social Emergency Fund (FSE) was born, aimed at mitigating the social effects of the célebre Supreme Decree 21060. The FSE was conceived as a transitory measure, but the success of its functioning – particularly in terms of budgetary execution – led it to be turned, in its second stage, into the Social Investment Fund (FIS), which little by little began to depend totally on donations from international cooperation (Urioste, 2002: 36).

Something similar occurred with the Peasant Development Fund (FDC). When the Agricultural Bank closed in 1985 the FDC was constituted in 1989, dependent on the Ministry of Peasant and Agricultural Affairs (MACA). Without giving it time to become the main source of finance for rural development, this instrument was used for party political ends and knew high levels of corruption. Despite the efforts of some of its executives, the poor performance of others occasioned several years of waste (ibid: 39).

In the 1990s new social actors emerged that posited well-defined socio-cultural demands, often oriented towards changes in daily life more than the taking of political power or economic demands. This is the case of the women's movement, which managed to have its claims for gender equality enshrined in new legislation on the rights of women.

The resurgence of the Guaraní people, after a century of historical amnesia, or in the words of Albó (1990:348) "from a project of biological and cultural self-negation", ended successfully with the conformation of its own organisation, the Assembly of the Guaraní People (APG). In February 1987 the APG was organised with its own, previously unknown, indigenous characteristics. Moreover it was able to encompass and even unite all the communities for the first time in Guaraní history[81]. In 1993 the government formally recognised the APG as the legitimate representative organisation of the Guaraní peoples, communities and captaincies of Bolivia.

Before forming the APG, the Guaraní had numerous problems with the CSUTCB, since the latter's classist union structure was an imposition that left no space for the ethnic character of Guaraní communal organisation, which considered both aspects necessary and complementary (Soliz, 1995). After its foundation, the APG became part of the CSUTCB. In this way the APG was a key referent in the CSUTCB's ability to deepen its discourse on complementarity between questions of class and ethnicity, and could represent claims for the diversity of Indigenous Peoples in the country. So, after a few months, in the III CSUTCB Congress of June 1987, the directorship of the confederation was already entrusted to the three great "nationalities": Quechua, Aymara and "Tupi-Guaraní", this latter representing over 30 lowland ethnic groups, whether of Tupi-Guaraní origin or not (ibid).

The indigenous peoples of the Beni organised themselves in 1987 in a "Central of Mojeño Indigenous Local Councils", creating various sub-centrals over the following years before founding the Central of Indigenous Peoples of the Beni (CGNP) in 1989. The principal stimulus for this organisation was the defence of their territories from the threat of encroachment by stockbreeders and loggers. A very important historical landmark appeared in the March for Territory and Dignity of August 1990 in which 800 participants – men, women and children – marched from Trinidad to La Paz. Thanks to this march the concept of indigenous territories in the Oriente was established, giving rise to the recognition of indigenous peoples' rights. Besides, a few months after the march, and without doubt thanks to it, Bolivia was one of the first countries to ratify Agreement 169 of the International Labour Organisation (ILO)[82].

The preparation and later realisation of memorial events opposed to the 500th Anniversary of the so-called "Arrival of the Europeans", in October 1992, was exploited in a very particular way by the indigenous population. One of the activities was to call an "Assembly of Nationalities". On the eve of the 12th of October 1992, they organised several massive marches towards the main cities. On the very day of the 500th Anniversary, the biggest march of all was carried out in the city of La Paz.

Indigenous multitudes from the Andes and the lowlands arrived in the city and, after numerous symbolic demonstrations near the main square Plaza Murillo (which was kept inaccessible and rigorously patrolled by the forces of law and order), they gathered in the Open Air Theatre where they proclaimed the institutionalisation of an Assembly of Nationalities. But when this moment of truth arrived, difficulties emerged that were attributable to the diverse political positions between and within the indigenous and peasant organisations that were present. Some wanted to establish the Assembly there and then with those present, while others maintained that the bases should be consulted beforehand. In the middle of these discussions there was a great rainstorm; everyone dispersed and then returned to their communities and departments. The matter was never spoken of again.

In 1992, the principal coca-growers' leader at that time, Evo Morales (of Aymara origin but established in the Cochabamba tropics), was defeated by the Aymara Block of the CSUTCB, headed by Paulino Guarachi and Félix Cárdenas. Years later, headed by Félix Santos and Román Loayza, Quechua-speakers began to have hegemony in the CSUTCB, with backing from the coca-growers' federations.

Finally new organisations emerged that were closer to the traditional Andean forms that "unionism" inherited from the MNR, which over the years have evolved into the Council of Ayllus and Markas of the Qullasuyu (CONAMAQ), formalised on the 22nd of March 1997.

The 1993 national elections resulted in a second triumph for Gonzalo Sánchez de Lozada (Goni), who this time had offered the vice-presidency to the former Katarist leader (and CIPCA worker) Víctor Hugo Cárdenas. The ascent of the pioneering Cárdenas to the vice-presidency was a landmark. This audacious and surprising alliance between indigenous peoples and neoliberals was not without its conflicts with some indigenous sectors, but it also facilitated greater development of the indigenous movement. Sánchez de Lozada and the MNR presented an ambitious Programme of structural changes that sought to consolidate the giro of Bolivia's turn towards a market economy. This meant an alliance with Max Fernández' Civic Solidarity Union (UCS) and with the Free Bolivia Movement (MBL) led by Antonio Aranibar and Miguel Urioste.

The group that was able to capitalise most on the direct election of new municipal governments, stimulated by the Law of Popular Participation (LPP) of 1994, was the coca-producers' movement, led by Evo Morales in alliance with the Single Union Federation of Peasant Workers of Cochabamba.

During the 500th anniversary events the idea began to emerge of a struggle, no longer only from the militant union ambit but also from the political sphere. The CSUTCB set out the creation of a "political instrument" as another arm of the peasant organisation (CORACA was already the economic arm). The coca-growers had decided to accept the new rules of the game and founded the Assembly by the Sovereignty of the Peoples, but when the new political arm was not recognised by the National Electoral Court, association was sought with the United Left. In this way, in the first municipal elections under the new law (December 1995), Evo Morales became the leader of the first political force in the rural area of the department of Cochabamba: he obtained almost 50 councillors and 10 mayors. This is the historical origin of the Movement to Socialism (MAS) under the leadership of Evo Morales, who in 2005 would be elected President of the Republic by absolute majority. Without exaggerating we can say that Evo Morales, as a son of the peasant union movement and of the coca-producers' movement, has been able to utilise the Law of Popular Participation as a trampoline from which to become national political leader.

The three fundamental pillars of Gonzalo Sánchez de Lozada's Programme were capitalisation, popular participation and educational reform. Capitalisation implied the sale of 51% of the actions of the six principal State companies, among them the public oil enterprise (YPFB), national telecommunications (ENTEL) and the airline

Lloyd Aéreo Boliviano (LAB). As we will see below, privatisation (euphemistically termed capitalisation) was at the root of the subsequent conflict over gas and hydrocarbon resources between 2002 and 2005.

Popular participation was turned into a Law that implied the establishment of municipalities, to which 20% of central State tributary income were assigned. Thus the possibility was opened to citizens of controlling the administration of their municipality's funds and of making decisions about them. Municipalities that used to receive a few thousand Bolivian pesos, or not even that, came to receive millions.[83]

On the other hand, with territorialisation, productive organisations (such as producers' associations, cooperatives and CORACA) were left outside the new decision-making panorama. Over the years, as practical experience was accumulated in the application of the LPP, this problem was overcome and now the productive organisations are part of the municipal dynamic.

Additionally, the government approved reforms to the Constitution, including the creation of a Defender of the People. With a mandate equivalent in other parts of the world to the Ombudsman and the National Commissions of Human Rights, the establishment of that office of Defender of the People has been one of the most successful elements of Bolivia's institutional and democratic reforms.

Towards the end of 1996, a few months before the change of government, the National Institute of Agrarian Reform Law (INRA) was approved. This was the most important step since the Agrarian Reform of 1953. It was necessary to close the National Council of Agrarian Reform (CNRA) and the National Institute of Colonisation (INC) because of the arbitrary way in which the land had been distributed (Urioste, 2003)[84]. The new INRA Law was designed between 1992 and 1996. While the 1953 Agrarian Reform was aimed at the country's Andean side, the INRA Law paid rather more attention to the lowlands of the Oriente (Kay and Urioste, 2005: 26).

The INRA Law initially set out to make the market for land more open and transparent, as suggested by the World Bank. But due to Bolivia's special conditions the INRA Law also included clauses favourable to small peasants. The Law retained the criterion of preferential property rights for peasants and indigenous people, and above all created the concept of Indigenous Communitarian Land (TCO) for awarding titles of collective property, as 'indigenous territories', to the original population. When it was promulgated in 1996, the stipulation was that the land property reorganisation should conclude in ten years. However, by 2005 only 18 million hectares, or 17% of the existing 107.47 million hectares had gone through this phase, while 30% were in process and 53% had not been reorganised (see also the following chapter).

CURRENTS OF THOUGHT

Within this historical panorama, NGOs that worked in rural development began to have other functions. Democracy at political level and the structural adjustment at economic level meant that NGOs had to redefine their role. Similarly, the cooperation agencies also began to redefine their relations with NGOs. The fact that CIPCA is part of this history makes it necessary for us to look closely at currents of thought at that time on the new role of NGOs. This will be followed by a more detailed analysis of two important themes on the 1990s development agenda: environment and gender.

NGOs in a democratic context

Born during military dictatorships and originally inspired by a consciousness-raising approach of popular education and action-research, some NGOs had, during the 1990s, become experienced and professional institutions. During these same years they had also become organised into functional and thematic networks. Attempts have been made to reproduce as public policies many of the ideas and experiences coming from these NGOs. Examples are programmes of micro credit, irrigation, intercultural and bilingual education, promotion of productive organisation, food security, adequate technologies and local management.

The objectives of NGOs, expressed according to structural change (awareness-raising and organisation) had evolved in the 1990s towards objectives that sought to combine the political-organisational dimension with concrete proposals for improvements in living conditions and economic development. Just as in previous years, the history of CIPCA has not been carried out in an ideological and theoretical vacuum. The members of CIPCA have been both receptors and innovators of these new ideas on the role of NGOs.

While democracy was consolidated in the second half of the 1980s, the number of NGOs financed by international cooperation increased dramaticly. The European Co-Financing Agencies (ACF), supportive of Latin American NGOs working under military regimes (Chile, Argentina, Brazil, Uruguay, Bolivia) also changed their institutional profile. In previous years, there was no formal monitoring of what NGOs were doing and there were almost no site visits. The directors and staff of ACFs and NGOs were, more than anything else, a group of supportive friends. There would be perhaps one visit a year, no so much to supervise or evaluate the work's progress, but rather to display international solidarity. In NOVIB, for example, the Latin America department was the most powerful and the group of intellectuals concentrated there managed a large part of the rest of NOVIB[85].

After 1985 this situation changed definitively. A process of internal professionalization occurred within not only in NGOs, but also agencies.

Francisco Matzusaki, ex director of CIPCA Santa Cruz, remembers how it was before:

When Oriol Gelpí handed me the management of CIPCA Santa Cruz, he left me a box, a black mission box with 48,000 dollars in it. He told me: take this, you can use it for whatever project you like.

The sums made available for the financing of NGOs also increased considerably. While the former NGOs managed to increase their budgets, many new NGOs also sprang up. Thus, by 1990 more than 400 NGOs were identifiable in Bolivia, of which a third were involved in activities of agricultural development. In 1997, the NGO registry mentioned 800 institutions, of which just over half worked in the rural area[86]. NGOs were increasingly sought after, as interlocutors, by organisms of international cooperation.

Apart from finance from private cooperation agencies, towards the end of the 80s there was a considerable increase in funding from development banks – the World Bank and Inter-American Development Bank, and multilateral entities such as the European Union. For example, in order to channel the Fund for Peasant Development (FDC), the international cooperation imposed the condition that the transfer of part of its resources should be made through the administration of NGOs (Urioste 2002: 39).

Another "hype" within the international cooperation agencies was the idea that grassroots organisations could execute development projects without the intervention of NGOs. Thus considerable amounts rapidly began to be channelled to the peasant organisations. Taking advantage of this juncture, the leaders of the grassroots organisations began to object to the presence of NGOs, saying that "their personnel were using the money for holiday trips to Europe or the USA and for too high salaries".

At the same time, there was great expectation of what NGOs were able to perform. A World Bank internal memorandum, for example, established norms for relationships between the Bank and NGOs[87]. In a report on NGOs in Bolivia, the WB recommended greater efforts to integrate NGOs in the policies aimed at relieving poverty since, by their criteria, these institutions were important as intermediaries between the government and the base groups. They could contribute to making the social services more accessible to the poor (World Bank, 1990).

Thus, little by little, demands were made from NGOs for what should have been demanded from the State: responsibility for the rural development. And later NGOs were criticised for not having achieved development results. Cooperation agencies began to evaluate the success of NGO activities according to the efficient and effective generation of economic benefits (preferably expressed in terms of increased income) in favour of the groups with which they worked.

In synthesis, NGOs found themselves in an almost impossible situation:
- grassroots organisations wanted also to be NGOs and began to compete with them;
- some representatives of the agencies of co-financing wanted to do away with NGOs and began to finance the grassroots organisations directly;
- other agencies, above all the multilateral and bilateral ones, began to increase finance to NGOs;
- finally, all the agencies demanded direct and short-term impact in the economic growth of the impoverished population.

Environment and sustainable development

The advocates of appropriate technology promoted technologies with a 'human face', having rejected western technology and the negative effects associated with it in western countries. Among others, such effects included environmental contamination and the exhaustion of renewable natural resources (such as forests). Thus, in the western countries, the theory of conservation and handling of natural resources began to have such importance that – on a par with the focus of 'small is beautiful'– rural development proposals began to appear that contributed to improvements in neither production nor productivity of peasant plots. The demands for clean production – so necessary and justified in the rich countries– were imposed also on poor peasant and indigenous families, as if these were the great contaminators of the environment. The agro-ecological focus evolved towards a holistic and systemic focus of the relations between human beings and the ecosystem. Within this focus, agrarian production was only considered possible as long as it remained in harmony with the laws of nature. The most important principle of agro-ecology was biodiversity.

In the late 1980s the so-called Brundtland Report was published, contributing a new definition to the concept of sustainable development. This new definition has had great influence on thinking about development and is still valid to this day: "sustainable development is a development that satisfies the needs of the present without compromising those of future generations" (Brundtland Report, 1987). Sustainable development puts emphasis on the conflict between the growth of needs and the limitation of natural resources. So, the new definition of sustainable development departs from two basic elements: the absolute scarcity of resources and intergenerational equity. Besides, the Brundtland Report affirms correctly that sustainable development is more than the conservation of natural resources or care for ecology. In order to achieve sustainability, there are several strategies: the eradication of poverty, the sustainable use of natural resources, the ordering of territory, technological development compatible with social and natural reality, social organisation and mobilisation, and state reforms.

Without denying the importance of the need to conserve nature, any reduction of rural development proposals to mere conservation means not knowing that sustainable development has many more aspects than the purely ecological. Thus, talk of environmental conservation has gradually lessened. Instead, attention is being given more and more to proposals for sustainable development, emphasising the rational use of natural resources and interpreting this as a collection of components that embraces economic, environmental, organisational, social, technological and cultural factors (CIPCA-NOVIB, 1998).

Gender

Peasant women, miners' wives and housewives have always played a prominent role in Bolivia's political struggles. These were the kind of women who, in 1977, forced the military regime to restore democracy with their massive Hunger Strike in the Archbishopric of La Paz. However, only in the 1990s was a specific economic and social policy established that took women's needs into account. It was the government of Sánchez de Lozada that established the first Gender Secretary within the Vice-ministry of Ethnic, Gender and Generational Affairs. Until those years, all the attention given to the situation of women was based on the traditional image of mother and wife, in which food donations played a crucial role. Utilising mothers' clubs as the best way to channel foods, it emphasised only the reproductive role of women (the family's providers of food) at the same time as their role as economic actors was undervalued. Towards the end of the 1980s there were more than 6,000 mothers' clubs with an average of about 50 members. Some 300,000 women were organised and coordinated so as to channel the food aid. As a consequence, rural development proposals saw peasant women almost exclusively as housewives and recipients of food in stead of producers of stapple food (Prudencio, 1991).

The theme 'woman and development' has been on the agenda of development organisations since the late 1970s. Also, specific activities were introduced in CIPCA in the early 1980s that involved and benefitted peasant and indigenous women. At the beginning, development models saw women as simply passive objects instead of important actors in economic development. Once a shift was made in accepting women not only in their reproductive role, policy makers and intellectuals only recognised women's productive role for satisfying basic needs and in the context of an economy of self-sufficiency. After the 1980s a third focus emerged, of woman and development, which recognised the importance of integrating women into the development process in order to strengthen the national economy. It was supposed that their integration would make the process more efficient and effective. This instrumental focus was based on the (mistaken) appreciation that the women were not, as yet, 'integrated' and that women's work still had not contributed to national development. However, all these points of view failed to see the inequality of power between men and women in the economic and social spheres, in public and private life. The focus of 'empowerment' emerged at the end of the 1980s as a reaction to women's not being recognised as economic and social actors on a par with men. It was based on the comprehension that structural inequality between the sexes can be reverted, reinforcing women's empowerment. Thus in the 1990s the concept of 'women and development' was replaced by the new concept of 'gender and development', emphasising the need to achieve equality and equity between men and women in all spheres of public and private life (Gianotten et al. 1994: 11-12).

The anthropological theory of Andean complementarity and the supposed reciprocity between man and women (*chachawarmi* in Aymara) implies – supposedly – equality between the sexes. This complementarity would also be reflected in private and public life – the spheres corresponding to women and men respectively. So, according to this theory, unequal power relations and modalities of exploitation do not exist in Andean peasant families; rather there is complementarity within private life as well as between life in private and public spheres. Based on an analysis of the mutual dependency between men and women, the principle of complementarity was presented, not as a normative ideal but as a reality that, however, only exists in the minds of anthropologists, and not in the everyday lives of indigenous women, who suffer exploitation, exclusion and – in many cases – domestic violence (for a critical analysis of this theory see Harris, 1985).

If it is true that complementarity implies mutual dependency, it does not automatically imply equality. In attributing mythical gender equality to indigenous cultures, aspects such as discrimination, physical violence and unequal power relations disappear in the analysis. But in real life, the complementarity is asymmetrical, based on a hierarchical system and an underestimation of all that is feminine. "The conversion of indigenous culture into something mythical – to a large extent the work of intellectuals – does not clarify the position of the peasant woman; rather, it is a pretext to ignore the unequal power relations predominant in families and in communities" (Gianotten et al., 1994: 28).

CIPCA was influenced by these different currents, initially taking a more anthropological posture but evolving, through acquaintance with the facts, towards recognition of the unequal power relations between men and women. CIPCA mentioned explicitly its rejection of the ideas of 'first-world feminists', because "these approaches are not adjusted to the socio-economic reality of the Bolivian peasantry" (Decennial Plan: 19). Thanks to the insistence of the women that worked in NGOs dedicated to the theme of gender – in alliance with their colleagues in international cooperation agencies –, it was possible to overcome this prejudice.

THE INTERNAL ORGANISATION OF CIPCA

After 1988, when the Decennial Plan was initiated, there was a significant increase in the wealth of reports, internal evaluations and documents, principally thanks to the new PME instrument. CIPCA's central library has developed a special section dedicated to all the internal production of CIPCA, which currently has more than 2,000 documents without counting other texts, many of purely local reach, which are held in each regional office.

CIPCA understood that its role as an NGO made sense primarily as a support to the popular movement, in particular to the indigenous peasants movement, which were acquiring their own weight and developing their own organisation as part of a broader popular historical project. CIPCA saw itself as one of many actors performing a function in which other participants were the state, political parties and the popular movement itself. In those years CIPCA supported the idea that a large part of its role had to be transferred to the peasant movement itself. Likewise CIPCA was of the opinion that certain roles that it then played in a subsidiary capacity would have to be transferred to other actors such as the state, private banks or service companies. By 2005 the demand for transference had disappeared from discussions, since which time NGOs are considered as important and indispensable actors in the construction of civil society. But in 1988, the theme of transference was still very much a presence in CIPCA's internal debates and those of the co-financing agencies.

The following sections will examine first the institution's most significant internal changes, leaving for the second part the analysis of concrete activities and the advances made in practice towards their objectives. Although it is not the aim of this book to relate in great detail the changes in CIPCA's internal organisational structure, this chapter will pause a little more on this theme, because many of the measures taken in the late 1980s are also still valid in 2005.

Objectives and strategy
Within CIPCA discussion continued on the mentality of the indigenous peasants

and whether this was conservative or, on the contrary, modernising. On the one hand, the ancestral values of communal organisation were respected and even enshrined; on the other hand, there were people who argued that the small producers had a conservative mentality, resistant to change.

In the Decennial Plan it is mentioned that the ancestral cultural tradition is not alone in generating determined attitudes and values. The same is also true of the division of production into subsistence plots, which gives rise to characteristics like individualism, distrust, astuteness and the predisposition to produce for survival, resorting to great diversification of production on a small scale. With this in mind, CIPCA proposed the CDT model in order to increase production and productivity and, at the same time, to change the peasantry's individualistic mentality. This mentality was considered a brake on the rise in production and on the building of an alternative historical project.

The Decennial Plan explicitly mentioned the articulation of the three dimensions of work: "the conformation of a solid and unitary peasant organisation is indispensable in order to achieve peasant power. But if this is not part of an equally solid economic base, the peasant organisation will not attain real power to exert pressure. And vice versa, a simple economic advance, not accompanied by adequate organisation, would lead to a simple individualist developmentalism. In both these cases, the educational dimension guarantees that the subjects should face their reality critically and develop a historic project in search of an alternative society." Thus the synthetic formulation of the CIPCA mission "to generate peasant power" coincided greatly with which the cooperation agencies tend to conceive as "economic, social and political empowerment".

The external evaluation of late 1991 (Schwember et al., 1991) had already emphasised that CIPCA should perform a more active role as a "public" (as distinct from "official") institution, so as to make known its experience at broader levels, including official institutions. This recommendation was reiterated in the following evaluation at the end of 1995 (Mejía et al., 1995). After 1995 a new working area emerged: advocacy and lobby to influencing public policies for rural development at both local (municipal) level and nationally (see the following chapter).

The change of emphasis towards ever higher levels was the fruit of an experience gained over the years and contributed to CIPCA's constant improvement in carrying out its broader mission. However it has also been very opportune that this expansion has been realised without losing a foothold in the local (communal and municipal) peasant and indigenous reality. This experience, linked more to the grassroots organisations, is what has given and continues to give credibility to the proposals of CIPCA at higher levels.

Work zones

During the years 1987-1995 CIPCA kept working in the same zones as in previous years. However, as a result of the external evaluation of 1995 the decision was made to carry out a profound evaluation of the region of La Paz, which provoked a total rethinking of CIPCA's work, including the decision to open new zones. This change will be dealt with in the following chapter. In the other regions there have also been some changes, but not with implications as drastic as in the La Paz region.

Until 1996 CIPCA worked in the following zones:

Regional La Paz (Altiplano)	Ayo Ayo Jesús de Machaqa Santiago de Machaqa
Regional Cochabamba (Andean valleys)	Tiraque Sacabamba Alturas de Sacaba
Regional Santa Cruz (areas of colonisation)	Antofagasta El Chore San Julián
Regional Cordillera (Chaco) 88	Charagua Camiri

Managerial aspects

After long discussions with some of the 1986 financing agencies and external evaluators, CIPCA had consolidated its vocation as a unitary national body with diverse regional offices. Another measure that in the long term has had very good results has been not to accept the indefinite permanence of members of staff in any post. The founders have had the good sense not to consider the institution as their eternal property[89].

In the methodological sphere the above-mentioned System of Planning, Monitoring and Evaluation (PSE) has been the principal innovation of the Decennial Plan. The *annual evaluation* was an intense moment of high participation from all personnel. These are the steps to be followed in the annual evaluation:
• collection of data in the field, jointly with local people;
• discussion of the results in each team, concentrating above all on those indicators

in which it proved most difficult to advance towards the triennial goal. The key question was: is this a question simply of a slow pace or rather of a mistaken path? The themes were selected that were judged worthiest of a general discussion with the rest of the personnel;
- a general meeting of all the staff, for a deeper understanding of the reasons for good or bad results.

The PME process has added rigour to action. The main criticism is perhaps the excessive refinement with which the whole system is improved. Despite good intentions, the collection of so much data has demanded a lot of work during the end of each managerial period and has not contributed to reach the intended results more rapidly and more sustainably.

Another problematic principle was to ensure peasant-indigenous participation in formal planning moments, above all when this implied discussions with the staff. Between persons who speak other languages and use another form of logic, the task of achieving active participation among equals proved very complicated. A better experience has been the participation of the grassroots population in the whole process of base line studies and micro-regional plans, which in turn were considered privileged instruments for the strengthening of the peasant-indigenous organisations of the area studied. The process was far more local and the thematic itself stimulated greater participation. In the early years, CIPCA dreamed of greater participation from the peasants and their organisations in the CIPCA management committee itself. But in reality it could never work out, except through the occasional participation of individuals of peasant and indigenous origin, who were already part of the same institution. Successive reflections and diverse experiences, within and outside CIPCA, were making it ever clearer that this kind of participation was not necessarily the right way. It was indeed necessary to develop excellent relations between the institution and the grassroots organisations; but these were a separate entity, with their own dynamic. For both, it was necessary to avoid confusing their respective roles.

Activities

In the following we will not deal with each region separately, because the main activities have been developed in all the regions under the same principles. The philosophy governing elements such as the CDT, the economic activities, education as an instrument for generating a critical conscience, a unitary peasant organisation, the proposal for a popular historical project for all the country, was an institutional philosophy, put into practice with only minor differences in each office, due to the regional contexts.

CDT: THE GREAT DREAM

Perhaps there has been no other theme so extensively analysed and debated in the history of CIPCA as its proposal for work communities, better known as CDT. Reflection on this theme and its implications go back many years before 1987, and as late as 1995 it was still generating seminars, documents, evaluations and permanent adjustments[90].

The previous years

Almost since its origins in the 1970s CIPCA, which then worked only in La Paz, fomented the creation of associated productive groups instead of support to individual producers. There were practical and theoretical reasons. The first was that of being able to attend to more people with less effort. The second was aimed at arguments in favour of a socialist model, very present in the (few) NGOs then in existence. Although real experiences were still minuscule, it was hoped that they might get closer, even in a very embryonic way, to this ideal. One avoided talking of 'cooperative' because this experience had previously had many blunders in the Aymara region.

One successful experience from the 1980s was that of the Murumamani community, in Achacachi. The CIPCA staff did not want to adhere to the North American '*trickle down*' methodology, which involved working with some innovative peasants in the hope that the others would automatically follow. Then, instead of working with the more far-sighted peasants, the proposal was to work with the whole community, organising associated groups.

At the other end of the country, and on its own initiative, the Jesuits of Charagua supported the community of El Espino, which had just had a hard struggle to defend its communal territory. The works began in 1976, when the "Statutes of the El Espino Work Community" was drawn up. This name, used then for the first time, better expressed what was intended and was more in line with the cultural reality, displacing the more conventional cooperative model. Since then these experiences have multiplied. In 1983 a pamphlet was published entitled the 10 *commandments of the work community*; and in 1986 a first analysis was distributed[91] (see the previous chapter).

Key components

Behind the common name there were experiences that differed according to the reality of each place. In La Paz, for example, after the mass participation demanded by the Drought Plan of 1983-84, an attempt was made to use the whole community as a platform and expand the CDT under the direct leadership of its traditional authorities, hoping that they would assume their role within these new productive activities. In the Guaraní world the process was rather the reverse: the participating nucleus in the CDT was what gave greater dynamism to the whole communal organisation. Something comparable occurred in Santa Cruz but with a different emphasis: faced with a 'bureaucratising' or perhaps 'politicking' union, it was hoped that the productive association of a small group would open new horizons for the communal organisation. In Cochabamba, where the property was much more individualised and fragmented, people began to speak of a 'Cochabamba-style CDT, a term intended to underline the difficulty of putting lands together for production. As a contrast to this tendency it was possible to mention the example of Khuluyu, also in Cochabamba, where participants had grouped lands for an innovative fruit-growing project without losing their individual property.

Each focus and variant was the object of heated discussions, taking of postures and internal seminars so as to better to understand a theme that appealed simultaneously to the economic, organisational and ideological dimensions. As a starting point it was reiterated that the community is the basic cell towards a new social model. With this basis, the following definition and characteristics of the work community were adopted:

It is a social and economic organisation that:
- embraces the entire peasant community;
- holds as collective property the means of production;
- has the capacity to cover without risk the consumption and needs of the participating families;
- generates surpluses that permit the accumulation of social capital and guarantee the development of the CDT's productive strengths;
- combines and articulates its common production with that of particular families in a rationalised manner.

Most of the associated projects were lacking in some of these characteristics, by which the previous definition marked more an ideal to be aimed at rather than a reality.

Evolution over the years 1987-1996

After two years it was considered necessary to collect the rich experience accumulated until then at a more operative level. In November 1989 a voluminous work of 180 pages was published entitled *Bases for a functional and legal structure of the CDT*.

This text collected and ordered all the documents and experiences of the regional offices up to that moment, differentiating between common elements and the particular emphasis given to each place. Because of its detail and size it was the most complete systematisation of what the CDT was and what it set out to be. Particularly significant is the greater emphasis on the ideological aspects of the entire model; in other words, the CDT continues to see itself as the embryo of an ideal society that it wanted to build.

The Santa Cruz regional office, in whose zones of colonisation the peasants were much more market-oriented and the traditional community organisation was also much more weakened, was the most explicit, saying it was necessary to 'perforate the CDT model'. With that expression, heavily criticised by other CIPCA offices, it sought above all to underline the need to take production at family level more into account.

Chiqui Núñez, an agronomist at CIPCA Santa Cruz who previously worked in Charagua, remembers:

We in Charagua had a very strange idea of the Santa Cruz people. We accused them of being followers of the Green Revolution. They thought big: they worked with people who owned 20-30 hectares, while we in Charagua were working with families that had only 0.5 hectares. They had even bought a harvester for 30,000 dollars!

In the month of October 1991 various events were organised to celebrate 20 years of CIPCA. In Jesús de Machaqa, La Paz, the I National Encounter of CDTs was held (they then totalled 135). Representatives from all across the country, some of whom had travelled several days, got to know one another, interchanged experiences and celebrated together. Another, more formal event, was an open seminar that brought together peasant-indigenous leaders and specialists from all over the country to discuss the future of the peasant community. Naturally, one of the themes was the CDT and the 20 years of CIPCA, the CDT continuing to be an important point of its strategy and showed a healthy vitality.

Pedro Carballo (ex-leader of the Khuluyu community) remembered in 1992:

We had been working more or less ten years with CIPCA. We had a medium-sized plot, the help of CIPCA engineers and fertilisers. During the government of Hernán Siles Suazo (1982-1985) we had two work groups. But with the economic crisis (hyperinflation), the harvest was devalued and this demoralised the people. It was a complete disaster, after so much sacrifice. It was necessary to take another path: use all the plots. Now we have 7 hectares of fruit trees, artichoke and triticale. Now there are 30 people in the work group.

Despite the practical conflicts, emphasis remained on the priority and advantages of associated production, insisting more and more on better articulation with family production. Tension between the associated and family tendencies was seen in the debate over whether or not to accept family credit. The defenders of associated production saw in family production a model only for personal consumption and not for the market. It is a pity that the warning by Marcos Recolons – "without family plot there can be no CDT" – was lost in the subsequent discussions.

The model deflates and transforms

After the first years of implementation of the triennial plan 1994-1996, emphasis on the parameters of success began to be placed more on the technical side and much less on organisational form, insisting on the associated model only if it proved technically interesting.

In 1995 the second external evaluation was conducted. The evaluators again concentrated on the CDT model. They confirmed the weakening of the model and recommended updating the central concepts. (Mejía et al., 1995):

"At the outset, there is no doubt that the model's ideological element had considerable weight. Many CIPCA leaders and workers saw the model as a slow but realistic path towards a community peasantry. (…) the experience has demonstrated that this communality occurs only in exceptional conditions, as in the case of Cordillera where there is no tradition of private property in a strict sense; even temporarily, as in the case of Khuluyu, in which they have gone back to 'privatising' lands once contributed for communal cultivation. (…) As a result there is much less talk these days in CIPCA of the CDT model and criticisms are even heard of the insistence on a model whose limitations were evident. However, its defenders salvage positive aspects of the accumulated experience, of which at least three stand out: (a) the importance for the activities of technical assistance and training; (b) peasant credit, which at family level is very small-scale, high-risk and difficult to administer, becomes feasible, effective and efficient; and (c) commercialisation is negotiated and managed by the group."

It was clear that, in the field teams and in the communities themselves, the desire was to gain more space for family productive activities. But there were also people in CIPCA who feared that going down this path would mean the disappearance of the ideal, cherished for so long, of eventually transforming the peasant mode of production.[92]

It is also important to remember that, since 1994, very special national conditions were taking shape. The Law of Popular Participation and other institutional reforms were now transforming the scenario. The rapid and necessary adaptation of CIPCA to the new situation has also brought to a second or perhaps third plane elements which a few years before was still at the centre of the agenda.

In the new strategic plan for the years 1997-2001, written in March 1996, there is no longer mention of the CDT, not even as one of the opportunities or strengths with which to face the new challenge of contributing to the reorientation of the peasant economy towards sustainable development.

The dream of the CDT, as a transforming motor of indigenous peasant society, had accompanied and motivated CIPCA over twenty years. It was a dream that mobilised; around it many productive and community projects could be given impetus. It is worth recalling that the original proposal for the Guaraní area was one that did take into account the interrelation between family and associative models. Besides, it was also an adequate proposal to break with patronage. It was a correct path to consolidate the settling of the Guaraní people as farmers, thus managing to halt the annual exodus to the sugar harvest.

Finally one should not forget that organisations come and go. People organise so as to achieve some objective. Once this objective is reached, the organisation is dissolved and a new one constructed. This process is permanent and does not automatically mean that the organisation has not been adequate for its specific moment in history.

To conclude this analysis of the CDT it is also opportune to recount some funny experiences, which show that concrete work in the countryside was and still is work for human beings.

El Espino villagers[93]:

"Over time we have learned to adopt new forms of sale. The sale of soya was interesting. In Villamontes, in the factory, they had never seen villagers like us bringing soya in qualities associated with landowners. They didn't believe us. They questioned us: whose was the soya, had some owner sent us? They asked us if we were landlords and at the same time labourers. When we said that we worked in a kind of cooperative, only then did they believe us. Before that they wouldn't let us in, not even five metres."

Eduardo Acevedo, CIPCA solicitor and since 2004 director of CIPCA Cochabamba:

"We dreamed of creating a socialist model, but when the work did not advance as we wanted, CIPCA felt in control of the situation and acted at times like a landowner. The work groups functioned only when CIPCA led the work. On the other hand, the peasants were mocking CIPCA; for example, the fattening centres only functioned when CIPCA visited the community. The peasants collected manure from the field and threw it in the corral. That way they could show the CIPCA staff that the corral was functioning. But one day we paid a visit unannounced: the corral was empty and the cows were yoked and working."

"There was a mistaken analysis of the community: people thought it was a millenary collective organisation. On the peasants' side, there was a lot of distrust. The CDTs were seen as communist organisations. People wondered where CIPCA brought the money from, why they did it. They feared that some day CIPCA was going to take the land from them."

Guido Valdez, agronomist of CIPCA La Paz:

"The fundamental err was having introduced at the same time a new organisational model, new technology, products unknown on the Altiplano (intensive crops like vegetables), collective credit and a new productive logic. I remember that families had simply appropriated of the cows, when they were still communal farms, and they had distributed them. Abandoned communal henhouses were not uncommon, either; one had been turned into a school and others even into chapels."

Adjusting the economic dimension

At the beginning of the Decennial Plan CIPCA had a productive strategic plan for each of the regions where it was working. These plans, which in many cases were nothing more than a collection of intuitions on what direction to follow in the economic development of the region, were considered a sufficient basis to initiate the work of economic improvement.[94]

Common points of the productive proposals

The productive plans set out in the 1990s were strongly influenced by the circumstances of the moment. Around 1987, agriculture in Bolivia confronted two great challenges: strong political pressure to incorporate into a market economy, and the acceleration of urban migration from the countryside. The former was manifested in the *boom* in Santa Cruz agribusiness and the latter could be felt in the rapid growth of the main cities on the central axis: La Paz, Cochabamba and Santa Cruz.

In a certain way the CIPCA plans enclosed a counter-philosophy in the face of the most visible threat at that time: urban migration. So as to ensure the stability of the population it was crucial to look for activities that, as well as being economically viable, would generate permanent work. Bear in mind that this conception did not consider what the peasant families always had practiced: complementarity between income in the countryside and the city as a strategy of peasant survival (we will return to this theme). The failure to consider a possible complementarity of economic income often obliged the creation of solutions that were too forced.

The second strategy was aimed at the incorporation of the peasant to the market and had two components: diversification and support for transformation-commercialisation. The idea that supported this strategy was that, if the peasant's income came from diverse products, this would mean better defence against the fluctuations of the market.

However, for different reasons, all these strategies could not always be executed. The principal reason was that in order to achieve diversification it was important to introduce new productive activities. This involved a cost in time and investments, for which finance had to be obtained. Another factor, which without doubt contributed to these proposals not materialising, was the lack of conviction and, in some cases, knowledge on the part of technicians about the way the new proposals had to be implemented.

The technology on offer on the Altiplano was not viable at the beginning. In Ayo Ayo the peasants had to take on the management of three dairy farms and three sets of greenhouses; in Jesús de Machaqa three dairy farms and greenhouses and in Santiago of Machaqa a sheep farm, a dairy farm and greenhouses. These constructions meant large investments on the part of CIPCA and some of them took over three years to build. We will cite the mid-term evaluation of 1999 with a historical review of this experience:

"the projects were non-viable since they weren't only a question of cutting-edge technology totally alien to the conditions of the area, but were also based on the mistaken conception that collective management was akin to the logic of production on the Altiplano as the peasant was organised in communities... the initial reaction was to complement the investments made with additional investments to make the project viable, which in turn led to other investments that only meant that they became still more economically unviable (...) Finally between 1994 and 1995 the farms were closed and the debts paid with the machinery and equipment that had been acquired"(Alemán et al., 1999: 84).

If it is true that the collective farming model was a mistake, supporting dairy production on the Altiplano was not so misguided. If a heavy investment in dairy production had been accompanied by public policies in its favour, the Altiplano could probably have been an important producer of milk for the consumption of the inhabitants of the capital. Note that in 2005 there were already several successful associations of dairy producers, such as those in Pucarani, Viacha and Ayo Ayo.

The same could be said of the greenhouses. The greenhouses are a good example of organisational evolution. In some of the first experiences the possibility had been tried out as a communal enterprise, with the participation of all the families. It did not work because of organisational problems and because the benefit per participant proved insignificant. New calculations were made and the ratio of surface to participant was significantly broadened so as to make for greater economic motivation, which implied a notable reduction in the participants. The reference to the community as a whole proved less and less important but did not prevent its status being maintained as an associated group, made up of people, families or otherwise, that now had prior knowledge or experience of working together. This associated dimension has continued to be functional for the construction of all the infrastructure and its maintenance; mechanisms of raising and repayment of credits; the organisation of certain joint or rotational tasks; and the commercialisation of the product. However, on the other hand, so as to stimulate each participant and diminish the risks, the option taken was that each family would become responsible for a particular greenhouse (even marking them with the family name for greater stimulus) within a group of 10 or 20. Besides, the technical innovation of drip irrigation considerably lessened the risk of failure due to some participant's negligence.

One of the criticisms that can be read in the evaluations and articles on the greenhouses is that this technological innovation has only served for the few peasant families already accommodated. So the old argument returned that, politically, it was not correct to support the 'richest' in the community.

The examples show the importance of an activity that can have impact in the sense that proposals and innovations at micro level (like that of NGOs) are finally accepted at macro level. Conversely, the work of NGOs is frustrating when public policies are not in favour of small producers and when – mistakenly – blame is put on the NGOs for a lack of impressive results and for not having drastically changed the rural economy.

Another unresolved matter of debate was how much an NGO can or should invest in the economy of the poor. Influenced by the trend towards demanding an efficient and effective development management, the two external evaluations of 1995 and 1999 criticised the proposals' cost-benefit ratio. Without wishing to resume the polemic, it is opportune to mention that, in the two evaluations, cost-benefit analyses were badly set out, based only on certain variables and indicators. Besides, they were based on suppositions of efficiency and efficacy that were not well-argued or fully calculated[95]. And what has never calculated is the amount of governmental investments and subsidies for small peasants in contrast with subsidies for large agro-business enterprises.

One difficulty that dragged along through all these years was a lack of clarity in the role of the department of education in the transfer of new technology. No regional training office developed an efficient training model to be adapted to CIPCA's productive proposal. In Santa Cruz and Cordillera this shortcoming was partially remedied through agreements with other institutions.

The experimental stations

Before the 1990s CIPCA had already established experimental stations in La Paz, Cochabamba and Charagua. As well as validating or developing new technologies, the stations were often a privileged place for the training of CIPCA technicians. Through the thesis-work system, CIPCA utilised these experimental stations as a place of recruitment for new technicians, which had been trained both in new technologies and in CIPCA's working method. In some cases, thanks to the collaboration of foreign advisers, cutting-edge technology was developed in these experimental stations.

A celebrated anecdote:

There was an air cargo of apple-tree seedlings prepared with artificial hibernation (because in Cochabamba there is no clear division of seasons). Very precise arrangements had already been made with Lufthansa by the time restrictions that the seedlings could survive. But on the day the plane arrived in Bolivia, the cargo did not include the long-awaited seedlings. Checks were made and it was found that the shipment had been delayed because of a much more important State reason: preference had been given to sending an immense load of brand-new banknotes printed in Europe, with new values due to the galloping devaluation that the country was suffering. Due to this unforeseen delay, the seedlings arrived on the following flight, fortunately none the worse for wear.

The Demonstration Station at Qurpa (Altiplano) played an important role as a centre of multiplication and distribution of seedlings for Altiplano communities. It was later utilised by CIPCA to develop crop technology in greenhouses, one of the main components of the CIPCA La Paz productive proposal.

A problem that frequently cropped up in the CIPCA experimental stations was the lack of diffusion of results within technical teams. Often the advances made in the experimental station were only handled by the technician in charge of the experiment. This problem meant that there were long delays in spreading the results of experiments: often these did not become widely-known at all, since the only person who knew about them was far away from the extension work.

Another important problem to consider was the cost to CIPCA of launching and maintaining so many experimental stations. Often the financing agencies failed to consider the importance of this work and were not very sympathetic when it came to approving the budget, forgetting that at that time the State was barely interested in experimental research, so necessary for the economic development of the country. As CIPCA could not find financing, it tried out a sound alternative in the nursery in Viloma (Cochabamba) converting part of the experimental station into a company SRL (Society of Limited Responsibility) for the production and sale of seedlings of fruit trees[96].

Irrigation

At the start of the 1990s CIPCA had very little experience in irrigation. It could only point to some limited experience in Cochabamba. Nonetheless, it was already aware that, where the land was scarce, the situation could only be improved through the introduction of irrigation since, in this way, the harvest could be assured and intensity of soil use increased. Besides, some of the economic proposals could only be borne out with the introduction of irrigation. This was the case, for example, with the fruit trees and vegetables in Cochabamba and Camiri. In line with this reasoning, the external evaluation of 1991 also emphasised the need for irrigation.

Indeed, irrigation projects were carried out in all the regions except Santa Cruz, and, if not all the projects were equally successful or striking; they represented investment in an activity that proved positive for peasant families. In 1990 CIPCA La Paz began to study the water potential in the subsoil in the work zones of the Altiplano. As a result of this study the greenhouse projects were redesigned, incorporating a drip-irrigation component. This innovation was a fundamental factor in the consolidation of the greenhouses, which, at that time, were about to be abandoned.

In the Chaco, which has always suffered from drought, water projects were supported by the Peasant Development Fund. The Cochabamba office created several projects for lining canals in Tiraque. Other trial projects, which met with relative success, involved lateral irrigation. This latter was a very simple design that has permitted the introduction of concepts of soil protection.

The experience of Sacabamba (regional Cochabamba) presented many problems at the beginning. The annual evaluations showed few results. CIPCA began to deliberate over whether to abandon the area. The technicians supported the idea of leaving, offering the argument that "the people did not respond". Marcos Recolons, who has always been very insistent, replied: "CIPCA exists where there is no alternative. One way or another, we have that find an alternative." In the late 1980s, the peasants of the Cantón Ch'allaqe – made up of five communities – had reached the conclusion that the only option it had to improve its production and economy was to construct a dam that would allow them to accumulate rainwater to irrigate their plots. Several alternatives were analysed but discarded for economic reasons. At the end of 1993 the management committee addressed the matter, looking to adopt a definitive decision. The insistence of Marcos Recolons tipped the scales in its favour and meant that the peasants' dream of having irrigation would materialise years later. If the solution was to construct a dam, a dam had to be constructed. In 1994, with its own resources, CIPCA drew up the design for an irrigation system at Ch'iara Qhochi, which was executed in the following years (1997-2000) once the corresponding finance was managed and obtained.

The most important aspect of these experiences is that CIPCA became aware that there are places where the economy of the peasants cannot be improved without investing in infrastructure for irrigation.

Commercialisation

Logically, productive proposals had to be accompanied by actions that guaranteed the arrival of products to market in conditions that were advantageous for the peasant. For the first time the theme of the market was formally included in CIPCA's productive proposals[97].

In accordance with this logic, departments were created in all the regional offices with the task of supporting commercialisation. It was soon realised that this was no easy matter and the position of coordinator of commercialisation was created, in the national office, with the function of advising the regional in this new task and define common policies for all CIPCA.

In chronological order, the first case of commercialisation appeared in La Paz in 1989 with the name of Agricultural Products of the Altiplano (PADA). The following year, in Santa Cruz, the office Commerce of the Oriente (OCO) was created, and that same year in Charagua, the Guaraní Trading Company. Finally, the Peasant Products of the Valley Trading Company (PROCAVA) was created in Cochabamba in 1993.

PADA initially had a strong component of institutional financial support, in the hope that it would become self-supporting along with an increase in the volume of commercialised production. It was not so easy. There were diverse problems of financial mishandling, exacerbated by a lack of business sense. Finally, the retailer specialised in greenhouse lettuces and entered into an agreement with the Credit Fund (FONDECO), CIPCA's new credit entity (see below).

The existence of PADA has proved fundamental in ensuring the viability of the few productive alternatives found so far on the Altiplano. Although their methods and demands do not always satisfy the producers, they are recognised as its channel and guarantee in placing the product on the market. It was also the effective stimulus for maintaining certain quality indicators. But its process towards self-financing proved slower than initially expected.

There remains the question, then, whether initial expectations were too unrealistic or whether the actors involved in PADA were unaware of its potential to be turned into a viable commercialisation entity. What is beyond doubt is that the demands made by financial and development agencies to the small producers to become self-supporting in a very short time, are demands that are never or very rarely made to medium or large producers.

PADA was on the agenda in almost all the CIPCA management committee meetings. Serious observations were made with respect to the sustainability of PADA, among other things because part of the PADA staff's wages were paid by CIPCA. PADA would have to set out a strategy of sustainability.

The story is different in the other regional offices. In Santa Cruz, the Trading Company of the Oriente (OCO) office was created in 1990, intended also to support the Guaraní Trading Company in Cordillera. But neither of them managed to catch on, largely because other channels of commercialisation existed in those regions. The attempts made in Cochabamba, above all to commercialise CDT fruits, came later. In 1993, within the regional office, the PROCAVA shop was inaugurated but not consolidated, partly due to other channels already existing and partly because of a lack of adequate staff.

In the case of Cochabamba it was soon realised that the 'retail' commercialisation model was not working. As it was one of the most important agricultural markets in the country, retail commercialisation made no sense in Cochabamba, since there existed great quantity of wholesalers and brokers that functioned far more efficiently. These were complemented by a vast network of *rescatistas*[98], some of them of simple survival, that were circulating in the communities with sound knowledge of the local and temporal variations in prices, offers and demands. This experience is another reminder that the traditional system of the rescatism, very much despised because it apparently functioned on the basis of exploitation of the peasant, carried out and continues to carry out rather an important role in the peasants' access to the market.

Experiences in transformation

In La Paz, three medium-sized transformation projects were built: the balanced food mill, the cheese factory at Ayo Ayo and the slaughterhouse at Jesús de Machaqa. However, the first two did not manage to function as expected and the slaughterhouse did not even get going at all. This latter was a gift from Spanish cooperation, but was accepted on the basis of the utopian idea that all these new productive companies could be left in the hands of communal organisations.

An important bugbear, one that negatively affected the formation of SRL-type companies with peasant organisation participation, was the incompatibility between the traditional way in which grassroots leaders are elected and the responsibilities that they had to assume in their new "businesses". The duties in grassroots organisations are assigned rotationally over short periods, but the project required instead people with charisma who could carry the project forward during a time greater than the duration of their positions.

In Cochabamba many studies were made of the processing and conservation of vegetables, but this never resulted in an industrial project. All that was achieved was to teach producers the way to turn their products into other items with greater added value[99], some of which are still being produced today. In Charagua some attempts were made at transformation of maize. Finally in 1990 a "star" project was installed in Santa Cruz. This was the rice mill La Campana, in which CIPCA was a member, together with a private businessman (ex-CIPCA) and the peasants of Antofagasta.

The success of La Campana awoke in CIPCA a "fever" for industrialisation. Everyone sought to extend the SRL model tried out in La Campana. The setup was certainly novel in CIPCA and responded to the need to find new alternatives to increase the peasants' income, raising the added value of their production. One might conclude that CIPCA proved itself to be very advanced in putting this idea into practice, since the start of the 21st century would see the new fashion for 'socially responsible companies', that promote a strategic alliance between private businessmen and peasants.

At some point is was suggested within CIPCA that these trading companies and transformation industries might also be an interesting way to help finance the institution, since at that time the changes that had occurred in European countries led one to expect a drastic fall in external aid to Bolivia over the following years[100]. Besides, the agencies of co-financing demanded the so-called self-financing of NGOs, mistakenly demanding that NGOs should embark on business activities with the aim of generating earnings for the institution. Very soon CIPCA realised that the idea of self-financing was a 'chimera' which would never materialise.

The credit component

Almost from the start, CIPCA had proposed the existence of a rotating fund that, by design, should make up an integral part of all projects. The rotating fund, if worked with an interest rate different to that of the market, was to all appearances a commitment to an economic loan, which had to be repaid. This mechanism was also considered important as an educational instrument. At the outset there was no clear idea of how the rotating fund should function and, consciously or otherwise, errors had been committed that were quite reminiscent of the demonised 'charity' model. Besides, no rules had been prepared as to how the fund should be 'rotated'. Due more to a lack of knowledge of the credit system's workings on the part of the technicians than to non-fulfilment by the peasants, the rotating funds quickly turned into lost funds.

This problem was subject to long discussions, which ended with the decision to create a separate entity, which was named Communal Development Fund

(FONDECO). The best reason for making this change was the need for each party to carry out its task without letting itself be influenced by other considerations. FONDECO was to be a system of credit preferential to small peasants, with institutional sustainability. The rest of CIPCA had the job of doing effective promotion work. If FONDECO was born in the bosom of CIPCA, its vocation, from the very beginning, was that of becoming an independent, autonomous entity specialising in the administration of rural credit.

After a year's preparation the office was inaugurated at the beginning of 1991. A large part of the initial work consisted of "cleansing" the previous rotating fund portfolio, writing off debts that were considered non-payable so that the new entity might be born without deficits from the past. The resources previously gathered by CIPCA for credit were transferred to the administration of FONDECO, while CIPCA still handled the funds earmarked for subsidies.

Until 1995 FONDECO remained a part of CIPCA, with a rank equivalent to that of a fifth regional office and the right to a place on the management committee. However, when it changed its legal status to that of a non profit-making civil association, independent of the Company of Jesus, CIPCA and FONDECO became separate institutions, each one acquiring its own legal status.

It should be clarified that FONDECO was not the only credit institution in Bolivia willing to lend services to micro businesses and small agricultural producers. There was also the National Ecumenical Development Association (ANED), founded back in 1978. In the second half of the 1980s several other institutions were founded, such as the Foundation for the Promotion and Development of Micro-Enterprises (PRODEM), the Foundation for Development Alternatives (FADES) and the Institute of Support for Small Productive Units (IDEPRO)[101].

The creation of FONDECO as an entity specialised in credit freed the CIPCA staff from an activity that interfered with their main work. However, finding a constructive understanding between the two entities was a very complicated task and there have been many misunderstandings between the staff of the two institutions, due mainly to the different forms of logic they employed. CIPCA was a promotional body and FONDECO a credit institution: the logic of the promoter, generally more responsive to the peasant's needs, was different from that of the financier, more sensitive to the security of its loans. So as to show solvency as a credit agency, FONDECO could only work with people financially apt for credit, while CIPCA staff also wanted to work with people who could not be subject to credit. These tensions between the two institutions were matters of permanent discussion in the CIPCA management committee.

The conflicts between CIPCA and FONDECO were quite serious and also influenced relations with peasant families. According to the CIPCA version, FONDECO did not correctly perform its task as a credit entity (informing, promoting, training and charging opportunely) and expected CIPCA to do these things. For this reason relations deteriorated almost to vanishing point. At the end CIPCA and the debtor communities drew up a proposal with several options to negotiate the debt, but FONDECO did not accept it, leaving the communities with debts that blocked the access to future credit actions.

An observation that should be made is that, as FONDECO consolidated, its credit portfolio shifted increasingly towards the Santa Cruz sector where CIPCA worked alongside peasants with higher incomes. Disagreements with the regions and the more depressed sectors began with divergences over interest rates and it is easy to demonstrate that, under certain conditions, agricultural profits were not enough to cover commercial interest. This situation was aggravated by an exaggeratedly high commercial interest in Bolivia, because of the structural adjustment. But the problem was not only interest; some innovative projects assumed important transformations in the peasants' economic base, which represented investments of time and risks impossible for peasant families to take on.

During the 1990s several crises appeared in sectors with limited resources in La Paz, Cochabamba and El Chaco, above all concerning the handling of credits authorised for investment. On the other hand, a municipality like San Julián (colonisers) had very low arrears. As a palliative measure FONDECO proposed to CIPCA the writing-off of several credits that had become irrecoverable.

Tomasa Aramayo, from the captaincy of Iupaguasu and until 2005 vice-President of the APG, summed up this whole problematic very well:

"At the beginning CIPCA did good work and we received a lot of moral and economic support. But when the non-repayable changed to credit, the problems began. Large sums had been invested based on plans that were not made by us. We didn't know how to manage them and we didn't understand for what activities. The locals began to slip into debt. CIPCA-FONDECO had turned into a new boss. Again the villagers felt semi-captive. FONDECO gobbled up all the earnings. The debt couldn't be repaid and FONDECO began to impound the goods. A trial was opened. So it was that Nelly Romero [President of the APG from 2002 to 2005] decided that CIPCA could not enter the zone of Iupaguasu. Deficits have been written off for some time, but a small debt still exists. Pancho Matzusaki acted as mediator, proposing that the debt be repaid, but promising that the money recuperated would be invested in the communities themselves. Now the matter remains of annulling the document which says that CIPCA cannot enter the zone."

An additional problem was that in the cooperation agencies it was now common to demand that activities should only be supported that were profitable in the short term and that were financed under the modality of credit. However, the fact that the profits from a project would not suffice to repay the investment required to put it into action does not mean that it automatically ceased to be profitable. It might be, despite this, the best alternative for the peasants of a certain region, as occurred with the greenhouses on the Altiplano. There may even be situations in which an agricultural activity barely covers the operating costs. In other countries, for reasons of governability, subsidies for certain productive rural sectors continues, despite the support implying the transfer of funds from other economic sectors. If this is not done, the food supply could be endangered or serious social problems might arise, such as those occasioned by uncontrollable levels of migration from the countryside to the city[102].

The cooperation agencies' idea that credit automatically meant sustainable aid – as opposed to charitable or assistentialist aid – was mistaken, and has meant many failures in the use of credit. Without having sufficient economic and financial knowledge, it was believed that the use of credit was synonymous with development, in so far as any type of subsidy was equivalent to assistentialism, as well as being unaware that certain subsidies can mean an important incentive for the economic development of a given zone.[103]

Micro-regional plans: the organisational motor

The compilation of base-line studies and micro-regional plans not only has required strong peasant participation, but has also given rise to the emergence of new forms of organisation.

The micro-regional plan: an organisational instrument?

In the economic sphere, the high priority of the CDT model concentrated most the work in specific communities without reference to a broader area. However, one of the most important instruments in the organisational sphere has been in these years the micro-regional plans. The concept of micro-region began to be used in La Paz after the emergency plan during the drought (1983-84) which involved all the communities of a particular area or province.

The term was also used in Cordillera, in a somewhat different sense, after its diagnostic and regional plan PDCC (1986-1987). With these and other antecedents, the feeling was gaining currency in CIPCA that this micro-regional level was a privileged entity within which to develop actions, it being a hinge between internal communal and inter-communal activities and those that with which the organisation faces other institutions.[104]

After the experiences in Cordillera and La Paz, CIPCA drew up a manual for base-line studies and – later – another for Micro Regional Plans (PMR). The two central characteristics were that (1) the grassroots organisations had to be involved from the diagnostic design to the elaboration and execution of the plan, so that they might acquire a greater knowledge of their own reality and increase their capacity of negotiation; and (2) high levels of inter-institutional cooperation were demanded with other NGOs and with the State.

The diagnostics of Tiraque and Sacabamba proved key in the transition of these micro-regions to municipalities and in drawing up the first municipal development plans. In Santa Cruz the diagnostics served largely as documents for the new municipalities of colonisers, such as San Julián. The experience of La Paz saw various difficulties, perhaps because it involved the permanent staff of the institution much less, leaving a good part of the work to external consultants.

To sum up some critical points regarding the drawing-up of base-line studies; the first is that their cost was very high[105], for which reason they did not prove to be an instrument that could be applied everywhere or with great frequency. The second critical point was that too often these studies or development plans were drawn up despite good previous studies already existing. Making diagnostics became an activity in itself, as a kind of self-training exercise. Thirdly, base-line studies consumed too much time, and rural populations wasted hours, weeks and months participating in their creation, providing data on their economic situation that were nothing new for them because they lived it on a daily basis.

It is also worth pointing out that a good diagnostic is not always necessary in order to conduct a successful activity. In Ayo Ayo a diagnostic had been done that had little participative content. However, a milk-producers' association managed to implement a good project that is functioning adequately since 1993. In Jesús de Machaqa, on the contrary, an excellent diagnostic was made, but it did not materialise into a consensual plan of micro-regional development that could guide inter-institutional work over the following years.

The implementation of the micro-regional plans (PMR) also encountered some difficulties. In the first place, the micro-region was like no-man's land, because the State was almost absent after having implemented the adjustment policy. In defining a territory that did not always coincide with public administration as a micro-region, it lacked an executive counterpart, capable of to carrying plans and projects forward, including the fundraising necessary for their implementation. On the other hand, it can be mentioned as positive that the plans permitted interesting agreements between NGOs and grassroots organisations, and managed a first dialogue with some State entities such as the IBTA and the Departmental Development Corporations

(CORDE). After 1994, the role of these coordinators changed substantially with the application of the new Law of Popular Participation (LPP) in which the municipality appears as mainly responsible for the local rural development.

From micro-regional plans to municipal plans

The possibilities and risks of the PMR have resulted – unintentionally – in an excellent way of preparing grassroots organisations to act in the new municipal scenario founded with the 1994 Law of Popular Participation. This new juncture presented new dilemmas for the NGOs. Initially, some of these even felt threatened by the possibility of losing "control" over what they had previously considered their "territory". And later the dilemma arose of whether they had to coordinate with the new municipal actor or to follow working only with the peasant organisations[106].

CIPCA also considered all these questions from the very beginning of the Popular Participation LAW (LPP). Already in 1994, even before the law was approved, it had various conversations with the chief creators of this legal initiative. In the management committee of February 1994 the Law of Popular Participation was discussed. Carlos Hugo Molina, who at that time was Vice-Minister of Popular Participation and the LPP's most important architect, was invited. In April the same year CIPCA organised a national seminar in Cochabamba to establish its position. The dilemmas were expressed in the internal document *Popular participation and micro-region*. An old dilemma regarding micro-regional plans again arose, also for CIPCA[107]: did they lead to indigenous peasant power and government or to greater power for state institutions?

A clear example of how diagnostics and micro-regional planning contributed to plans for municipal development is the case of the municipality of Tiraque (Cochabamba), where the micro-regional diagnostic gave origin to a municipal investment plan, presented – at the Sánchez de Lozada government's invitation – in the Governmental Palace. This constituted one of the examples of the planning method for municipal development that the government wanted to foment.

Popular Historical Project: the ideological dimension

In the ideological area the principal instruments developed over these years was the Popular Historical Project or PHP. The term 'historical project', then very commonly used on the left, referred to a proposal applicable to both country and society. The added term 'popular', broader than 'peasant' or 'indigenous' wanted to emphasise that this proposal could not exclusively deal with one of the component social sectors. However, in the developed proposal was underlined, naturally, the peasant and indigenous perspective. In the presentation of the book that had an important impact in all the country it was expressed as follows: "how do you conceive a Bolivian society in which the peasantry and the native peoples feel at last to be fully participant citizens".

The Popular Historical Project: a national proposal

The PHP was the last great activity of CIPCA in the ideological arena. The idea of the PHP, however, was born from very practical reasoning. The education teams had never finally clarified their aims once and for all, oscillating constantly between being simply pedagogical helpers for agricultural technicians (for example, giving didactic explanations or preparing pamphlets to introduce some agricultural item), emphasising rather the personal and critical growth of each peasant participant, or launching into ideological considerations and broader policies. Options for one pole or the other were made in accordance with the inclinations of each Regional Director. On several occasions there were encounters between educators and radio communicators who sought to establish a clearer framework regarding its multiple function. And it was in those encounters that the idea was gathering strength of the need for a theoretical conceptual framework for the work of awareness-raising.

The definition of 'popular historical project' showed that this was a case of another great dream, comparable to that of the CDT. This latter used local concerns as a starting-point, in the hope that by beginning to construct small productive communities with other forms of internal relationship it was possible, little by little, to transform society as a whole. The other instrument, the PMRs, remained in a more operative sphere without great theoretical considerations. Finally, the PHP started off from large considerations, the utopia of an ideal country which it wanted to move towards. It incorporated other more local elements, such as the CDT (here called 'productive self-managing units') and the micro-region, as one of the basic units of organisation and planning.

The creation of the PHP was a work of three-year operation, initiated in 1988, with success in carrying out a series of regional workshops with broad participation of leaders of the peasant and indigenous organisations. Its results were compared in a first national seminar, which decided to draw up a first joint document. This was returned to the regional offices for a new round of workshops, followed by a second national encounter. From there, a commission prepared a new version that was presented as a working document for a workshop restricted to national leaders of both the indigenous peasant sector and the political sphere. Finally, in May 1991, the book *For a different Bolivia, contributions for a popular historical project* was published, which was presented in its dust jacket as "a provocation to the public debate about an urgent theme, but one constantly passed over."

Unexpected echoes in the country

During the entire process a certain change of focus occurred. What had begun as an instrument aimed at helping education teams to orient their work in the countryside, ended up being a text oriented towards a public debate for the country's political class.

It is symptomatic that that official presentation of the book was held in the Universidad Mayor de San Andrés (UMSA), something that CIPCA had never done in the past, and that the book later became the object of numerous debates in the press. Some saw it as a breath of fresh air, others as a collection of harebrained ideas. There was always someone to question if it was the first letter of presentation of a new phase, in which CIPCA was planning a more direct participation in Bolivian politics, perhaps through some new political party. Naturally, this was not that what was intended. But these reactions showed that something had been achieved in terms of putting a new thematic on the public agenda.

Something that had not even been suspected was that a significant group of personalities who had participated in the 1991 workshop would, barely two years later, perform important duties in government functions and, in their way, would incorporate into the legal reforms some of the themes debated in that PHP proposal: land and territory, popular participation, bilingual intercultural education, pluricultural State. It was perhaps the first time that CIPCA had been involved, without having planned to do so, in what later would be called advocacy and lobby. On the other hand, it was not the first time that innovations and creative ideas from CIPCA and other NGOs would find an echo in government. Nor should it be forgotten that during that first Sánchez de Lozada government there were many NGO professionals who went on to be government members in important posts such as ministers, vice-ministers or secretaries. This kind of impact is rarely considered a positive result of NGOs.

The book has served also in workshops for indigenous peasant leaders at national level, for example, to discuss themes such as class and ethnic origin, land and territory, self-management, State, nation and ethnic nations, assembly of nationalities, etc. An interesting result for CIPCA was that the CSUTCB, whose executive secretary participated also in the workshop of 1991, asked for authorisation to present it as its own project.

It is surprising that the theme of regional autonomy, in the political foreground in 2004-2005, was already proposed in the book. The two fundamental lines of the book were: (1) a society without class exploitation and neither a state-oriented nor centralised economy, but rather recognising regional and cultural specificities, and (2) a multinational State, respectful of cultural differences and recognising the territories, authorities and margins of autonomy of the communities and of their groupings in forming the 'nationalities' constitutive of this multinational State. These ideas have been challenged in the political debates of the years 2000 (see the following chapter).

An instrument for the local teams?

The most paradoxical element in this process was perhaps that, with the final product, what had set this whole PHP exercise in motion moved on to a second or third plane: equipping the education teams with an instrument for organisational work at local, regional and national levels.

The education teams had become intensely involved, together with the grassroots organisations, in regional debates and workshops prior to the publication of the book; however, its use later became less common in everyday work with the bases. A complementary publication had been foreseen; a series of pamphlets that set out the same proposal and debate as the PHP, but couched in more popular terms for rural communities. For this purpose an inter-regional team of educators was appointed, but its work proved to be very slow; only in 1994 was the first of the planned pamphlets published. It was certainly very well presented, but by that time it was too late, given the new directions in which the country and the world were moving.

The new political and economic context, both national and global, contributed without doubt to the disenchantment with utopias and, as such, did not create a favourable climate for this thematic. Alliances between parties began to be drawn increasingly according to pragmatic calculations and no longer through ideas, principles or programmes[108]. In fact, the new political climate contributed to puncturing dreams and utopias in almost all institutions, both public and private. CIPCA was no exception.

The PHP experience proved positive nationally but had little success at local levels. In the first sphere it showed CIPCA its possibilities to influence the drawing up of national policies favourable to the countryside, a line of work that would be seen developing more over the following years. In contrast, on a more local sphere, the thematic had not managed to catch on. At this level much more concrete preoccupations were instead imposing themselves, which were of local and immediate interest.

Radio as educational support

CIPCA has had a long history in the use of radio for more extensive coverage, above all in the educational ideological area. There have been significant differences in the use of this instrument according to eras and regions, due partly to CIPCA having always preferred to work in agreement with other radios and not through its own station, so as to simplify its already over-complex administrative management.

In the early 1990s CIPCA developed a communicational strategy that distinguished three levels: (1) the more local radios had to lend support to the PMR; (2) Regional radios permitted amplification of the proposals of CIPCA and contributed, on the way, to strengthening cultural identity; (3) programmes in national radio stations had to contribute to indigenous peasant unity as well as aiming to spread interest in the rural problematic among the remaining sectors of society. There have been distinct results on the three levels.

The main experience at *local level* has been Radio Machaqa, inaugurated in 1991. It is the only of property of CIPCA, together with the local parish. It achieved very good direct popular participation: in 1992 1,026 people participated and in 1994, barely two years later, there were already 5,590, of which 2,237 were female, above all young women.

Pascuala Parra Villca, CIPCA communications technician in La Paz, remembers:

"Radio Machaqa was a crazy idea that came from Iván Arias and it was born to accompany the Micro-Regional Plan. I was the first woman presenter in that radio station. The men were furious and told me they would get me out of the place, which they never did. One night there was a storm and the lady in charge had switched off the electricity to avoid fires. But she did not warn me and I stayed there another hour broadcasting while the radio was not on the air."

The experience was very positive with regard to the education of local presenters and scriptwriters, through a programme of small grants. But it did not manage to consolidate the network of communicators, or overcome the practical problems of self-management, including the financial.

Also worth mentioning is the successful experience with life radio programmes during weekly fairs in the different communities. The news was meant for those who attended the fairs and played an important role in setting prices for the products sold in the weekly markets.

At *regional level,* Cochabamba began to exercise leadership in this labour, thanks to a new agreement with Radio San Rafael. The Programme *Llaqta Qhapari*, initiated in 1983, went on to have a bigger audience in the countryside. The Single Union Federation of Peasant Workers of Cochabamba soon began to consider it as its mouthpiece. Various Quechua-language radios of the region entered the channel to re-broadcast it.

In La Paz there was also a certain recovery after 1992, with a change of partner that entailed leaving Radio Fides, which had a smaller audience in the countryside around La Paz, and returning to Radio San Gabriel, specialising in the Aymara audience with which there was already an excellent relationship in the 1970s. However it never reproduced the vigour and influence of its early years, because a certain radio specialisation already existed in other institutions. For this reason CIPCA decreased its activity in this sphere, its staff being reduced to a minimum after 1996.

At *national level* there were – three times a week – small informative programmes on the well-known Radio Fides. However, in the long term it has not been possible to maintain this level of diffusion, largely due to a lack of adequate financial and human resources.

The efficiency of CIPCA's work in radio has depended to a large extent on two factors: (1) the solidity of agreements with radio stations that already had a broad rural audience and (2) the creativity and commitment of those responsible. On the other hand, the maintenance of good programmes was rather expensive, both in renting radio airspace and in human resources. For this reason the radio component suffered notable cuts during the late 1990s.

Publications, research and library

CIPCA has had publications of two styles: one formal and academic, the other popular in nature. But in both cases the objective was to transmit and share the results of its research and its own experience with others. In the 1990s the public was still relatively restricted: the readers most directly sought-after were other actors committed to the quest for an alternative society. Over the following years the type of audience differed in accordance to the desired impact: they varied between government employees, employees of NGOs, university students, peasants and indigenous people and businessmen.

Anthropological research, so prevalent in the early years, decreased little by little. Agricultural experimentations and innovations demanded more technical studies. The avoidance of merely academic research continued; instead priority was given to research-action linked to praxis and, wherever possible, to active peasant participation.

In 1987 a librarian was hired to order the stored documents, which had not been cared for since the dictatorship of García Meza. Over the years, the library had grown to the point that in 1988 it was necessary to install the Micro-Isis Programme to organise it; this meant that the library became one of the first libraries in Bolivia to have its documentation digitalised. At the beginning, the librarian was responsible only for organising the documents without offering services to third parties. This proved impossible, because of the number of people who were coming to knock on the door. Then it was decided that service could be given to the public, but only to researchers and not to students. This measure did not work, either, because few researchers came but there were many students.

In 1991 CIPCA La Paz acquired a building in El Alto and the library was moved to its ground floor. Once the library was installed in El Alto, more attention was given to secondary school students than to researchers. Between 1999 and 2000, for example, there were 30,000 consultations.

New themes: the environment and gender

By the early 1990s, these two themes were already on the CIPCA agenda for debate, but the CIPCA staff showed certain resistance in accepting either thematic, due to the following reasons:

- both the ecological theme and the gender theme were considered to have been imposed by the cooperation agencies;
- in the case of environment, the criticism was that the rich countries had consumed all the planet's wealth and now the poor countries would have to suffer the consequences, restricting the development of modern agriculture;
- the gender theme presented other complications: it was criticised as an imposition by feminists from the European urban middle class. Moreover, men in NGOs did not want spend their time, for example, training peasant women, who were considered only as mothers and housewives.

Environment

Resistance to the acceptance of new ideas concerning the environment was gradually giving way to a critical position vis-à-vis ecological problems. Professionals in general, whether from finance agencies, universities or NGOs, adopted the position of looking for development alternatives that were economically profitable, ecologically viable and socially desirable. In other words, sustainable development steadily grew in importance. However there has always been a certain pressure from some finance agencies to keep implementing romantic agro-ecological proposals with few possibilities of economic development.

The external evaluation of 1991 confirmed that Bolivian peasant cultures are hardly aggressive towards the environment (very slow rotation in the use of soils, subsistence consumption with little waste, religious respect for the land, etc.), but that demographic pressure and poverty are turning them into depradators, as shown, for example, by deforestation on the Altiplano[109].

In the 1990s CIPCA was already working in four distinct ecosystems: the Altiplano, the Andean valley slopes, the Chaco and the humid sub-tropical plains. As distinct as these four ecosystems are, they also have some aspects in common; one example is their fragility and the natural restrictions they present for any increased exploitation of resources. Besides, the population settled in these systems is the poorest in the country. This poverty was probably what also made some NGOs, including CIPCA, initially reluctant to include explicit environmental considerations in their development proposals.

Only after 1991 did CIPCA begin to develop various activities explicitly related to care for the environment:
- education in natural resources and environment, not only to peasant families, but also to children in rural schools;
- the development of an evaluation methodology of environmental impact;
- systematic monitoring of environmental indicators.

We might mention various concrete projects from those years that took restrictive environmental conditions into account: improvement of pasture and handling of flocks; the agricultural potential in the Chaco; rational handling of herding areas, with techniques that avoided the degradation of pastures; irrigation by spray technique in the Andean valleys; soil conservation and agro-forestry.

Gender

In the early years the idea was prevalent in CIPCA that the sum total of its action applied to the peasantry, men and women. As such, the beneficiaries of this action were all the members of the community and no special attention was given to any sector of the population. All this came under the supposition that the situations of different sectors of the population were similar: common needs and equitable results, independently of social class and/or sex. When the decision was made to develop actions within the framework of the 'promotion of women', they became beneficiaries of precise actions aimed above all at strengthening their domestic image (Crespo, 1993: 252-53).

Towards 1988 CIPCA began a concerted effort to overcome this deficiency, incorporating the feminine problematic more explicitly in its work. The main point of departure in dealing with this problematic was a seminar held in August 1988. Previously, each regional office had prepared specific diagnostics on the situation of rural women. According to CIPCA staff, the Aymara were apparently more dualist, considering the couple as the fundamental unit. On the other hand Guaraní men, despite having a matrilocal system, exercised an authoritarian role and questioned the opportunity of giving greater roles to women. According to regional staff in Cochabamba, Quechua women would have a high level of participation, thanks to the economic and commercial roles they performed; and lastly, the coloniser women, in the middle of an apparently more modern economy, proved to be the most isolated.

The result of the seminar was the broadened management committee's approval of a policies document on 'the problematic of women in the work of CIPCA'. The document's main recommendations:
- support for women's active participation in community economic programmes;
- design and implementation of CDT projects in a way that includes active participation by women;
- foment organisational entities particularly for women, organically articulated toward peasant organisation at all levels;
- promotion of women's active participation in the communal assembly;
- promotion of women's active participation in any peasant organisation portfolio;
- promotion of awareness-raising among men of the rights and problematic of women;
- support for the peasant women's organisations in making its demands by directly petitioning State institutions and programmes.

One of the most debated aspects of the 1988 seminar was whether specific women's organisations should be fomented or whether they should simply be incorporated directly into already-existing peasant organisations, at their various levels. The option taken was for the first alternative, precisely to strengthen this discriminated sector, but underlining that it should be a convergent rather than a parallel process, towards the active participation of women in the "matrix-headquarters" organisation of the communities.

Another of the most debated subjects was whether women should be responsible for specific tasks within the CDT or even to have their own work groups and access to specific credits for them. It was decided that this latter option could be a useful training mechanism to increase their knowledge in matters sometimes considered only for men. Furthermore, FONDECO accepted the idea of giving small freely-available credits precisely intended for women.

After 1993 CIPCA decided, although not with absolute certainty, to incorporate into the national office a gender specialist to include specific gender-differentiated objectives, goals and indicators in its triennial plan 1994-1996. Mónica Crespo was given the task of conducting a profound revision of the institutional culture that supposed, in the words of Hugo Fernández "dismantling certainties and identifying challenges"[110].

One of the ideological detours that had to be negotiated was the supposed need to respect the particular culture of the peasant-indigenous population at all times. On various occasions the defence of traditional values had been used as an argument against the gender perspective. However, this consideration was not used when it came to projecting and developing actions of technological transference or agricultural innovations. Some women quite rightly criticised this position, arguing that it would be difficult, if not impossible, to have an impact on the position of women, "without affecting the common sense validated by culture, that was expressed in forms of social relationship, habits, beliefs and attitudes." (Cottle and Ruiz, 1993: 3).

After 1993 it was defined as a general criterion that all CIPCA's everyday activity had to display a special sensitivity towards equitable relations between men and women. A gender focus was assumed institutionally, acknowledging the importance of gender relations, that (peasant and indigenous) men and women, being different, had a distinct vision of reality and that the needs and specific interests of each gender should therefore be taken into account.

The creation of a gender consciousness within CIPCA, above all in men, has not been a simple process. Consciously or unconsciously there was a good deal of resistance, at times shared by the male members of the grassroots organisations themselves. In one case, the field team relegated the female promoter, who was a local *cholita* (an Indian or mestiza woman in traditional dress), to the role of cook in the CIPCA house. In order to remedy this resistance to gender discussion a special group for permanent reflection and support was set up in each regional office, in which both women and men participated, thus emphasising that gender was everybody's business and not something that could be delegated to (female) specialists.

Surprisingly in Cordillera, where at the beginning there had been considerable opposition from the APG itself to female participation, women had achieved full incorporation into the CDT, even at directive levels. Similarly, in five communities had achieved a participation in communal organisation previously monopolised by men[111].

Some data on the participation of men and women in educational events show that the objective of having equilibrium in the number of men and women was still far from being achieved. We will see in the following chapter that the tendency of always having fewer women than men has continued over subsequent years; not even in 2005 had a percentage of 50% men and 50% women been reached in educational matters.

CONCLUSION

Despite the greater importance given to the economic dimension, CIPCA was still very strongly inclined towards a structural transformation of society through the CDT. Also the popular historical project, *For a different Bolivia*, was a proposal for the

| | La Paz | | Cochabamba | | Santa Cruz | | Cordillera | |
	Men	Women	Men	Women	Men	Women	Men	Women
1988	1495	303	1270	782	no data	no data		
1989	3970	1502	6576	1655	1831	409	1557	165
1990	2192		6192	3118	1986	846	1020	245
1991	1902	644	5364	2490	877	321	1455	1093
1992	3184	2233	2549	1026	1724	663	7949	2648
1993	489	710	3447	1336	2285	603	1892	1041
1994	901	89	4240	1552	3070	709	3782	1663

construction of a new society. On the other hand, technical proposals were rather based on modernising agriculture. CIPCA never considered peasant technology as a product of a millenarian culture that was worthy in itself and required no changes. Then, at a technical productive level modern proposals appeared, while at organisational level there was an insistence on romantic solutions.

In the final years of the Decennial Plan important changes occurred in the country and in CIPCA. The Law of Popular Participation demanded a rethinking of CIPCA on the role of the State in development, especially the role of the municipalities. Likewise, the Land Reform Law and the new organisational modality of Indigenous Communitarian Land (TCO) implied a rethinking of CIPCA on land ownership, especially in the Oriente. After 1997, a new phase began in Bolivian history, in which the struggle against exclusion according to class, ethnicity and gender was beginning to yield positive results.

CHAPTER V
CIPCA CONSOLIDATED
1996–2005

In the second half of the 1990s there were a series of legal advances that seemed totally unreachable when CIPCA began in 1971. In August 1994 the Political Constitution of the State (CPE), was modified, defining Bolivia as a "multiethnic and pluricultural" country (CPE, article 1) and introducing the concept of "Indigenous Communitarian Land", including the concept of "territory" and recognising the resources, customs and forms of internal government of the indigenous communities (CPE, article 171). The Law of Popular Participation recognised the legal status of the communities in their multiple local forms. The Law of Educational Reform indicated interculturality and bilingualism as basic pillars of education. The INRA Law recognised the right to collective ownership of the land for the lowland indigenous people and finally the Forestry Law guaranteed native peoples the exclusive right to exploit logging resources in the Communitarian Lands of Origin (Albó, 1999: 479).

However, these legal advances and constitutional achievements have still not had sufficient expression in everyday life. Economic policies have remained unfavourable to indigenous peasant families. Poverty has persisted in the countryside. The setting in motion of the INRA Law and the Forestry Law have been criticised and obstructed by the big cattle-ranchers and loggers; the process of reorganisation has progressed very slowly; ethnocentrism and regionalism on the

Altiplano, in Santa Cruz and Tarija have endangered the very future of the country.

Although the Law of Popular Participation was approved in 1994 and the INRA Law in 1996 and although these laws were discussed within CIPCA even before their legal approval, the challenges of municipal development and reorganisation were only incorporated into the institutional life of CIPCA after the first strategic plan (1997-2001). For this reason, detailed discussion of these new laws and ideas of rural development and popular participation has been left until this chapter.

It is no exaggeration to say that after 2000 an accelerated process has began to establish new power correlations in Bolivia, in which the different social actors have assumed other roles and functions in society, both politically and at social and cultural levels. It goes without doubt that the results of these process has never been seen in Bolivia nor in Latin America.

HISTORICAL OVERVIEW

In 1997 Hugo Banzer won the elections with 22%. Thanks to the alliance[112] with the MIR, the UCS, CONDEPA and New Republican Strength (NFR)[113], in August 1997 Hugo Banzer and Jorge (Tuto) Quiroga were installed as president and vice-president of the Republic. It should be mentioned that, in these same national elections, four Quechua peasant leaders from the Department of Cochabamba achieved deputations: Evo Morales, the undisputed leader of the coca-producers, Félix Sánchez, Néstor Guzmán and Román Loayza, all of them from the brand-new Assembly for the Peoples' Sovereignty (ASP).

One month later, Banzer convened a national dialogue to legitimise his programmatic proposal based on four pillars: 1) dignity: relative to the total eradication of excess coca; 2) opportunity: linked to the economic growth, with a goal of 7% growth by the end of the mandate; 3) equity: relative to the struggle against poverty; and 4) institutionality: relating to the strengthening of the judicial system and democracy.

Of these four pillars, the one that developed most systematically was the first, called "dignity" because it was ostensibly aimed at liberating the country from the drug-trafficking 'stigma'. In reality, "dignity" activities focused on the eradication of coca leaf cultivations, with the ultimate objective of "coca zero", which surpassed even United States expectations. It managed effectively to reduce part of the cultivated area[114] but not the activities of the drug-trafficker.

In 2000 another National Dialogue had to be held: a consultation process previous to the redaction of a Poverty Reduction Strategy Paper *(PRSP)*, one of the conditions of the World Bank for having part of the external debt written off for

Heavily Indebted Poor Countries (HIPC,). With the vacillation of the government, that didn't consider it an apt moment for consultation, the Catholic Church, which had actively collaborated with international efforts to have the debt written off, held the Foro Jubileo (Jubilee Forum) 2000 with the participation of broad sectors of society: federations of workers and miners, peasant and indigenous organisations, representatives of political parties, Non-Governmental Organisations.

Faced with the pressure exerted by the issue raised in the Foro Jubileo, the government decided to convene the National Dialogue 2000, structured in three discussion panels: economic, social and political. The one which functioned most effectively was the social, due perhaps to the antecedent of the Foro Jubileo and to the broad participation it had. The economic panel centred on short-term questions that had nothing to do with any development strategy, and the policy served to isolate urgent themes of political reform that emerged from the climate of conflict between social movements and government.

The results of the National Dialogue included the Bolivian Poverty Reduction Strategy Paper (PRSP), aimed at satisfying the conditions of the multilateral organisms, and the Law of National Dialogue, which formalised the destination of HIPC funds to the municipalities according to their level of poverty. Despite its failings the document was approved by the World Bank and the International Monetary Fund, institutions responsible for the HIPC Programme, faced with the need to demonstrate advances in the initiative at global level. An official evaluation, carried out by the government of Carlos Mesa in 2003, concluded that the strategy had not helped to reduce poverty (UDAPE, 2003). In 2004, as a result of a new consultation prescribed by Law, the name of the document was changed to that of Bolivian Development Strategy.

The climate of conflict between social movements and government was becoming ever more acute during the first years of the decade. The initial spark came in April 2000 as a result of speculative charges for drinking water in the city of Cochabamba, by a multinational company. This gave rise to huge popular mobilisations, which then broadened also to other sectors and included other grievances. The most directly political echo of the "Water War" in the indigenous and peasant movement was a wrangle between two leaders, Evo Morales, of the coca growers, and Felipe Quispe[115], of Aymara communities on the Altiplano, who provoked successive roadblocks in their respective areas of influence. These actions involved old sectorial demands mixed with issues pertaining to their own struggle for hegemony over the movement. In the lowlands, the organisation of colonisers and those most explicitly indigenous in nature – CIDOB –, were also in confrontation with a branch closer to MAS, called Oriental Block. This block was created in 2000 and over the years it managed to group together many lowland indigenous organisations.

Tuto Quiroga, who assumed the presidency in 2001 after the resignation of Banzer because of illness, governed for a year during which there were no changes of a political nature. At the beginning of 2002, as the result of a decree prohibiting the legal commercialisation of the Chapare coca leaf, there was a massive march of coca-producers from the tropic of Cochabamba, provoking a conflict with the police in which two policemen died. Evo Morales was expelled from Parliament, accused (without proof) of being to blame for these deaths, with the aim of de-legitimising him. But this expulsion instead won him greater sympathy, and his party grew exponentially toward the 2002 elections. The population was totally sick and tired of the traditional parties' political and economic manipulations.

The elections of 2002 were won by the MNR, the MAS[116] and the NFR. Evo Morales took second place – less than 2% behind the victor, Sánchez de Lozada – with 18 parliamentarians and a political projection that now extended far beyond the coca theme. Felipe Quispe, who had also formed his own party, the Pachakuti Indigenous Movement (MIP), attained another six representatives, all them Aymaras from the department of La Paz. For the first time in the parliamentary history of Bolivia a considerable quantity of people of indigenous origin had been elected. Finally, the parliament elected Gonzalo Sánchez de Lozada as president and Carlos Mesa Gisbert, an independent journalist, as vice-president.

Two months before these elections, lowland indigenous peoples linked with the Block Oriente, in alliance with highland organisations including CONAMAQ, carried out the fourth peasant-indigenous march "For popular sovereignty, land, territory and natural resources". The chief demand on this occasion was that the government should convene a Constituent Assembly, with the idea that this would mean greater recognition for Indigenous Peoples, as had occurred in recent Constituent Assemblies of neighbouring countries[117]. At that pre-electoral moment, such a request seemed extemporaneous because the majority of the urban and rural population was totally caught up in the electoral campaign. However, seen with hindsight, that march proved prophetic and was far from in vain, since the outgoing government came to approve a law recognising the need to reform the Constitution, which would later facilitate the convening of the Constituent Assembly.

Above all, the indigenous movements on the eastern plains not only postulated claims for land and territory, but also demanded participation as full citizens in Bolivian society. Unfortunately these new organisations, for example the Coordinator of the Indigenous Peoples of the Beni (CGNP) and the Coordinator of the Ethnic Peoples of Santa Cruz (CPESC), were not understood by the veteran organisations like the COB, the CSUTCB and inclusive the CIDOB. CPESC was about to form part of the Oriental Block. Meanwhile, under the leadership of Angel Durán, a new social movement emerged in the Chaco called the Movement without Land (MST) which in 2002 split into two factions, one headed by Angel Durán himself and the other, more closely tied to MAS, led by Moisés Tórrez.

In his second mandate, Sánchez de Lozada proved much weaker, more conservative and inefficient than in his previous period. This was due among other reasons to his conflictive alliance with MIR, a coalition without which, nevertheless, he would have been unable to govern. He had to navigate through a growing storm of social conflicts that left him increasingly dependent on the repressive capabilities of the army. MAS and MIP played an important role in social mobilisations, both in the countryside and in the city, particularly in El Alto. Little by little the neighbourhood committees of El Alto, agglomerated in the Federation of Neighbourhood Committees (FEJUVE) and the Regional Workers' Central of El Alto (COR, belonging to the COB) began to play an important role in street demonstrations. Important leaders of these organisations were Abel Mamani, Jaime Solares and Roberto de la Cruz.

Into the foreground came the handling of a strategic natural resource: gas, which had become the country's main wealth, but was now in the hands of multinational companies. Advanced negotiations for gas to be exported to the United States through Chile – the country that deprived Bolivia of its sea outlet – touched other raw nerves and national sentiments. This matter, with its intense nationalist element, transcended both rural and indigenous concerns, but paradoxically it mobilised primarily the popular sectors.

It should be underlined that since they began their parliamentary incursions in 1997, the peasant and indigenous politicians have never ceased to be at the same time leaders of their corresponding grassroots organisations, even when they also occupied seats in Parliament. The representative Evo was still coordinating the six organisations of coca-producers; his ally Román Loayza was at the same time senator and executive secretary of one of the two CSUTCBs, very close to MAS; and Felipe Quispe was simultaneously a parliamentary representative and executive secretary of the other CSUTCB, more centred in La Paz and tied to the MIP. When their struggle in parliament was blocked almost automatically by the governing coalition's so-called 'parliamentary bulldozer', they returned to the streets and the roadblocks, in a manner that the other political sectors criticised for still being too 'unionist', while the grassroots complained that they were forgetting their more local demands and acting like any politician, thinking only of their personal interests. Former leaders criticised the union organisation as resembling an organisation for fighting, for roadblocks, for protest rather than proposals.

In October 2003 came a *coup de grace* that owed much to the repressive activity of the government, which had even resorted to calling in special army troops at the cost of some 60 deaths and over 200 wounded among the civil population of Warisata, El Alto and the south of La Paz. With this the Vice-President Carlos Mesa, who deplored the use of force, dissociated himself from the rest of the government, a significant sector of the middle class joined the protests and, finally, President Sánchez de Lozada was to present his resignation and escape from the country.

Constitutional succession required that the government passed into the hands of ex-Vice-President Mesa. His respond to the demands he faced was to establish a national agenda, dubbed the October Agenda, which included as priority matters the revision of the Law of Hydrocarbons, the referendum on gas and the call for a Constituent Assembly. During the first months of Mesa's government there was a certain informal alliance with the popular movements and MAS, due to a mutual need in parliament which outweighed their notable differences.

During this first stage, Mesa promulgated a constitutional change that broke the monopoly of the political parties. Among the most important changes was the possibility of calling a Constituent Assembly and the openness of the political system to citizens' groups and indigenous peoples. The new Law of Citizens' Groups and Indigenous Peoples stipulated that the quota of women could not be lower than 50% for the authorisation of lists of candidates from citizens' groups and/or indigenous peoples. The promised gas referendum was also held, with a result favourable to the five proposals of the government, which later proved too ambiguous for them to be implemented.

However, the control of the public administration remained in the hands of the traditional political parties (MNR and MIR), which also obstructed all parliamentary work. The MNR, MIR and NFR were not prepared to do constructive parliamentary work. MAS withdrew its tacit support for the government and Mesa began to face opposition from all sides. The most hostile came from parliamentarians from the traditional parties displaced in October 2003, which were the most dogged and effective in blocking proposals made by the Executive.

The weakness of the Mesa government was also taken advantage of by the regionalist movement of Santa Cruz. If it is true that this civic movement had had various moments of importance in the XX century, it had been cut adrift as a result of the new role assigned to the municipalities by the LPP. However, after 2004 it enjoyed resurgence as a political force of magnitude, among other things because of the demand for departmental autonomy, as well as the defence of the regional royalties from gas exports. It was joined by the oligarchy of Tarija, in an attempt to expand the movement to the lowlands as a whole. The Santa Cruz élite played with fire and the old spark of *camba – colla* animosity caught ablaze.

In 2005 the situation with the 'Gas War' worsened. President Mesa presented his proposal for a Law of Hydrocarbons, which was rejected by Parliament, while the social sectors accused the government of defending the interests of the transnational company. Also the civic committees of Santa Cruz and Tarija opposed the Law of Hydrocarbons and pressed at the same time for a referendum on autonomies. With the great success of the local manifestation for autonomy and *cruceñidad* (Santa Cruz essentiality), held on the 28th of January 2005, the civic committee of Santa Cruz was eager to declare autonomy unilaterally. The idea of constituting a broader alliance of the "half-moon" was closer than ever.[118]

The popular sectors that had previously given Mesa a degree of truce again began to generate roadblocks, marches and other social conflicts, each one in accordance with its most immediate sectorial demands, at times with maximalist touches from the left that were reminiscent of the UDP years.

The President was unable to follow a clear line, coherent with the promises he made at the beginning of his mandate. In his desperation, from the first months of 2005 he retreated into most conservative postures and at one moment went so far as to launch a strong public diatribe against Evo Morales and Abel Mamani. A week later he climbed down, but his oscillations heightened the impression that the country was beginning to drift and that the President – faithful to the end to his condemnation of violent repression – had now exhausted his governmental resources.

Finally, on the 6th of June 2005, he presented his irrevocable resignation and, after various ineffectual attempts by the traditional parties to occupy the post by constitutional succession, it passed into the hands of the President of the Supreme Court of Justice, Eduardo Rodríguez Veltzé, whose mandate was to call general elections as soon as possible. In this way a certain social truce was reached that finally, following various vicissitudes, ended on the 18th of December with the holding of general elections. These resulted in an overwhelming triumph for Evo Morales and MAS, whose 54% of the vote dwarfed the 28% obtained by his closest rival, ex-president Tuto Quiroga.

For the first time in 500 years an indigenous person had reached the presidency, and did so with an indisputable and impeccable electoral victory unequalled since the restoration of democracy. But this new chapter as yet does not come into our history.

CURRENTS OF THOUGHT

To understand the new context in which CIPCA will act in this latter period, it is indispensable to explain something more of how political change had also occurred in the configuration of the most relevant social actors.

Role of the State and civil society

In the first place the relations of NGOs with the grassroots organisations and with the government have changed substantially. As we saw in the previous chapter, NGOs had to redefine the role of protest and denunciation they had played in the era of military dictatorships. During the first years of democracy, this role changed into a contestatory and pro-active position and, finally, the NGO posture was to have a third characteristic: active participation in state entities.

There were changes in the definition of the role of the government, in the process of decentralisation and de-concentration of governmental institutions, in the economic model that, since 1985, had been ruled by the principles of the free market, and in the construction of a democratic society interested in sustainable development. Then, as well as assuming an autonomous and independent position, CIPCA had to establish a new relationship with government, and in particular with local government.

Since the late 1980s, the indigenous peoples of the lowlands emerged as social actors, with a dynamic and very specific struggle to be included in society. Their demand for a recognised identity of their own has had great influence on other peasant sectors of indigenous origin. Little by little, both in the grassroots organisations and in NGOs, a change occurred in the discourse: emphasis shifted from peasants to indigenous or native peoples, and from class identity to ethnic identity.

Within some grassroots organisations and some NGO it is also possible to find *indigenista* focuses that are romantic rather than constructive, and may even be seen as fundamentalist. There are union leaders who are able to move a lot of people, but their discourse can be belligerent instead of proactive. Unfortunately, there are also cooperation agencies with *indigenista* politics that do not differentiate sufficiently between indigenous fundamentalism and indigenous movements which struggle to have their identity and culture respected, without disrespecting the identities and the culture of others.

After the year 2000 there was also an appreciable resurgence of regional organisations, in most cases directed by regional élites. The civic committees of Santa Cruz and Tarija are among those who have, in this way, become important political actors.

But within this panorama of new social actors, the most important would be municipal government. With the Law of Popular Participation, approximately 20% of the resources of the National General Treasury were directed towards the municipalities, having also conferred special roles of vigilance by peasant and indigenous communities and neighbourhood committees. It should be pointed out that two currents of thought existed: a 'municipalist' perspective and a 'ruralist' vision. The final result showed a preference for the municipal perspective, rather than being a specific tool for rural development.

Analysing the process, we might conclude that the peasant-indigenous population has broadened its presence from the social and union sphere to the administrative and municipal. Many leaders gave up their posts to instead become municipal authorities, with greater or lesser success, and, from there they also went on to some other levels. In any case, the fact of linking up, and even coming to exercise public power at those local levels, albeit not exempt from errors and conflicts, has permitted numerous grassroots leaders to have a first experience and apprenticeship in the management and exercise of power, which will soon be useful to them when they have access to superior levels.

It is encouraging to see the number of people of indigenous origin which began to have representation within the municipal governments. In the first municipal elections, held under the norms of new LPP, there were at least 500 peasants and indigenous people elected as councillors and mayors. Likewise, it is interesting to underline that the new municipal sphere has opened a space of greater public participation for women. Although they still constitute a minority, in the 1999 municipal elections 36% of those elected were women. The proportion of indigenous people (those who identify themselves as such and who speak the indigenous language from childhood) among those elected was lower (28%) and the non-indigenous proportion (self-identified as such, speaking only Spanish) reached 47%[119].

Local development and popular participation

As we indicated previously, since the 1990s Bolivia has experienced a process of reforms that has led to the country legally reinforcing its condition as a country with an institutionalised parliamentary democracy. Similarly, the 1994 Reform of the Political Constitution of the State (CPE) culminated with the incorporation of a new article that defined Bolivia as a multiethnic and pluricultural country. With this modification, new curricular content began to develop within the Educational Reform, local and cultural-specific ways of administering the TCOs were established, and groups of municipalities were constituted which, indeed, were principally made up of indigenous people. Similarly, the constitution obliged public policies to incorporate gender criteria in their conceptual focus.

As precursors and sources of inspiration for these laws we can mention the following (Urioste 2002: 158-159):

• The Fundamental Agrarian Law project, presented by the CSUTCB in 1984. One of the claims made in this proposal was recognition for peasant communities as units of autonomous government, with productive capacity.

• The project for a Law of Indigenous Peoples, drawn up by the CIDOB in 1990 in which elements were considered such as administrative political autonomy and full rights to all natural resources by the indigenous territories. This initiative was later articulated in the new Land Law (INRA Law).

• Another source of inspiration came with the electoral programmes of the MNR and the MBL for the 1993 elections. In the MNR's "Plan for All" one of the points mentioned was the decentralisation of political power. In 1991 the MBL had presented a project for a Law of Communities that advocated, among other things, the recognition of territorial jurisdiction for the peasant communities and the direct grant to these communities of 10% of tributary co-participation.

• CIPCA's 1991 book *For a different Bolivia* proposed a restructuration of the State from a regional perspective.

Through the LPP, the State broadened the jurisdiction and competence of the 311 municipalities, transferring 20% of national income to them, which was distributed proportionally according to the number of inhabitants per municipality. In order to have access to these resources of co-participation, the municipalities had to draw up their municipal budget in accordance with the Municipal Development Plan (PDM) and the Annual Operative Plan (POA), as well as effecting an accountability report from the previous administration. Subject to the LPP the indigenous communities, indigenous peoples, peasant communities and neighbourhood committees, have been recognised, promoted and consolidated as part of the legal, political and economic life of the country. The recognition of the legal status of all of them as 'territorial organisations' (OTB) implied that they would be considered as subjects to citizens' rights and duties. Vigilance Committees were created in each municipality as organs of social control.

Luis Saucedo Tapia, Municipal Mayor of Charagua between 1995 and 1999[120]:

"The municipality received land tax from two types of people: those indigenous peoples who paid nothing, and those who say they pay, the stockbreeders and the landowners. The municipality never saw these taxes: even before the approval of the Law of Popular Participation, its annual income was around 30,000 Bolivian pesos:

in all, we had three employees. And I say this because I have had the delightful experience of being a mayor before and after the LPP (...) whereas we used to have no income, we had nothing, on the other hand we could move like fish in water. Who was going to go that far to control an expenditure of 30,000 Bolivian pesos? (...) We have to recognise that, in the past, the State was absent in the rural municipalities. There was no government, not even municipal. The Regional Development Corporation only appeared once in a while, it did whatever it liked. With the new Law of Popular Participation the moment came to face up to a form of planning that was very difficult to put into practice. The municipality has had 2,300,000 pesos' income from popular participation. Not 30,000 as before. With these two million, in projects that are being carried out, we have generated a further six million." (Saucedo Tapia, s.f.: 99-103).

Omar Quiroga, a CIPCA agronomist, remembers:

"In 1995, after entering an electoral process to elect councillors and mayors throughout the country, two of the three captaincies of the Assembly of the Guaraní people (APG) that belong to the municipality of Charagua – Parapitiguasu and Charagua North – reflected on how to participate in this contest and decided to form a pact with the MBL. They asked Lucho Saucedo to be their candidate for mayor. The electoral campaign began and it culminated, months later, with a narrow victory for the MNR which obtained 943 votes as against 907 for the MBL. With the backing of the APG, Lucho forged an alliance with his great friend Prof. Abelardo Vargas, an ADN militant, who despite instructions given to him by the departmental leaders of ADN to support the MNR, preferred to endorse his dear friend. In this way, Lucho became mayor with the historical backing of the Guaraní communities and of an important urban sector of the municipality." (Cipca Notes No. 148, March 2006).

CIPCA was quite critical from the start. It was feared that the peasant organisation could become disarticulated and that the Law was rather deceitful. Another criticism was that it demanded many responsibilities from the people and gave little money (only 20%). Within CIPCA there were different postures, some were in agreement in supporting it; while others, did not look kindly on that "accursed Law".

The villagers of Jesús de Machaqa became involved, in the most unexpected way, in the final stage of the Law's creation (Ticona and Albó, 1997: 281-86):

"In February 1994 the principal *Mallkus* of Machaqa visited Vice-President Víctor Hugo Cárdenas to invite him to the *marka* to commemorate the anniversary of the uprising and massacre of the 12th March 1921. The vice-president accepted immediately. But soon the government attempted to put another face on the visit, seeing it as an excellent opportunity to present an image of peasant support for the Law of Popular Participation. Palace advisors calculated that it could attract some 20,000 people and suggested that, together with the vice-president, President Gonzalo Sánchez de Lozada himself should go to Jesús de Machaqa.

What followed was wilful mutual unintelligibility. For the Jesús de Machaqa people, the visit gave a high profile to a civic event whose axis was the traditional resistance of the native communities in the face of its oppressors. But the governmental delegation sought peasant support rather than a law proposal. So it was that the discourse – in Spanish – of the local *jach'a mallku* included some phrases that were more audacious than prudent, praising the courage of the Aymara and mentioning their distrust of (any) government because of corruption and false promises. The presidential committee, in contrast, moved in accordance to a different logic. The vice-president's response concentrated on an explanation, in Aymara, of the benefits of the imminent law. But when the President's turn came, the content and the tone of his discourse were quite negative, because he had interpreted the discourse of the *mallku* as a direct attack on him and his government. He said: "It appears that you don't want this law. It seems that we were mistaken and we were wasting our time, because we come here and the only thing the authority does is read a long list of demands and threats, and don't refer to what is worthwhile... if you don't want this law, we won't make it and we'll carry on as before... Why have you invited me if you did not want to listen to me?"

In April 1994 CIPCA organised a national seminar to fix its position. CIPCA decided to support the new Law and even one of its key collaborators, Carlos de la Riva, moved for a while to the Departmental Secretariat of Popular Participation, in Cochabamba.

The INRA Land Reform was most ambiguous, with both favourable and unfavourable elements for small producers. It recognised the same types of property already included in the Agrarian Reform of 1952 – the peasant plot, the small property, the medium-sized property and the agricultural enterprise – and added communitarian lands of origin and communal properties. The peasant plot and smallholding were considered inalienable, indivisible and nonseizable; they were not liable for land taxes and could not be sold. The middle-sized property and the agricultural enterprise were taxable and could be sold. The TCOs and community properties were considered inalienable, indivisibles, nonseizable, collective, and non-taxable. The lands that belonged to communities, indigenous peoples and family plots could not be used as a mortgage guarantee.

The land reform process began with great enthusiasm but, through political pressure from the rural élites (stockbreeders and loggers) it was carried out with low levels of efficiency, a great deal of bureaucracy and little effectiveness. After nine years of the INRA Law less than 20% of the lands had been reorganised. In 2005 lands were not expropriated even for their redistribution (only for carrying out works of public interest) nor were lands returned to State ownership[121].

Peasant economy

Ideas on the peasant economy were slow to arrive in Bolivia[122]. Although there were individuals who from the late 1970s became interested in the resurgence of the peasant economy, institutionally there was not much interest in studying it more deeply. In Bolivia, for example, there is no faculty of economics where it is possible to study and research the peasant economy. In CIPCA the emphasis on the CDT also absorbed reflections that made it not possible to theorise more deeply on the family economy.

Although interest in the peasant economy only emerged in the 1980s (see for example Figueroa, 1981), the debate concerning the subject is not new. In the 1920s there was already debate in the Soviet Union over the particularities of the economic rationality of peasant production and organisation. It was above all the economist Chayanov who developed innovative theory on the peasant economy. According to Archetti (1979), the Argentine anthropologist who introduced study of the peasant economy in Latin America, social scientists rediscovered the works of Chayanov because the social sciences needed a theoretical analysis that did not ignore the specific economic context in which the peasants are immersed. Neither the culturalist focus nor the Marxists currents attributed to the peasantry the potential to participate in the development process. Both perceived the peasantry as a traditional anachronism (see also chapter I).

Chayanov (1979: 90) developed a new analytical category: "the economic unity of a family of peasants or artisans that does not employ salaried workers and that only uses the work of members of the family itself. This family unit has a particular economic rationality."

The main characteristics of the peasant economy are (ibid: 95-110):
- in the peasant economic unit, the 'businessman' and the laborer are the same person. Then, as in any family company, the benefits that the peasant may have as a businessman, using for example a machine that saves manpower, are negated in his guise as a worker;
- the peasant may fulfil different productive activities: these may range from agricultural exploitation to artisanal or commercial activity and may involve the temporary abandonment of farming;
- the economic evaluation of peasant production produces a qualitative assessment:

the satisfaction of the needs of consumption by the unit of production which, at the same time, is the unit of consumption.

One of the main problems for the peasants is not having access to good lands. Over the course of history, many of the peasants have been displaced to low quality, marginal lands and to areas geographically distant from markets where, to make things worse, there was not even minimal productive or communications infrastructure. In such cases peasant families can barely satisfy their basic needs with what they obtain from their agricultural activities. Depending on the local and regional circumstances, the peasants are always involved in a wide variety of activities: agricultural, so as to satisfy alimentary and financial needs; commerce; artisanal activities for domestic use and for sale. Peasants also do paid work, as temporary migrant agricultural workers, or in mining, construction or services.

Thus the non-agricultural activities undertaken by peasant families constitute not complementary activities but integral activities. They are governed by a logic designed to support the lives (or guarantee the survival) of the peasant domestic unit.

Finally, the peasantry is not a homogeneous social class; there is economic differentiation within the peasantry, due to which a collective production mode is unthinkable. Furthermore, peasant families generally have few interests in common. However, relations with society at large are similar across the social sector as a whole. This is where the role of the peasant organisation comes in, not only for protest and political action but also for economic organisation (whether communal, associative or other).

Under the conditions in which the peasants are active (on marginal lands), they can only exercise control over natural resources and defend their interests in a global society if they manage to organise themselves at greater levels. Their economy is not eminently individualist, but neither is it correct to suppose that peasant families have an automatic disposition towards collective organisation. The peasant economy must be considered in its family (individual) dimension and in its collective dimension. The peasant unit cannot be conceived as isolated from of other similar units; it always appears as part of a broader group of units with which it shares a common territorial base. This 'local collectivity' may be the Andean peasant community, the Mexican *ejido*, the Amazonian indigenous community or some local organisation (formal or informal). In synthesis, any analysis of the peasant economy cannot be limited to the study of the family unit, but has to incorporate territorial collectivity.

One has to consider the peasant economy as a dialectical unit between the individual and the collective. In the case of Altiplano and Andean valley communities, it is the communal organisation that guarantees the usufruct or individual ownership of the land, the usufruct of the collective lands, the joint execution of works of infrastructure and of services that cannot be performed by individual families. In this way peasant organisation has a cultural function regarding collective identity. Other ethnic groups, like the Guaraní or Moxeño, have similar communal organisations, while colonisers in the Oriente have replicated their former organisation: the union. Family units mostly concentrate on production and reproduction, while communal organisation gives a framework for the reproduction of the whole system in its various dimensions.

To complete the picture, it is necessary to add the growing impact of the migratory factor, including the sustainability of the peasant economy. CIPCA already gave this attention in the specific case of the Altiplano in the series *Chukiyawu, the Aymara face of La Paz* (1981-87). However, since the year 2000 remittances from migrants who live (often illegally) in Argentina, the USA and Spain have become more and more substantial.

Among those dedicated to rural development in Latin America, whether in NGOs or in universities, there is still both pessimism and optimism regarding the possibility of development in the peasant economy. Among the pessimistic visions, there is a predominant scepticism regarding economic profitability, given the fragile agro-ecological and geographical conditions and the market conditions.

Business management

Since the start of 1992 there has been audible support for application of the business management model to NGOs. Professionals in cooperation agencies and NGOs felt pressurised to show tangible and quantitative results of development actions. In this way, as a new "cure-all" remedy, organisational development appeared on the agenda of international cooperation. It should not be forgotten that, in the discourse of the development agencies, NGOs were already considered more as their local operators than as independent, proactive organisms.

Often NGOs have commenced their actions voluntarily and informally, charging them with a profound experiential sense and constituting true work communities. Then, many groups have proceeded to act in a way that was certainly organic and rational, but also schematic. It was necessary to purify the task and make it more professional. However, the accent laced excessively on organisation and the fulfilment of strict stages and organigrams, has been imperceptibly leaving aside something of the spirit and the primary goals that constitute the keystone of identity and group vocation. Thus objectives with social and humanist content were transforming into objectives that pointed to institutional strengthening and quantitative aspects: goals and activities related to better technical functioning, economic-financial stability, more effective administration, drawing-up of payrolls, organigrams, reports, preparation of projects, computerised monitoring systems and evaluation, etc. (Berreta, 1992: 37).

Berreta's criticism is still valid today. Moreover, this emphasis on the organisational development of NGOs ran the risk of turning into an objective in itself. The fundamental role of NGOs – the strengthening of civil society – which, after all, is a political objective, was relegated to a marginal question. Computerised models of planning and monitoring were implemented, the peasants and indigenous were considered as 'clients' of NGOs, and assistance and training services became 'products' that could be bought and sold. Business jargon was introduced into the vocabulary of NGOs: client[123], product, *targets*, measurement of client satisfaction, management of human resources, *balanced scorecards*, strategic planning[124], planning by objectives, conflict management, risk management, knowledge management, etc. It is striking that the introduction of these business instruments into NGOs is almost always outdated, coming some ten years later when private companies are experimenting with other instruments.

For many employees it seems difficult to accept that reality is not controllable through instruments of management, above all when the work implies a permanent interactive dialogue with human interlocutors who also have their own priorities, visions and objectives. It seems difficult to accept that human beings – fortunately – do not allow themselves to be controlled. On the other hand the very positive idea has to be mentioned of taking into account the satisfaction of the base groups with which one works, since this helps to continually reconsider the work and avoid imposing ideas inconsiderately. Similarly there is merit in the initiative of signing agreements with OC-OIs to define the functions, tasks and responsibilities of each party – the NGO and the grassroots organisation – thus clearly showing the interdependence of both.

Over the last ten years, NGOs have been commonly criticised for not having been able to present quantitative results in poverty relief. NGOs are blamed for the rural population still being just as poor as thirty years ago. The demand for efficiency and efficacy emerged to combat the problem of this lack of convincing results. Then, so that NGOs might fulfil their functions more efficaciously and efficiently, one of the recommendations made of the cooperation agencies was that they should adapt to a business management focus. However, once NGOs have ceased to be informal groups and have turned into formal organisations, it is certainly necessary to formalise their organisational structure, staff recruitment policy and financial policy, as well as their administrative systems. However, it is not correct to consider this recommendation as a rural development panacea. Although more efficient and effective institutional management is a condition necessary to ensure the survival of NGOs, it is certainly not enough on its own. An NGO's rationale cannot be sustained by the management of the organisation as such, but by its social role which consists, fundamentally, in contributing an institutionality with defiant, proactive capacity and contestatory power. Let us look at the history of CIPCA between the years 1996-2005.

INTERNAL ORGANISATION

In 1995 an external evaluation was carried out, and in 1996 there was broad internal consultation within CIPCA. Based on this consultation and in accordance with the guidelines of the two most important cooperation agencies, CIPCA set out its new policies. Both NOVIB and EED had agreed with CIPCA to move on from financing by project to institutional financing. In this way, since 1997 CIPCA has presented three quinquennial plans: Strategic Plans 1997-2001, 2001-2005 and 2005-2010[125].

New legal status

The most important fact of institutional life was a legal measure: the transformation from 'CIPCA Company of Jesus' to 'CIPCA Civil Association'. Since its foundation in 1971, CIPCA had functioned legally thanks to a foundational document by which the Company of Jesus of Bolivia created this affiliated institution. It conferred a high degree of autonomy but in the final instance depended on it[126].

In January 1995 the foundational accord was signed that made CIPCA a new civil association and in the beginning of 1996 the first meeting of the new assembly of founder members was held.[127] In 1971 CIPCA was one of few NGOs that worked in rural zones with the peasant organisations. In 1995 there were around 800 known NGOs, of which some 500 were officially registered. The total finance of NGOs in that same year was more than 200 million dollars (Mejía et al., 1995: 7). Within national NGOs, CIPCA was probably one of the biggest in the country, in terms of its national coverage as well as its budget capacity and staff numbers.

Strategy, mission and challenges

When the CDT model was abandoned, it was decided that the level of economic-productive intervention was to be the peasant family as member of a community. Perhaps the law of the pendulum meant that any good that had also been achieved with the previous associative model was overly ignored. Thus for several years CIPCA showed no interest in working with economic organisations, such as associations of producers. However, reality soon obliged it also to undertake economic activities beyond the family nucleus.

During these years it was also necessary to clarify which levels of action would be chosen, and in what thematic spheres they would work. The emphasis was changing, with attention shifting towards increasingly high levels: from the community to the micro-region or municipality, the department and the country as a whole. Apart from seeking to have an influence at different levels – from the peasant family micro-level to the public policy macro-level – CIPCA also made the decision to expand its system of relationships and inter-institutional coordination with private and public entities.

CIPCA, as an institution opposed to the State, was disappearing. CIPCA was consolidating, though, as an organisation of civil society with contestatory, proactive power. In 1996 there was an innovatory and defiant political and institutional context that permitted the reconsideration of CIPCA's strategy: the new legal status of CIPCA, second-generation reforms (Law of Popular Participation and Land Reform Law), the new boom in international cooperation and the new instruments of institutional financing of NOVIB and EED which made it possible for CIPCA to enter a new phase of its institutional life.

The option taken by CIPCA at its foundation in 1971 was to contribute – from the field of social sciences – to the development of the peasantry, since this sector constituted the majority of the country's population yet suffered extreme poverty and social, cultural and political marginalisation[128].

In 2005 CIPCA considered it necessary to adjust its mission according to changes that had come about in the political environment. The years 2000-2005 were very turbulent, to such a point that there were moments in which political problems put the country's very democracy at risk. The CIPCA assembly agreed an updated formulation of its mission: "contribute to the political, economic and cultural strengthening of peasants and indigenous peoples – both men and women – and, from this perspective, participate in the construction of a democratic, intercultural, equitable and economically sustainable Bolivia."

CIPCA drew up its first strategic plan in 1997, when the small peasant producer was still ignored by the State. The viability of small producers depended increasingly on their means of access to different markets. Only through strong investments in productive infrastructure, and improvement of human capital, could peasant production manage to be competitive in the national market and maintain its position as provider of basic foods. The INRA Law had been passed barely a year before the first quinquennial plan, but CIPCA made this its own from the start by incorporating into the plan the important but conflictive theme of land and territory, referring explicitly to the growing territorial demand from the indigenous people.

Unavoidably, the municipality had become the new scenario of rural development plans. In the December 1995 municipal elections – the first under the new law – peasants and indigenous people participated much more than in the past, not only as electors but also as elected and – with 36% – as elected women.

The leadership of the Bolivian Workers' Central, a great social actor up to ten years before, had somewhat receded. The CSUTCB partly filled the vacuum left by the miners and workers, although it still had difficulties finding its role in the new situation. Moreover, a new actor had emerged in the peasant movement: the lowland indigenous peoples.

This is the environment that CIPCA took into account for the formulation of institutional challenges for the 1997-2001 and 2001-2005 strategic plans:
1 Contribute to the strengthening of the peasant and indigenous organisations so that they might respond to new challenges.
2 Support the peasant and indigenous communities in gaining access to, and property of, land and territory; also in the exercise of their rights over the resources found in these lands.
3 Contribute to the sustainable development of the peasant and indigenous economy.
4 Strengthening, in the municipal sphere, the exercise of citizens' rights, participation and social control among men and women.
5 Influence the municipal governments and other institutions in the municipal sphere to promote sustainable rural development in an efficient manner.
6 Influence the concerted formulation and execution of national and departmental policies affecting rural development.

Over the years 2002-2005 there were many political, economic and cultural conflicts in Bolivia that, despite the results of the 2005 elections, were not resolved in the short term. These ethnic and intercultural problems were what prompted CIPCA to carry out an analysis which culminated in the approval of a new mission and, as a consequence, a new content of institutional challenges.

It is worthwhile giving a brief summary of the key factors in the political environment that brought CIPCA to reformulate its institutional challenges (CIPCA, 2004: 9-11):

Democratic consolidation. The Bolivian scenario, over 22 years of democracy, has shown important political and social advances: minimal power quotas have been established in favour of women; municipal governments have been consolidated with political participation and social control; there are incipient processes of decentralisation; pluriculturality and ethnic diversity have been recognised; reforms to the Political Constitution of the State have been incorporated to broaden democratic participation without party mediation. In the social sphere, the coverage and quality of some basic services have been broadened, such as education, health and basic reorganisation. This democratic consolidation is nevertheless weak, partly due to a crisis in political parties, which have been losing legitimacy through their constant shenanigans, corporatism and cronyism, as well as their systematic avoidance of any dialogue with the population. The corruption, ineffectiveness, bureaucracy and moral crisis that characterise the handling of the public affairs are the reasons the main parties obtained such a low score in the opinion polls[129].

Tension between dualisms, polarities and complementarities. Bolivian reality is still marked by contradictions, dualities, complex articulations and complementarities in various senses. From a geographical perspective, the Andean west, the valleys and the eastern plains at times are counterpoised (discourses, postures, proposals, models) but also complement each other in many ways (access, commerce, migration, temporary jobs, etc.). However, from a socioeconomic perspective there is clearly a poor majority and a rich minority, separated by a gap that is widening all the time. It is common to speak of the 'two Bolivias', referring to the contradictions shown by some of the aforementioned indicators. Hence, Bolivia is a country that is feebly articulated, in terms both of its geographical aspects and its social and economic factors.

Few advances in the distribution of wealth. Almost two decades after decree 21060, which implanted a free market economy, its advances have been practically irrelevant for the great majority of the Bolivian population, which has not been able to improve its economic situation. In this model, the small rural producers were not, and still are not, taken into account as significant producers. The time has come to transform the economic stability, large investments, credit systems and facilities that are available to companies into income for the common people. Government policy until the end of 2005 timidly proposed a redefinition of concepts such as territoriality, property and the use of natural resources, as an indissoluble part of rural development policy. Unfortunately, these proposals for change have mostly remained at the level of discourse[130].

Insertion into globalisation. Whereas one has to recognise some positive aspects of globalisation and the opportunities it brings to various spheres (economic, information and communication spheres), nevertheless elements of discrimination and exclusion can be perceived in this same phenomenon. Whatever the case, the country has to face up to globalisation and gradually enter into it. Meanwhile there is the challenge of working, from below and from the local, towards another globalisation; one with an emphasis on rights, leading to a world with greater equality, improved justice and better economic development.

As a response to this new environment and based on the lessons learned in previous years, CIPCA set itself five institutional challenges for the years 2005-2010:
1 Democratic indigenous and peasant organisations.
2 Land property rights, territory and natural resources.
3 Sustainable rural economy.
4 Intercultural democracy and efficacy in local and intermediate government institutions.
5 Public policies favourable to peasants and indigenous peoples.

There is no doubt that these challenges, which will be worked on during the years 2005-2010, have been correctly identified for both the country and CIPCA. 35 years of experience, of lessons learned, both right and wrong decisions, positive and unexpected results, strengths and weaknesses, have meant that CIPCA has been, still is and will continue to be an important factor in Bolivian society.

Management model

Once CIPCA was legally constituted as a civil non profit-making association, the following organs of deliberation and decision were established: a members' assembly, the board, a executive management committee, the general directorship, regional offices, a special unit for lobby and advocacy (UAP), the library[131] and PADA.[132]

With the opening in 1997 of two new offices in Moxos and Riberalta, CIPCA reached a national coverage that included the country's main agro-ecological zones, in five of the nine departments. [133]

A positive characteristic of the 1997-2005 management model was institutional credibility, by the real and not merely formal role of controller exerted by the Assembly and the Board. One could similarly stress decentralisation and the corresponding autonomy of the regional offices. Relations between the general direction and the regional offices were based on dialogue and constant consultation.

However, due to their own informal and non-systematic nature, the *ad hoc* initiatives for certain themes of political and strategic importance did not manage to constitute a space of institutional reflection. For this reason the mid-term evaluation of 2004 proposed greater formal coordination between the regional offices, as well as coordination between these offices and the general directorship (Armani, 2004: 35). In other words, the pendulum had swung, in recent years, more towards regional autonomy than to centralised leadership, a mode typical of the management of Luis Alegre.

So it was that in 1997 the UAP was created as a linear unit whose chief mandate was to influence public policies and the public debate in favour of rural development and the improved position of the peasants and indigenous people. In the first years the work of this unit was most centred on communication and diffusion, while in the last five years, the impact of its research and contribution to the public debate has increased considerably.

Financial and human resources

In 1997 CIPCA's budget was more than 3 million dollars a year, while it had 125 employees on the staff payroll. From its birth until 1998 CIPCA had known only growth in staff and finance. However, in 1999 it had to face measures such as a critical reduction in financing, which forced staff reductions. The crisis was so serious that there was even the possibility of selling off some assets from the regional offices.

The priorities of the cooperation agencies did not coincide with the new context. The agencies were late in adapting to the new priorities and were not prepared to finance specific projects for the municipalities; the CIPCA management committee decided to maintain the new focus utilising institutional funds and making cuts in any not considered a priority. Because of these problems, CIPCA had a budgetary deficit for three consecutive years.

While solutions to the crisis were sought, there was a debate over whether CIPCA could or should generate a greater quantity of its own resources participating in the consultancies market and in public competition (tenders). There was calculation of the risk that would be run in having to adapt to the tastes and priorities of the finance agencies, with the final consequence that the contractors, and not CIPCA, would be those who set the pace and the institutional dynamic. This would probably have distanced CIPCA from its mission. It opted to continue as an NGO, maintaining its autonomy in defining its mission and mandate, a decision that had the painful consequence of forcing the institution to part with very valuable personnel.

At the end of 2004 CIPCA again had 110 employees on its staff payroll. NOVIB and EED had approved the 2005-2010 strategic plan, whose total amount was almost 12 million Euros for five years, of which NOVIB brought in around €1,800,000 (for three years) and EED €920,000 (for six years).[134]

The most important human resources policies are:

-CIPCA only carries out consultancies and other activities financed by local sources if they are related to the mission, challenges and policies of the institution;

-CIPCA respects the party-political opinions of the members of the institution, but requires that work is not used for party ends;

-CIPCA seeks to contribute positively to intercultural and gender relations. As such, in its organisation and internal regime, it recognises cultural values and gender differences, respecting and fomenting their expression;

-CIPCA earmarks a minimum of 2% of its total wage bill for staff training and interchange of experiences.

Systematisation and knowledge management

Despite different external evaluations having recommended better systematisation of experiences and – in the current jargon – greater knowledge management, there is no doubt that CIPCA has always been an exemplary institution as regards the systemisation and generation of knowledge. It seems to be a mantra that development cooperation agencies continually repeat, without realising that CIPCA does indeed systematise, does learn from its experiences and does seek to socialise knowledge. Moreover, it is one of the few NGOs that have also managed to generate and spread new knowledge. If the reader had the chance to visit the CIPCA library, s/he would realise that it is one of the best social sciences libraries anywhere in Bolivia. This is also the institutional memory for the staff itself, not to mention students, researchers and future generations.

The various triennial and quinquennial plans have always been the expression of new working proposals, a result of systematisation based on previous experience. On the other hand, it must not be forgotten that adequate systematisation requires a certain distance, which means that it is difficult for the staff that is 'in the action' to analyse and write at the same time. And when finance was requested so that someone from the outside might take on certain studies that were more intellectual and academic, often the agencies would not want to finance them. They would use the argument that this type of cerebral work did not produce concrete, immediate and tangible results in the reduction of poverty.

If we analyse the current definition of knowledge management, the conclusion is inevitable that CIPCA has been doing it for many years, perhaps without having used the concept[135] (which was not even known at that time). CIPCA has also developed an interactive webpage to and has established an excellent distribution channel called *Cipca Notas* (CIPCA notes) in which staff contribute writings on themes of their own specialisation that are circulated by e-mail. Every year there is at least one thematic workshop on institutional policies and staff have the right to follow an individual training plan, consisting of elements such as temporary out-placements, internal training and study grants.

In the 1990s research was more concentrated on technical studies and micro-regional diagnostics. After 2000, under the new director general's management, CIPCA began to reactivate social research, giving some staff members the opportunity to systematise various experiences from CIPCA's institutional life. Some items that should be mentioned are a study on the income of peasant families, a systematisation of sustainable rural development proposals and a collection of life stories from some peasant and indigenous leaders.

WORK ZONES

In the late 1990s there was a strong discussion between NGOs and the cooperation agencies about an NGO's cycle of intervention in a given zone and/or with a specific population. This debate had a bearing on CIPCA's decision to reorganise work in its zones of influence, in the four previous regions. Besides, in the case of CIPCA La Paz a crisis of exhaustion had arisen which was not possible to overcome without drastically renewing work on the Altiplano, among other things through a base-line study of new zones.

In the 1997-2001 strategic plan the following organisational challenge had been formulated: "define the cycle of institutional intervention and make sure that it contains an effective strategy of transference and appropriation". This challenge provoked considerable discussion among the staff, members of the board and representatives of the development cooperation agencies.

It is not clear when and how this debate began. What is certain is that there were opinions in the world of development cooperation which sustained that an NGO could not work in any zone for an indefinite time. This was seen as unsustainable and, besides, incompatible with realistic planning. The NGO had to plan its intervention in such a way that, at any given moment, it could transfer the activities it was carrying out in grassroots organisations or local institutions. Another argument that influenced this position was that the NGO had to be capable of identifying the concrete results it was seeking and situate them precisely in time. When the NGO was not capable of achieving the foreseen results systematically and over a prolonged period, it had to be honest, admit its failure and either conclude its activities or totally reformulate them. It was not correct to go on doing more of the same thing, either through simple inertia or using the facile argument that people needed the help.

In March 1999 this problematic was broadly discussed in the Assembly, when people wanted to know of the advances in defining the cycle of institutional intervention, and how CIPCA thought it might assure an effective strategy of transference and appropriation. The Assembly asked the regional directors to identify those zones thought to have adequately fulfilled institutional objectives as a result of applying the Decennial Plan. In these zones it would be necessary to plan a final exit phase, of a maximum duration of three years. At the same moment a process had to be initiated to define new zones of intervention. All future work had to establish clearly the period of intervention.

A sample of opinions expressed at that moment:
- There was no need to leave the work in San Julián because so much had already been done that it would have been a shame to withdraw when the work was beginning to go better.
- The work in Antofagasta could be abandoned because the peasant organisation was fully consolidated.
- Regarding the results in Santiago de Machaqa, some assembly members wondered why the place had been classed at that time as a work zone, considering its economic and organisational weakness.
- In Jesús de Machaqa there were few results, partly because there was still the problem of it not being a municipality and because of all kind of internal political conflicts; however, the option of withdrawal arose precisely at a moment in which there was the possibility of getting positive results.
- The decision to withdraw from Tiraque and Jesús de Machaqa had to do also with the fact that CIPCA wanted to show the financing agencies that these zones were not considered as its "fiefdoms", which was a very common criticism in those years.

In these opinions it is notable that the discussion made little sense, because the same arguments were used both for staying in one zone and for withdrawing from another: cultural, economic, political, topical and programmatic factors all played a role[136].

Currently the theme of the cycle of intervention has totally disappeared from debates among NGOs and development cooperation agencies. Similarly CIPCA, after having made adjustments, no longer considered ten years' activity as a norm, but rather discussed the theme of whether or not to continue working in a zone according to the problematic, rather than being based on artificial periods.

Throughout all the political events of the 1990s, CIPCA felt the need to make a proposal of its own to help improve the lot of lowlands indigenous people. Its presence in only the Guaraní region was not sufficient. Thus CIPCA began to work in the Amazonian zone with an indigenous problematic quite distinct from that of the Altiplano, the valleys, the Chaco or the integrated region of Santa Cruz.

After five years of deliberations, the CIPCA board decided to take on the risk of creating two new offices: in 1997 it opened an office in San Ignacio de Moxos (CIPCA

Beni) and other in Riberalta (CIPCA North) for Pando and part of the department of Beni.

In December 2005 CIPCA worked in the following municipalities and/or TCOs:

Regional La Paz	Guaqui, Ancoraimes, Ayo Ayo, Viacha, Apolobamba
Regional Cochabamba	Community of Municipalities of the Caine Basin: Sacabamba, Anzaldo, Toro Toro (Potosí), Acasio (Potosí)
Regional Cordillera	Charagua, Gutiérrez, Camiri, Huacareta, Boyuibe TCO: Charagua North, Parapitiguasu, Isoso
Regional Santa Cruz	Santa Rosa, Urubichá
Regional Beni	San Ignacio de Moxos, Santa Ana de Yacuma TCO: TIM and TIMI
Regional North	Riberalta (rural area), Guayaramerín (rural area) Pando: Gonzalo Moreno, San Pedro Río Orthon and Río Madre de Dios

REGIONAL OFFICES

A this stage in writing CIPCA's history, it is opportune to sum up the perspective of the regional offices, both old and new, so as to grasp how historical continuity and institutional unity has led CIPCA to adapt, in all kinds of ways, to the characteristics of each moment and place.

CIPCA La Paz[137]

In 1995 the evaluation (Mejía, 1995) recommended that a more profound evaluation be undertaken of the regional office of La Paz with particular impact in the technical-economic area. Undeniable achievements were recognised, such as the greenhouses built on one of the few productive alternatives viable on the Altiplano, the decisive support given to the CSUTCB, and support at local level for the peasant communities. On the other hand, it was mentioned that staff motivation had diminished; the impression existed that the old mystique and passion had been lost, and that the tendency was to do more of the same. The CIPCA board took the recommendation seriously and requested an internal evaluation of the CIPCA La Paz performance (Crespo et al., 1996). The evaluation's recommendations were taken into account and a rethink of the La Paz office was the result.

As regards gender there was a lot of debate in the La Paz team. The evaluation document (ibid: 5) indicated that in La Paz resistance had been stronger than in the other regions. To begin with, an explicit gender focus was not clearly understood, nor accepted. It was argued that Aymara culture was based on the complementarity of the family unit, with egalitarian roles and rights among its members. Within this vision, it was thought that the new focus would divide the family. There was little will to examine the viability of work from a gender perspective. Over the years it was possible to convince those concerned members and finally it has been recognised that also in the Aymara world there is gender inequality, expressed in fewer opportunities for women in the public life, domestic violence, etc.

So as to reconsider its productive proposal for the Altiplano, CIPCA took seriously the endless criticism it had received, both directly and indirectly. There was the criticism, for example, that the greenhouses needed too much capital investment and, as such, were not sustainable. It was also argued that the dairy cattle were not competitive with those in other regions of Bolivia and the world[138]. The La Paz regional office opted finally for the family economy level, with which it certainly had interesting positive experiences, like sustainable soil management through the construction of live fencing and terraces, seed selection and control of the Andean weevil. Micro-irrigation systems and agro-ecological production played a dynamic and important role in the two zones in which their activities were concentrated, Guaqui and Ancoraimes, whilst it ceased to work in Ayo Ayo.

One of the criticisms of this regional office at the end of the 90s was that it had centred its activities in two small municipalities that were unrepresentative of the Altiplano. The office extended its range to include the municipalities of Viacha, Pelechuco, Curva and Charazani (in the highlands and valleys with populations speaking Aymara and Quechua, in the north of the department). In this way, CIPCA La Paz has resumed a regular relation with associations of small breeders of bovines, in Viacha, and of camelids in the other municipalities.

Organisationally, CIPCA La Paz is one of the offices that advanced most in participative management models for municipal governments and in the promotion of social control, principally articulating the peasant organisation with municipal management. Subsequently both CIPCA La Paz and the municipalities of Guaqui and Ancoraimes were recognised for their contribution to popular participation. There are increasing numbers of people of Aymara origin elected as mayors, councillors and/or members of vigilance committees. In the 2004 Ancoraimes municipal elections, for example, they obtained 38% of the votes (3 councillors).

Gender quotas and the decision of Altiplano women to advance more decisively in public positions have also had positive results.

Justina Machaqa, an Ancoraimes councillor, remembers:

"In 2000, we Ancoraimes women, organised ourselves into the Sub Federation of Peasant Women "Bartolina Sisa" of Ancoraimes (SFMCBSA). We managed to get a Gender Agenda drawn up and allied ourselves with strategic actors for the incorporation of women's demands in the Annual Operative Plan. In 2002 I was the only woman in the Vigilance Committee; in 2005 there were already two women as representatives for the women's organisations and I was elected councillor for the municipality.

The men use us women to present projects to the institutions, because there is a higher probability that the projects will be approved when they are presented by women."

At higher levels, the question persists of how to maintain equilibrium between leaders and bases. The leaders of the CSUTCB, of the Single Union Federation of Peasant Workers of La Paz "Tupac Katari" (FSUTCLP-TK) and of the Departmental Federation of Peasant Women of La Paz "Bartolina Sisa" (FDMCLP- BS) at times think more about their own professional careers as leaders than about their function as representatives of their bases.

Two initiatives are worth mentioning. Firstly, CIPCA La Paz decided to formalise relations with the peasant organisations by signing of agreements in which the rights and obligations of each party are stipulated. Similarly, in its work of organisational strengthening, CIPCA La Paz also included themes that refer to the organisations' internal democracy.

CIPCA Cochabamba[139]

The Cochabamba regional office covers the peasant problematic in the Andean valleys, an area of temperate climate, very fragmented landscape and dense Quechua-speaking population. In the preceding phase CIPCA had worked in the municipalities of Tiraque and Sacabamba, but it then solemnly withdrew from Tiraque and since 1998 has concentrated on the new challenge of constituting and consolidating the Association of Municipalities of the Caine Basin (MMCC), to which Sacabamba also belongs[140]. With the good experience of this municipality, it wanted to expand its action in its natural zone of influence. CIPCA got involved in the Association of Municipalities' problems, running the risk that its activities might prove more beneficial to the interests of the rural élite than to those of the great majority of the poor population. However it proved to be a successful experience, among other things because, in the Community's governing bodies, peasant representatives also participate together with the municipal authorities. They were also able to awaken the interest of the prefectures of Cochabamba and Potosí by seconding the proposals of the Asociation of Municipalities. This pioneering experience has become an example of coordination, and effective participation of municipal governments and peasant organisations.

On the productive side the Cochabamba office had worked for years on the introduction of fruit trees, apple and peach, based on the results of previously mentioned research. In all nearly 30 hectares of fruit trees were planted in Tiraque. Importance was also given to an improvement in rearing livestock (cattle and sheep), and an association of stockbreeding promoters was constituted that provided services to Tiraqueand the neighbouring municipalities. On several occasions this association won the tender of the vaccination campaign organised by the Departmental Service of Agriculture and Livestock (SEDAG) of the Prefecture of Cochabamba, competing with other companies and service providers. Only in the last six years has CIPCA begun to work on both the improvement of existing irrigation and micro-irrigation systems (two dams with finance from the Peasant Development Fund), and on innovations in pressurised irrigation. All this work was part of the Agricultural Development Plan which was drawn up, based on the micro-regional survey.

In these same years the first work began on the irrigation system at Ch'iara Qhochi in Sacabamba. The work on soil conservation and forest plantations were the first activities, for the project did not consist only of the construction of the infrastructure but also of the other components like forestation, conservation of cultivable and non-cultivable soils, organisation and agricultural production[141].

The participation of Don Gerardo Blanco, Mayor of Sacabamba during two consecutive spells (1996 to 2004) was very important. Together with many women and men from his community, he had supported this project which was crucial in order for the zone to recuperate development perspectives. Because of its magnitude, this irrigation project required financial support from central State, the departmental prefecture and the municipal government, as well as several sources of international cooperation. The final result is that there are more than 200 peasant families who produce under irrigation and obtain two harvests a year.

An irrigation technician remembers:

"There were four families affected (they later were compensated) that roundly opposed the construction of the dam, to such an extent that one of the ladies became famous for scaring us technicians away with a hail of rocks as we were about to do the preliminary works for the project. When the execution of the irrigation began, the lady was one of those leading the soil protection works. When reminded of her "exploits" with the technicians, she laughs graciously, without saying a word."

This experience was also innovative for CIPCA since, if some irrigation projects had been executed in Tiraque, this was a case of minor works. Ch'iara Qhochi meant new learning, since CIPCA had to liaise with various ministries of the central State, coordinate with the Prefecture, with the FDC, battle with the contracting companies, manage the expenditure in La Paz and coordinate with the municipality and the association of irrigators.

The results achieved in the transformation from unirrigated cultivation to crops under irrigation have served as a base from which to adjust the productive proposal of CIPCA Cochabamba, and have opened up new perspectives in the agricultural and livestock work in Sacabamba and Anzaldo, later broadened to include the Caine Basin Association of Municipalities.

The implementation of the productive proposal also implied the creation of producers' organisations: this occurred in 1997 in Sacabamba, and in 2001 with the foundation of the Association of Agricultural Producers of the Caine.

The following is from a chronicle by Bernardino Soliz (*From shepherdesses to farmers*, 2001):

"The implementation of the Ch'iara Qhochi irrigation project in Sacabamba is changing the traditional roles of peasant families. The change is more visible in the case of women.

Before, the women of the zone, with the help of children, had shepherding as their main (though not only) activity; 12 animals on average. From November onwards, besides, they had to work in sowing tubers and unirrigated cereals, followed by cultural labours and harvests. Agricultural activities finished in June, with the winnowing of wheat and barley.

When at last the day for watering arrived, they perhaps never thought that the water for irrigation would change forever many aspects of their lives and their everyday activities. Now they are dedicated more to irrigating the plots, which begins in the month of June. After this month it is necessary to tend to the crops until the harvest in November. Also in November the seasonal sowings begin and have to continue with the same activities of crop care practically almost until June.

As Doña Juana says: «In this season (November) we just used to have to eat whatever potatoes we could buy ... and that lasted us. But now we have plenty; in fact now we even take some to sell, which is good».

And what about the sheep? Most families have had to look for new ways to rear them. They tie them up where there is a bit of pasture and add forage and *phalaris*, which is multiplying all over the area. In other cases they give them *al partir* (share raising) to families that do not irrigate. Other families are already planning to get rid of their sheep and buy a couple of cows, which will provide not only manure but also milk with the alfalfa that they are cultivating now."

Another theme in which CIPCA Cochabamba has achieved great capacity is municipal development. Within the framework of popular participation – first in Tiraque and Sacabamba, then in the municipalities of the Caine Basin Association of Municipalities – it supported the political participation of the peasants in municipal government through their organisations. Increasing access to municipal government for peasant men and, gradually, also for women peasants, was quite successful if one considers the context of conflict and tensions with some elites of the urban centres. Managerial capacitiy increased, of the municipal authorities in general, and of the peasants in particular. This served CIPCA as a basis for taking on, along with the Universidad Mayor de San Simón (UMSS) and the Centre of Research and Popular Education (CINEP), a training and formation programme in municipal development in 35 municipalities of Cochabamba and North of Potosí.

Excipión Villarroel, an ex-leader tortured and imprisoned during the dictatorship of García Meza, remembers:

"Since the year 2000 many people have become mayors and councillors without having struggled politically. Young people who were born under democracy do not recognise previous struggles, they don't even know about them (.....) in the 1995 campaign the peasants did not want to present themselves as candidates for mayor and/or councillor, and now (2005) they all want to be mayors and councillors; there are fights and divisions."

During those years, internal conflicts and leadership squabbles increased within the peasant organisations; these led to the division of the Single Union Federation of Peasant Workers of Cochabamba (FSUTCC): on the one side Román Loayza and on the other Alejo Véliz[142]. Indeed, for some years there were two Federations. If until the mid 1990s coordination between CIPCA and the Federation was very close, the division meant that coordination became more and more difficult, to such a point that, for a while, CIPCA had to concentrate on more local levels, where the squabbles and conflicts had not appeared except in isolated cases.

Román Loayza, former general secretary of the CSUTCB and MAS senator, remembers:

"Every weekend we used to go to the countryside with CIPCA and CENDA. NGOs gave us mobility and we were trained in matters such as leadership and union independence. [The radio programme] *Llaqta Qhapari* was very important in all this. After the stage of union support came that of political support. In 1997 CIPCA supported me with the radio, in workshops, in my campaign as uninominal representative."

In 1997 the Departmental Federation of Irrigators' Committees (FEDECOR) was also constituted. Nearly thirteen thousand irrigators from the different valleys attended Congress, but the directorship of the FSUTCC opposed the creation of a new federation, knowing Cochabamba's propensity for divisionism in its grassroots organisations; the most it would accept was a Secretary of Irrigation within the FSUTCC and under its tutelage.

Internal disputes and difficulties in working with this level of peasant organisation partly influenced CIPCA's decision to concentrate on the Caine Association of Municipalities. Since 2004, conflicts and tensions within the peasant organisation have diminished. The Departmental Federation has re-established its mobilising capacity and has returned to coordinated work with CIPCA. Proof of this is seen, among other things, in the broad participation of leaders of the Departmental Federation and of the "Bartolinas", who are joined by local organisations in producing the radio programme *Lllaqta Qhapari*.

CIPCA Cordillera[143]

In the period 1997-2005, the Guaraní people experienced one of the biggest boosts in their history. The Assemblee of the Guaraní People (APG) used the INRA Law as a base for presenting 19 claims of TCO, of which 14 were admitted. Likewise, the Workshop for Guaraní Education and Communication, (Teko Guaraní) was the base for the introduction of bilingual teachers and educational systems under the direction and the control of its own authorities. Several of the initiatives introduced in the educational field by the Guaraní were then included in the Educational Reform at national level. Finally, the Law of Popular Participation was the legal framework within which the political participation of the Guaraní began to increase, obtaining seats in municipal governments, both in councillorships and in the directorship of some mayoralties.

The captaincies[144] grew from 18 to 24, which generated greater strength in the APG and, at the same time, obliged them to confront new problems such as that of leading the process of disengagement of the communities from their former landlords, mainly in the Chaco of Chuquisaca. The return of the oil companies forced it to acquire capacities for the adequate protection of communal lands and resources. Within this framework important negotiations were held that were later to benefit the entire population of the municipalities of the Chaco, where there was and still is oil activity.

In 1998 CIPCA established a new sub-regional office in Monteagudo (in the southeast of Chuquisaca), so as to give exclusive attention to the communities recently constituted by Guaraní people previously tied to the haciendas. The constitution of these communities entailed lands being acquired with resources obtained by the Church (or rather, by the Vicariate of Cuevo), CIPCA and other institutions, to hand them over as property to those Guaraní peoples who were prepared to leave the haciendas where they lived under landlords. Thus working relations have been established in eight new communities. The change was important for those families that until recently survived in a regime of feudal-style servitude. The greatest problem – one already mentioned in previous chapters – is that in some of these communities CIPCA and FONDECO did not know how to have an adequate credit policy for such special circumstances.

The APG consolidated its organisation at communal, regional and national level. The elections of leaders were stable and dynamic and – overcoming the resistance of the first years – the percentage of women elected for directive posts is now notable: 26% in communal directives, 23% in zonal directives and 40% in regional directives. CIPCA has trained 444 women who have occupied executive functions in the captaincies and communities. The APG was the first indigenous organisation at regional level to have had in its directive (2003-2005) a female president (Nelly Romero) and vice-president (Tomaza Aramayo). It is worth remembering that in 1988 CIPCA still thought that within the Guaraní culture, despite its matrilocal system, the males exercised an authoritarian role and questioned the opportunity of giving roles other than the traditional ones to women.

The Guaraní people was one of the first to appropriate the possibilities of the LPP by which, since the 1995 elections, the Guaraní have participated with varied success in different municipal governments. Charagua is one of the most successful. The Guaraní presence, jointly with the participation of other sectors, resulted in a municipality with stable governments and with important investments. CIPCA accompanied the municipal process through the formation of leaders, men and women, both in municipal management and in social control.

CIPCA Cordillera accompanied these demands for land and territory in three of the TCOs. The process of reorganisation, if it has strengthened the APG and generated the consolidation of certain captaincies such as Iti Kaaguasu, Yacuiba and Takobo Mora, it is also true that it has consumed a large part of the institution's resources, since these were slow processes, often distorted by INRA and in a framework of permanent conflicts with some of the ranch owners. It also meant the reorganisation of CIPCA, which had to contract lawyers and other professionals to carry out an adequate and permanent accompaniment to the process of reorganisation.

To consolidate the collective land ownership, the TCO management and CIPCA have begun to draw up Territorial Management Plans (GTI) that include, among other elements, an inventory of natural resources. These documents have been recognised by the municipalities as valid planning instruments. The idea is that these plans should be considered as a social contract that articulates various systems and procedures, which include legal security, land space zoning, the access to natural resources and their equitable and sustainable use within the framework of the implementation of public policies.

For several years new conflicts have arisen because the Guaraní territory coincides with the biggest gas reserves in Bolivia. There is also an overlap of interests between oil concessions and indigenous territories over the use of, and access to, natural resources. For the APG this has meant a new front, dealing with conflicts and disputes concerning these resources, both renewable and (above all) non-renewable. Some of the offices, especially Charagua, have accompanied the APG in its negotiations with the oil companies. The Territorial Management Plans were indispensable instruments when it came to negotiating compensations and development actions on the part of the oil companies.

Between 1997 and 2005 attention to the economic productive aspect of the CDTs has decreased and a new agenda was established which demanded a permanent mobilisation due to the expectation of (collective) property titles of the territories. Besides, the reconversion of the initial proposal of CDTs to one of a family nature was not readily adopted, either by the CIPCA staff or by the communities[145]. Despite this adverse context, a family plot proposal was consolidated, principally oriented towards the protection of soils, diversification and agro-ecological crops.

CIPCA Santa Cruz[146]

The Santa Cruz regional office historically directed its actions towards the organisation of communities recently established by peasant colonisers mostly originating from rural communities in Chuquisaca and Potosí. In the years 1997-2005 it started to also work with the indigenous organisations. The indigenous demands, in many cases, went beyond the limits of the department. The INRA Law exposed conflicts between indigenous people and "businessmen" and also between indigenous people and peasants. These conflicts generated greater concentration and articulation of the business groups with interests in land property and logging matters. This juncture meant that Santa Cruz became a referent for the whole Bolivian Oriente, both in its possibilities and its contradictions.

The Santa Cruz regional office concluded its activities in the colonisation zone of San Julián. In 1998 it abandoned productive support activities, and in 2000 it stopped supporting municipal management and social control. It maintained its presence in the other colonisation zone, the Municipality of Santa Rosa del Sara, and began activities in Urubichá, a municipality with local indigenous Guarayo population. At the beginning there was a certain resistance on the part of municipal authorities against working with CIPCA, due to its previous history of support to only peasant colonisers. Between 1997 and 2005 CIPCA has supported peasant communities and indigenous peoples with agroforestry, silvo-pastoral and community forest management proposals. In Urubichá, whose population owns a TCO, but is at the same time surrounded by stockbreeders, there were different disenchantments with the land entitlement programme, among other reasons because indigenous leaders, businessmen and State employees have trafficked with TCO lands.[147]

In the case of Santa Cruz, for both indigenous peasant organisations and the institutions that support them, the biggest challenge is providing development actions that simultaneously contain and embody alternatives to the extensive export agriculture based on the cultivation of soya, sunflowers and rice.[148]

But beyond its work in determined municipalities, an important change in the general focus of CIPCA Santa Cruz has broadened its influence in the departmental sphere and thence to the whole Bolivian Oriente, since in Santa Cruz there is a confluence of interests, often conflictive, of colonisers original from the Andean high lands, indigenous population from the low lands, oil company bosses, loggers, big landowners and stockbreeders. CIPCA Santa Cruz assumed the challenge of working in this reality, playing an articulating role between the four regional offices situated in the lowlands.[149]

In 1999 and 2001 peasant marches were held that consolidated the alliance of the called Oriental Block, in which the indigenous organisations of the Amazonian North, Beni, Santa Cruz and the Chaco are concentrated. The agenda of indigenous mobilisations had progressively extended its reach to the demand for acceleration in the land reorganisation process. New demands for the national agenda were presented: Gas Referendum, new law of hydrocarbons and the election of a Constituent Assembly.

In the years 2001 and 2002 the indigenous and peasants were in conflict with big landowners; the most serious of these occurred in the Forest Reserve of the Chore, in the TCO Monteverde (municipality of Conception) and in Pananti (municipality of Yacuiba, Tarija). Such conflicts escalate into violent confrontations which, in the case of Pananti, provoked the death of 6 members of the Movement without Land (MST) and of one of the attackers. This situation was accentuated by a slow and distorted process of application of the INRA Law.

Also worth mentioning are the fresh shoots of an exacerbated regionalism seeking to halt an 'Indian attack' from the highlands. The sectors that dominated before the so-called "*Media Luna*" group began stealthily manoeuvring towards independence for the Bolivian Oriente. They even furthered 'blood pacts' between fractions of Guarayo and Guaraní indigenous groups with stockbreeders and the

Chamber of Agriculture of the Oriente (CAO) for the defence of the lowlands against the 'invaders from the highlands'.

Communication in CIPCA Santa Cruz has had a renewed impulse after a new focus, which mainly incorporates the treatment of demands from indigenous and peasant organisations, and other themes that are found on the agenda of the social movements. This has made it possible that communication became an important instrument in countering the campaign against these demands unleashed by regional power groups, that contained messages loaded with regionalist feeling exacerbated by racism. CIPCA Santa Cruz then turned to the radio as a means of communication and, recognising its importance, broadcast the Programme "Land and Democracy" through local and regional stations. Finally, together with the Women's House, CIPCA Santa Cruz has constituted a network of communication named *Ondas Libres* (Free Waves) and has published a webpage with the same name[150].

CIPCA Beni[151]

In 1997 the Beni Regional Office began to work on the multiethnic territories of the plains of Moxos, an area characterised by an ecology and economy rich in flora and fauna, with numerous rivers and lagoons and flooding in the rainy season. These are territories mainly occupied by large cattle-raising haciendas. Although notable advances have been achieved in the productive sphere, the conflict over land and the resistance of the local power groups to the participation of indigenous people in public entities have configured a tense atmosphere for development perspectives for indigenous communities.

The local Catholic Church (the Jesuits and the Ursuline sisters) has played in the zone an important role of protection and promotion of indigenous peoples. In 1989, on the Jesuits' initiative, the Trading Company "Promotion of Moxos" (PRODEMO) was established in San Ignacio, offering credit and technical support to agricultural production. It paid high prices for rice and other products, with which it could lessen the influence of the dealers and helped to break dependency on the ranch.

When Oscar Bazoberry and Mónica Crespo made the survey, the Beni elite had said clearly that CIPCA could enter the zone (as if it were their property), but may not touch on certain themes. There were (and still are) very closed social relations and the cattle-raising elite was not capable of understanding that it also stood to benefit if the indigenous population were less poor and had more prospects. In 2003 a stockbreeder opined: "CIPCA is spoiling the indigenous: they send them to university; but the indigenous do not know how to study and, now, neither do they learn to work".

It is worth stressing the positive attitude of the financing agencies. They understood that it is a very conflictive zone and that it would not be easy for CIPCA to find an adequate working strategy. NOVIB, EED, *Fastenopfer* and Christian Aid accepted the initiative and recognised that the process of relationship was going to be very slow.

After 1998 PRODEMO was incorporated into CIPCA and has assumed the commercialisation of various products as a priority activity. PRODEMO was a point of reference in the communities for the purchase and sale of rice. It attempted to specialise in the commercialisation of alternative products, including maize, beans, chivé (yucca flour), chocolate, bees' honey, tamarind and vanilla. Finally, it was decided that it was preferable to specialise only in the commercialisation of chocolate. The first stock was gathered in 1999-2000 and by 2000-2001 30 trips by light plane had already been made to transport the products. PRODEMO has also developed sophisticated systems of sale by Internet, principally for the commercialisation of chocolate, a product that it could make self-supporting. The change of roles, from provider of technical advice to trader, was not at all understood in the communities; neither was the fixing of prices according to the market, skipping almost all subsidies.

A collateral problem was that the indigenous organisations had professional people as leaders who lived in the cities of Trinidad and Moxos. CIPCA sustains that it should have been the communities making decisions about their land and territory and not pseudo-leaders who no longer lived in the communities. After a year's work a big seminar was organised to draw up a proposal. Out of this, in 1998, came the idea of the territorial demand and the TCO TIMI (Moxos Ignaciano Indigenous Territory) was founded, as an addition to two previous territories that had already emerged from the I Indigenous March of 1990: the Indigenous Territory of the Isiboro Sécure National Park or TIPNIS (1990) and the Multiethnic Indigenous Territory or TIM (1990).

The organisation structure at community level is the local council (*Cabildo*), introduced by the Jesuit missions of the colonial era. This organisation, with the magistrate (*Corregidor*) at its head, is respected by all. There are a total of 108 communities in San Ignacio de Moxos, of which 18 correspond to the TIM and 18 to the TIMI. After various conflicts, the Central of Moxeños-Beni Ethnic Peoples (CPEM-B) emerged, with which CIPCA initiated a work of support at regional level. The participation of women in the indigenous organisations has always been minimal. However, little by little some women have gradually appeared in directive posts.

In the political scenario, the traditional parties have dominated the panorama over the last 20 years. Until recently they handled the municipality of San Ignacio de Moxos and they also controlled the civic committee, the educational system and the communications media. The relations of CIPCA with the municipality were practically non-existent until 2003, in which year the first cooperation agreement was signed. At the same time, though, there was exploitation of the conflicts between the local elite and CIPCA when, as a result of the assassination of the mayor – spuriously, since CIPCA had nothing to do with it – the CIPCA offices were completely destroyed, and the staff obliged to seek refuge in Trinidad. It seems that what basically most annoyed the local elite was the support that CIPCA gave to the indigenous organisation and to its demands for land reorganisation in the region. In these conflicts the parish priest, the Jesuit Enrique Jordá, and the Ursuline sisters also suffered physical aggression by some authorities and stockbreeders. In January 2004 the municipality suspended CIPCA's operating licence and closed down its installations. But CIPCA did not allow itself to be intimidated; it initiated legal proceedings against these measures and won. It has since resumed work in San Ignacio.

The process of organisation and indigenous demands for participation resulted in their organisation, CPEM-B, achieving something until then unheard of: two councillorships in the municipal elections of 2004. However, these political games not having obtained a majority, the indigenous organisation sought an alliance with the ADN, one of its eternal opponents, in order to make Sixto Bejarano Congo the first indigenous mayor of the Municipality of Moxos. This unexpected result of the last municipal elections generated a permanent tension in the municipality and in the management of Sixto, since the local élite was never able to digest the indigenous triumph. Through all these problems, CIPCA has given priority in Beni the challenge to achieve intercultural and multicultural democracy, since the opposed political forces would still be slow to value the richness of diversity and equity.

On the productive side, CIPCA Beni has emphasised the development of agroforestry systems, with the plantation of perennial crops such as chocolate, mara, citrus, tamarind and avocado. The demand for chocolate is so great that it proves impossible to attend to all the requests from communities. The agroforestry development approach has emerged precisely because of the possibilities offered by chocolate, and the need to bear in mind the sustainable use of the territory, still in the process of reorganisation.

CIPCA North[152]

The Regional North, whose headquarters are in Riberalta, was created in September 1997 with the objective of promoting the economic and social development of peasants and indigenous of the Bolivian northern Amazonian region, whose economy combines subsistence agriculture with silviculture and extractive activities from the forest.

During the first year, the work of CIPCA North was centred on the compilation and the study of technical, economic and sociocultural information on the region and the relationship with the indigenous and peasant organisations and with local institutions. In the second year, in accordance with the planning carried out with the Peasant Federations, the communities and the municipal governments of Riberalta and Gonzalo Moreno (Pando), productive projects began in the communities, as well as the training, technical assistance and support for the strengthening of the communal and higher-level organisations. Similarly, advice and support began to be provided to the municipal government of Gonzalo Moreno and to the vigilance committees of the municipalities of Riberalta and Gonzalo Moreno.

In 1999, in coordination with the Departmental Peasant Federations the process began of training and advice on the INRA Law with the aim of achieving land reorganisation and distribution to the peasant communities. Since the year 2000, CIPCA North, together with other institutions that made up the Inter-Institutional Commission of Support for the Process of Land Reorganisation, has concentrated on support for land demands from the peasant communities of Vaca Díez province (Beni) and the Department of Pando.[153]

Until 1985, the region's economy was based on the extraction of rubber and, on a lesser scale, of Brazil nut, activities carried out in the so-called *barracas*[154] by the same people, called *siringueros*[155], since these are two activities that occur at distinct times of year. They live with their families in permanent settlements on the riverbanks, or within the forest, in areas that are –illegally- possessed by *barraqueros*[156]. However, after 1985 the fall in the price of rubber unbalanced that type of arrangement, which was relatively stable although very exploitative[157]. The result was a strong impulse toward new processes of spontaneous agricultural colonisation and urbanisation. Since the Brazil nut was collected only during three months of the year, from January to March, the *barraqueros* could not keep the workers in their establishments, which meant that thousands of *siringueros* left the *barracas*, escaping from the feudal system. Many of them settled in rural communities and 'converted' into subsistence farmers or migrated to urban centres like Riberalta, Guayaramerín and Cobija, swelling the ranks of the poor on the urban margins.

Collection of the Brazil nut has thus become the work of temporary migrants in the *barracas*; however, a part of Brazil nut production also comes from the peasants and indigenous, who collect them in individual plots obtained in peasant communities, in communal lands and in the TCO.

As in almost all the lowland regions, the peasant communities are faced with problems of access to land ownership. In 1997, at the request of the Apostolic Vicariate of Pando, Mons. Luis Morgan Casey, CIPCA North carried out a study of the land tenancy situation and access to natural resources among the peasant communities of the Amazonian region. Simultaneously the bishops of the Bolivian Oriente gave the initiative for the Pastoral Letter entitled "Land, Bountiful Mother for All". Later, in 2002, CIPCA North drew up a detailed study of spatial necessities where it was decided that the minimal surface necessary for the peasant families in this region and particular ecology had to be 500 hectares.

Despite the promulgation of the Agrarian Reform in 1996, until 1999 INRA had done nothing to initiate the process of land reorganisation in the northern Amazonian region of the country. Meanwhile the *barraqueros*, capitalising on their economic and political power, obtained the approval of the Supreme Decree 25532 in October that year, through which they intended to convert the *barracas* into forest concessions of non-logging products, with which they wanted not only to prohibit thousands of peasants and indigenous from continuing to collect forest products (Brazil nut), but also, to prevent all possibility of access to the land for the peasants and indigenous who legally sought access to public lands.

Faced with this situation, the peasant and indigenous organisations, together with the support institutions, initiated a series of events and negotiations aimed at preventing the application of the mentioned decree. In order to confront the problem the Inter-Institutional Commission of Support for Land Reorganisation was organised. This entity was made up of all the peasant and indigenous organisations of the region, and the support institutions[158].

As a result of this Inter-Institutional Commission's pressure and negotiations INRA emitted the Administrative Resolution No. 078/2000, through which Land Reorganisation was decreed for the peasant communities. In addition, through Administrative Resolution No. 087/2000 it resolved to grant 500 hectares of land per family in the region's peasant communities involved in extractive activities. The Commission pledged support for the INRA's efforts to seek finance.

Despite these good results, the struggle of the organisations had to continue, seeking to overturn DS 25532, which turned the *barracas* which extracted rubber and Brazil nuts in northern Amazonia into forestry concessions. This meant recourse to the Defender of the People, an institution with which actions were coordinated that took two complementary paths: in 2000, the Commission presented the claim that this decree was unconstitutional. Parallel to these negotiations, in June of the same year, the Third Peasant–Indigenous March for "Land, Territory and Defence of Natural Resources" was also organised. This march began in Riberalta and concluded in the city of Montero in the Department of Santa Cruz, with the subscription of an agreement between national government and the country's peasant and indigenous organisations. The agreement contained 19 sections, among which was the government's commitment to derogate DS 25532 and, indeed, on the 10th of July 2000 DS No. 25838 was passed, through which the contested DS No. 25532 was abrogated.

Since 2001 CIPCA North has supported and advised municipal governments, first in the formulation of its Municipal Development Plans and, subsequently, by holding meetings to evaluate and draw up its Annual Operative Plans.

In the productive aspect, after 1999 agricultural and livestock projects were implemented that sought diversification of family production to as to achieve food security for the peasant families, and sustainable development based on the implementation of agroforestry systems that combine annual and perennial species, as well as non-timber species (beans, bananas, cacao, copoazú, caoba, cedar, Brazil nut, pejibaye, majo, asaí, avocado, achachairú, tamarind and citrus). Up to December 2004 more than 1,000 hectares of agroforestry systems in 62 communities had been implemented in seven municipalities, benefitting to 810 peasant families.

The acceptation of the productive proposal is reflected in the organisation of the agroforestry producers: in 2004 the Association of Agroforestry Producers of Northern Amazonian Bolivia (APARAB) was founded. Since 2005 associations at zonal and communal level have been created. APARAB has the mission of watching over the protection of natural resources and the promotion of sustainable productive activities.

ACTIVITIES

In previous sections we have given a summary of the main characteristics of the regional offices over the years 1996-2005. We have also presented the working strategy of CIPCA and the institutional challenges. In this strategy there are some striking aspects:
• Of the three classic dimensions of the CIPCA working methodology – education, organisation and production – education was no longer so explicitly present in institutional challenges. From the first strategic plan (1997-2001) CIPCA opted not to make training and formation a strategic line of action, but only one that was

functional to strategic challenges. However, if we revise the annual memoirs and the six-monthly reports of activities, we find an interesting list of training activities, and the production of educational booklets concerning all the important themes in the institution's everyday affairs.
- Research concentrated more on the generation and systematisation of knowledge, as well as some themes of national importance such as ibilingual intercultural education and international commerce. After 2003 research has resumed on an important line of work, thanks to the enthusiasm of the director general, Oscar Bazoberry, who has encouraged staff to undertake research and systematisation projects. There has never been such a variety of authors publishing with CIPCA.
- The two transversal themes, gender and environment, have had fluctuating treatment according to the specific interests of the staff. The environment has been taken into account in productive proposals since the start of the 1990s, although not with any great enthusiasm. The conditions of poverty suffered by populations of the different ecosystems where CIPCA operates have been a decisive factor in the ecological dimension not being a single, exclusive focus. But something that has always been present in productive proposals is, and remains, the need to incorporate principles and practices related to the rational and sustainable handling of natural resources. Within this perspective, the environmental theme has been totally integrated into agricultural, silvopastoral and non-timber forestry extraction proposals.

Thanks to internal policies, the number of women working in CIPCA has increased by 17% to 43%. So as to achieve gender equity it is necessary to maintain an explicit effort, because it is still not generally accepted that women are equal to men. Unfortunately the man-woman ratio in the grassroots organisations, municipal governments and councils, in the vigilance committees, in training days and other activities, was still unequal in 2005.

To finish this chronological history we will deal with the institutional challenges faced by the three strategic plans drawn up and implemented between 1997 and 2005.

Democratic peasant and indigenous organisations

We will begin with a observation by Aurelio Huallpa, Altiplano peasant leader, that shows the complexity of combining the native system and the formal legal system of peasant organisation:

"The rotation of posts according to the native system is fatal: many *mallkus* do not live in the community; they receive salaries in the city of La Paz where they work as teachers or public employees. By obligation they must exercise a duty of which they understand nothing and say that it is essential to respect the millenary system. For example, as *mallkus* they oppose the economic organisations because they say that these associations divide the community. The supposed *mallkus* did not want to receive CIPCA, because CIPCA would divide the community with its associative proposal."

For many years CIPCA has given more priority to the strengthening of capacities of the indigenous nd peasant organisations as political actors in the public sphere and less to the democratic functioning within the grassroots organisations themselves. And if it developed activities to improve the internal functioning, these were principally aimed at two themes: women's participation in the decision-making bodies of the organisations and financial-administrative management.

The grassroots organisations have achieved greater mobilisation capacity and greater presence in the political sphere at local, regional and national level. Above all the presence in the municipal government has increased considerably. but also the conformation of the national parliament has changed drastically since the national elections of 2002. As a final (and starting) point we can mention the election of the coca-growers' leader Evo Morales as President of the Republic.

There have also been achievements in the recognition of their ethnic identities. However, cronyism, political messianism and favouritism – such deep-rooted practices in the traditional political parties – begin to emerge openly in the indigenous and peasant organisations as well, as they begin to have national political influence.

With regard to internal democracy, differences are noticeable according to the organisational level. At local levels, where the indigenous peasants participate directly, the grassroots organisations are more democratic and participative, while at the higher levels there can be clashes between cults of personality and political interests.

With respect to the participation of women, processes can be observed that move at distinct speeds: there are organisations that have remained simply at discourse level for specific demands of the women; other organisations have already accepted feminine participation in decision-making. There are even organisations that have established and implemented policies that guarantee gender equity at all levels. These processes presuppose the recognition and valuing of women as actors in public spaces. However despite 25 years of gender policies, women's rights are still far from being recognised and respected as they should be in democratic societies, whether in Bolivia, Holland, Latin America or Europe.

It should be pointed out, as principal achievements of the work with indigenous and peasant organisations, the strengthening of their self-esteem and their being accepted as valid interlocutors with the State and society. In other words, CIPCA has contributed to a process of emancipation and inclusion of the peasant and indigenous population. However, it is essential to consider that self-affirmation and the strengthening of identity *per se* do not necessarily make people and collectives more democratic. This problem has been aggravated in the first years of the 21st century, originating from political problems related to gas and regional autonomies. Cultural and ethnic intransigencies among various social groups (whether in Santa Cruz or El Alto) have alerted CIPCA and obliged it to reflect upon and to reconsider its actions for the (re)construction of a multiethnic and pluricultural Bolivia. Much as there has been good progress in the strengthening of the peasants and indigenous organisations as political actors in the public domain, there is room for improvement in the internal democracy of peasant and indigenous organisations: "The strengthening of capacities like mobilisation, proposition and negotiation, although important, does not necessarily mean that organisations become more democratic, participative, with greater gender equality, with renovation of leadership or more open to interculturality" (Armani, 2004: 26).

CIPCA concluded, accurately, that with more democratic and more efficient grassroots organisations it would be possible to advance further in those matters that are still unresolved (such as the full exercise of citizenship, access to land property and natural resources) or that have been only partly worked on or subsumed (like interculturality or gender equity). Democratic organisations are vital in order to keep advancing in the collective and co-responsible construction of Bolivian democracy.

Land property rights, territory and natural resources

The INRA Law, promulgated on the 17th of October 1996, had without doubt ambiguous aspects, that were well exploited by influential landowners' groups, but it also had points in its favour, above all for the lowland indigenous peoples. In the first years, the government applied the law well, but with the change of government in August 1997 a premeditated bureaucratic stagnation occurred that was not resolved until 2005.

Throughout these years, CIPCA support for the reorganisation of land and property rights of the TCOs has become the main activity in the four lowland regional offices, accompanying concrete processes of reorganisation and, from the Santa Cruz office, participating in the debate over its regulation. CIPCA's accompaniment has brought important achievements, although it was confirmed that these are inconclusive processes stultified by bureaucratic tardiness and in several cases, such as that of Moxos, by conflicts with big landowners and a lack of political will on the part of INRA employees.

It is important to bear in mind that the land issue is highly sensitive and, in some way, the painful experience of Moxos is an expression of this political struggle. As a consequence of the looting of that office and subsequent threats, part of the Moxos staff resigned.

Despite all this, there are also positive results from the land reorganisation process. In Beni, the TCO TIM was entitled by decree on the 24th of September 1990 as a result of the first indigenous march for "Territory and Dignity". It concluded the field check of 457.870. However, there are many demarcations still in dispute. TIMI has demanded an area of 98.388 hectares. Reorganisation began with field checks in 2002 and until now provisional results show that, of the 89.802 hectares measured, 46.773 are considered exploitable by the TIMI, 39.296 are in favour of third parties and 3.732 are considered public domain.

In the Chaco, discussion continued regarding the modification of the technical norm that regulated animal density in medium-sized properties and large companies: the plan was to increase the surface from 5 to 25 hectares per head of cattle. Another problem was that INRA and the businessmen wanted to make compliance with the 'Social Economic Function' (FES) more flexible in medium-sized properties and large agricultural enterprises.

The APG, with its different captaincies, has demanded from the State the entitlement of 22 indigenous territories with a total of 9.866.452 hectares. Up to 2005, 13 TCOs had partially obtained their ownership with a total of only 767.952 hectares, while the TCO Charagua North obtained the reversion of 26.976 hectares. Additionally, CIPCA advised the APG in matters of defence of natural resources and negotiations with petrol companies and road-builders, which in various degrees affect the countryside and the environment of Guaraní communities.

Riberalta and Pando are notable for the predominantly precarious rights of its workers, with power concentrated in the hands of *barraqueros*. The land has traditionally been concentrated in their hands, with the local population working in the collection of both rubber and Brazil nut, under the working regimen of the aforementioned *habilito*, which entails total economic dependency on the landlord.

The most strategic factor in the process of land reorganisation has been the creation of the Support Commission, as a space for legal technical advice and an area for promoting dialogue instead of conflict. Despite strong pressure from the *barraqueros*, Brazil nut traders and other power groups, between 2000 and 2005 the Commission had achieved that 88 peasant communities obtained their property titles, acceding to 719.497 hectares for the benefit of 2.449 families. To this effect, legal promoters were trained to accompany the peasant federations and communities, who organised support brigades to oversee the INRA work. For their part, indigenous organisations have obtained collective ownership of three TCOs, gaining access to 804.497 hectares.

One very important source of support that should be mentioned is the coordinating role that the Santa Cruz office has played, facilitating support for different grassroots organisations and providing practical manuals to help the organisations in the processes of land reorganisation, utilising Geographic Information Systems (GIS).

Since 2003, indigenous territorial management has been CIPCA's new field of work. The implementation of plans for the management of natural resources is a necessary condition after having obtained ownership of land and territory. However, it is crucial to avoid repeating past errors, and take care not to awaken excessive expectations with the drawing-up of territorial management plans that are then not carried out due to a lack of financial resources or because they are not sufficiently applicable. It should not be forgotten that the micro-regional plans of the 1980s, drawn up with such a high degree of peasant and indigenous participation and with so much enthusiasm from CIPCA staff, were not always able to be implemented.

In general the process of land reorganisation is positively valued. Many organisations were born and strengthened in this process. Rural development and the role of natural resources became matters of debate. Without forgetting that the land is a limiting factor for rural development, it became clear that there is still oncentration of land ownership in few hands as well as a great demand from peasant and indigenous communities.

Unfortunately, at the same time, the land reform process was often co-opted by corporative groups that prevented adequate advance, for which reason land reorganisation ended up being highly indebted and costly, both for the institutions and for the State, but most of all for the peasant and indignous organisations.

Sustainable rural economy

The rural economy has always been confronted with a national and international economic environment adverse to the initiatives of small rural producers. Public policies have not been sufficient or adequate to develop the indigenous peasant economy. Despite this adverse context, successful economic initiatives and activities by small rural producers have increased; many of these ventures are market-oriented while others aim to cover self-consumption, although the creative combination of both tendencies is still constant. In this sense, the long and variegated experience of CIPCA, in diverse ecological contexts, has evolved, from group focus and business orientation tendencies, towards others that are , more family-oriented and above all aimed at ensuring environmental sustainability and diminishing the risks of market fluctuations. In both cases an effort has been made to combine production for the community's own consumption and adequate access to the market.

Since the first strategic plan in 1997-2001, work with CDTs has ceased and instead efforts have concentrated on implementing development proposals for peasant families. These proposals have taken the sustainable use of natural resources into account, as well as the fact that women are economic actors just like men. For both peasants and CIPCA's technical agronomists it has not been easy to change technology: the agronomists had had to change from cutting-edge technology to one that did not demand large investments. The peasants that were so used to a CIPCA with considerable investments (subsidies and credit) had to accept a different CIPCA, without a pile of money.

During the years 2002-2003 research was conducted aimed at evaluating the economic situation of the families that have put CIPCA's proposal into practice, comparing them with a control group of families from the same communities that did not implement the proposal. The results have been published in a book by José Luis Eyzaguirre (2006) *Composition of family income among indigenous peasants. A study in six regions of Bolivia*. This study is an excellent example of applied research, which not only has oriented the adjustments of productive proposals, but has also has helped CIPCA critically analyse the reach of its institutional strategy. CIPCA has also performed analyses of the results, which were published in Lorenzo Soliz' and Silvia Aguilar's 2005 book *Peasant production and peasant-indigenous economy*.

CIPCA has not wanted implement a proposal as if it were an obligatory manual for all the regional offices. Each strategy had a distinct emphasis according to the characteristics of each region[159]:

- On the *Altiplano* rotation of crops, implantation of live barriers, infiltration ditches, control of the Andean weevil, associated crops, sowing of pulses, milk production and forage production were prioritised.
- In the *valleys* the proposal concentrated in the transformation of unirrigated to irrigated production with four components: irrigation infrastructure (canals and reservoirs), production of vegetables and fruits, improvement of stockbreeding and commercialisation.
- In *Cordillera*, where agriculture mainly consists of unirrigated maize, beans and peanuts, it was proposed that the plots should be enclosed with wire and/or live fencing, and sowed in curved terraces; for livestock, proposals have been made for animals such as hair sheep, bovines and poultry.
- In *Santa Cruz* a proposal was made for the implementation and handling of agroforestry systems that combine annual crops (rice, maize, peanuts in Urubichá;

beans, yucca and rice in Santa Rosa), medium-term plantations (potato, pineapple, citrus) and long-term plantations (cacao, mara, cedar); the proposal included also infrastructure for pastures and animal health.

• In the *Beni* CIPCA had a lot of success in the production and commercialisation of native chocolate; the cacao was turning into the principal component of the system because of the density of plants to be introduced and because of this constituting a strategic item with national and international marketing potential; hair sheep were also introduced, as well as agroforestry systems with annual, mid-term and long-term crops.

• Finally, an achievement in *Riberalta* was that collectors of Brazil nut were converted into producers of Brazil nut and chocolate. The agroforestry system included rice, banana, vegetables, while cacao and copoazú were considered as medium-term plantations. Also in Riberalta chocolate, alongside the Brazil nut, is considered a strategic item.

From 2001 to 2005 CIPCA has been based on the following principles in supporting the peasant economy (Strategic Plan 2001-2005):

• The productive unit is generally the family, for which reason initiatives at this level are fundamental; however, families are also vulnerable if there are no organised entities to defend their interests and jointly confront critical aspects of their economy. Support to broader organisational structures would vary in accordance with the characteristics of each region;

• The viability of a capitalisation-oriented proposal will depend on access to the market and the existence of strategies and mechanisms of commercialisation. This means that CIPCA will propose alternatives and improvements in commercialisation and will facilitate alliances with entities such as already-established trading companies;

• Capital plays an important role in the development proposals, by which reason CIPCA places great importance on access to credit and other financial resources; however, credit must not be considered as a panacea for the whole rural sector; it often proves counterproductive if ability to return funds, or the feasibility of granting credit, are no taken into account;

• It is also crucial to support access to subsidy in the case of those items that can strengthen the productive potential of rural strata, whose economic level will not allow them to be subjects of credit.

These examples are forms of support that are mandatory for the State. CIPCA has channelled its efforts to commit state resources, but the slowness and insufficiency with which these funds are obtained show the need both for direct action on the part of CIPCA, and for political pressure.

The systematisation of the experience of rural development proposals (Soliz and Aguilar, 2005) and the study of the peasant economy (Eyzaguirre, 2006) have backed the status of peasant and indigenous families as still a productive strength, despite their having been ignored by the Bolivian State and public policies. There are still many myths and realities surrounding rural production. For example, it is often said that the rural area of small producers has no viability, above all on the Altiplano and in the valleys. It is also often said that peasant and indigenous families are no longer interested in agricultural activities and that they would prefer to dedicate themselves to (micro-) business activities in the cities. The systematisation and the study show however, that productive rural work continues to be important for peasant families because it still contributes significantly to the family income.

Intercultural democracy and efficacy in local and intermediary governments and institutions

The definition of this challenge has changed considerably over the years. Between 1997 and 2003 the influence of municipalisation was still felt as a result of the Popular Participation Law.

One of the important ideas behind decentralisation was that it could offer better instruments with which to combat poverty and promote local development. However, the decentralisation of the social policies has not automatically brought greater efficiency in the provision of social services. Much depended of managerial capacity at local level. Besides, many municipalities did not and still do not have sufficient human resources, administrative capacity or political structure for the planning and execution of social development projects.

The results of the first municipal elections were already encouraging enough to make it possible to speak of a real change in local power relations: more than 500 indigenous councillors (Albó, 1999). Discussion between NGOs turned around the question of whether they should support municipal governments, which were government entities, or whether NGOs only had to advise the vigilance committees as critical and contestatory entities of social control. The municipal government was considered a bastion of the local elite in a good number of Andean municipalities or totally controlled by the cattle-ranchers and big farmers in the majority of the lowlands.

The political and social inclusion of peasants and indigenous men and women in the local political system has still not been achieved completely, despite the broadening of the system having permitted the incorporation of the rural population in electoral contests. There is no doubt that the number of councillors and mayors of indigenous and peasant origin has increased. The percentage of women also steadily increases, despite resistance from men of all ethnic conditions and social classes. As an example, we can mention the elections in Cordillera: in 2004 six Guaraní women had achieved to be elected (as against eight Guaraní men), whilst in the 1995 elections there were no woman councillors.

Another discussion had to do with the role that NGOs had to play in drawing up Municipal Development Plans (PDM) and Annual Operative Plans (POA). There were NGOs that took on such clear leadership in creating these plans that they became entities with considerable power within the municipality. Also at the start, the role assumed by CIPCA was too executive.

Oscar Bazoberry remembers how a consultancy company contracted by the municipality of Charagua changed a small productive proposal presented by women into a great white elephant:

"The women had proposed a project for egg-laying hens. In the workshop, the consultancy firm indicated that in order for its demand to be important, it had to propose raising in sheds. Then, when the company proposed a shed, the women replied 'fine, that's ok'. The consultancy then said: 'but if you're going to have sheds, you need light. What if we include a motor in the proposal?' The women: yes, that's all right'. The consultancy: 'but if we include the acquisition of a motor, at the same time we can include a large motor for all the people'. The women: 'yes, yes that's good'. The consultancy: 'with that bigger motor, we can enlarge the sheds, but the hens would need a balanced diet'. The women: 'yes, yes, that's good too'. The consultancy: 'we can also include a factory to produce this balanced diet for the hens'. The women: 'yes, yes, yes'. And in the end the women never got their hens."

The members of the general assembly and the board of CIPCA warned several times that it should not do the jobs of other actors, that CIPCA could not be 100% functional to municipal government. It was necessary to take care that the work of the institution did not end up substituting other social actors. The board also observed that, in work with the municipalities, at times was not clear who was doing what. There was also the warning that the field staff, in its enthusiasm, should not confuse the institutional responsibilities of CIPCA, the municipal government and the grassroots organisations.

Since the year 2000, when the idea of the political instrument began to gain new strength, above all with the MAS party's electoral results getting better all the time, the question returned of whether an NGO like CIPCA could get involved in the party politics. The response was still 'no', although it was possible (and necessary) to support social organisations in gaining more power and inclusion in political life. It was established that CIPCA supported no individual candidates, but could advise the political organisation and those whom the organisation had selected as its political instrument. In the last municipal elections the decision was made, besides, to give special support to those indigenous organisations that had decided to present themselves as independent groupings. These organisations participated at a disadvantage because, if they lost, they would also lose their prestige. They were putting the name of the social organisation at stake.

Almost 10 years after having supported the process of popular participation and decentralisation, CIPCA has contributed – without a doubt – to there being higher levels of inclusion of peasant and indigenous men and women in local, regional and national political life. Here is a summary of appreciations from the last mid-term evaluation (Armani, 2004: 38-39):

"CIPCA has contributed considerably to the process of strengthening the exercise of citizens' rights at municipal level, but the pace and sustainability of this process are still generally limited. There have been important advances, recognised by the issue of identification cards, training and political education, as well as in the growing quality of peasant and indigenous participation in processes of planning, execution and social control (...) The election of peasants and indigenous people to municipal governments and councils has grown slowly and with acknowledged problems in the democratic quality of management. The most frustrating indicators have been those pertaining to the participation of women in the public domain, whether in municipal government, municipal councils or vigilance committees. In this case, progress has been slow and limited and they are still not consolidated."

However, apart from these positive results, there remain new challenges for the future. One of the most important will be the construction of a new civic culture. There is still resistance from the conventional political culture, but there has also been little emphasis on the need to create a sense of citizens' co-responsibility in the public space. Another of the challenges is how to constitute local public space, with the strengthening of ethnic identity, without reinforcing a corporatist ethnic-fundamentalist perspective.

The intercultural focus was present in CIPCA from its inception. However, the urgency of working on it explicitly only started to appear around 2000, when the ethnic and intercultural tensions were becoming more acute. After many years of training in organisational aspects, political strengthening and cultural self-esteem, indigenous peoples began to enjoy greater inclusion in local, regional and national political life. This inclusion, although incipient, began to worry the sectors that traditionally held power; they began to feel that they were going to lose their cultural, economic and political hegemony. Proof of these concerns have been seen in the events of San Ignacio de Moxos and the xenophobia of the Santa Cruz elite with their proclamation of a Camba Nation. The other tendency, that of greater political and cultural power for indigenous peoples, can also run the risk of falling into ethnic-fundamentalist approaches, whether coming from the indigenous leaders themselves, or from some NGOs that advised the grassroots organisations.

Here it is worth summarising some principles with respect to the issue of interculturality:

- In its support for native indigenous peoples CIPCA rejects all attitudes and expressions that denote contempt or discrimination.
- In each sphere of activity CIPCA foments the mutual interchange of knowledge, experiences and cultural products between members of diverse cultural traditions for the enrichment of all, avoiding impositions in a single direction.
- CIPCA involves itself in public activities and proposals that lead to a multiethnic, pluricultural and equitable society.

Despite that CIPCA has always taken into account the cultural dimension, it lacked a more profound institutional reflection of how put in practice the policy of interculturality. Intercultural democracy is incipient both in the State spheres and in society as a whole. The development of intercultural relations between culturally distinct groups and people should be considered as a fundamental value of democratic pluralism. However, there are still prevalent positions and exclusive postures on the part both of the economic elites and of the indigenous organisations. Achieving a culturally democratic society is, then, a challenge for the future, not only for CIPCA but for all Bolivia.

Public policies favourable to peasants and indigenous peoples

A first example of impact and political pressure has been – in 2000 the Water Panel proposed by the National Water Authority Law. With the participation of twelve institutions, CIPCA promoted a technical panel for inter-institutional coordination on the law and regulation governing the water resource, drawing up and distributing a proposal to this effect, and obtaining support in peasant and indigenous organisations and even in parliament. It should be mentioned that there was also inter-institutional coordination to exert political pressure from the Land Panel in Santa Cruz. However, inter-institutional coordination does not automatically make an impact in public policies. Besides, such coordination comes and goes according to the political moment; and there is nothing wrong with networks or forms of coordination disappearing when they have fulfilled their objectives, then giving way for new ones to appear, which have other names and serve other purposes.

CIPCA has had positive results in supporting demands from peasant and indigenous organisations. Backing political demands from the peasant movement on the Altiplano and in the Andean valleys has been quite complicated, because the same movement has been hampered by internal struggles and messianism that have always divided it into new factions. It is not easy to achieve proactive capacity and internal democratic management in the peasant-indigenous movements, among other reasons because of an excessive politicisation which may either be introspective or project from the organisations outwards. At times intransigent positions are taken up towards other social sectors which often react, upon seeing their privileged positions threatened, by increasing their own intransigence.

In terms of sustainable rural development, even fewer actions aimed at political pressure or impact on public policies have been noted, although the year 2005 has seen many diffusion activities through seminars, presentation of books, etc.[160]. Nevertheless, CIPCA is every day more present in debates and organises activities in which development policies are discussed. This pro-active and autonomous role is quite new. The positive result is that CIPCA has become a serious referent for the rural development problematic.

The systematisation of development proposals for peasant economies is a very fine example of concrete work in the regional offices, whose results may have a bearing on public policies at national level. Some other important achievements have been the draft for a law to include the working situation of the Brazil nut breakers in the General Labour Law, the Supreme Decree that foresees the granting of 500 hectares per family in the Amazonian north, and the proposal of animal density in lowland herding areas.

In the evaluation of 1995 it had already been concluded that it was necessary, as part of its role as facilitator of the peasant and indigenous movement, for CIPCA to assume a more active role of its own, as a social and political actor (Mejía, 1995: 45). This same recommendation, expressed in other words, was repeated in the external evaluation of 2004 (Armani, 2004: 45-46).

The key question is how best to exploit the organisational structure that had been so long defended: a general office with six regional offices united by the same mission and the same institutional mandates, but which execute different programmes in accordance with the specific context of each region. Both the national office and the regional offices could play an important role in the articulation of social movements, from regional to national ambits. This aspect, above all, began to become increasingly urgent after the year 2000, given the dispute over cultural and economic hegemony and the separatist proposals of some regions.

CIPCA has carried out many dissemination activities such as its radio programmes, webpage, *CipcaNotas*, and above all the publishing the results of research. CIPCA has also been present in the organisation of seminars and workshops on issues of economic, social, cultural and political interest. However, let us not forget that, however many spaces for reflection, debate and discussion are generated; it is always the decision of the policy makers whether or not to let themselves be inspired by new ideas. These decisions escape the influence of CIPCA.

With the election, in December 2005, of Evo Morales as President of the Republic and a Congress with representatives and senators from all social classes and diverse ethnic groups, Bolivia has entered a new historical moment. For CIPCA it means an important moment in which to influence, from civil society and with the active participation of indigenous people and peasants, the formation of national, regional and municipal public policies, generating impact upon the country's future imaginary. It is, then, still more opportune that favourable conditions be created beforehand so that CIPCA's proposals might invite discussion and debate, exerting influence on public policies.

PART III
DEBATES OF YESTERDAY, TODAY AND TOMORROW

We have reached the end of 35 years of institutional life. A life in which there have been several moments when the very existence of CIPCA has been in danger. There was aggression during the years of dictatorship and internal crises that put the institution's survival in danger. There have also been many external opinions on the *raison d'être* of CIPCA, casting doubt on the need for it still to exist. Some argue that an NGO like CIPCA should not be a permanent actor in society, while others do not see a future for CIPCA because it did not achieve concrete and convincing results in the struggle against poverty.

The previous pages are proof that CIPCA has a unique *raison d'être* and that it must continue to exist over the coming years. The following chapter sums up the most significant themes that are still debated, as well as some unanswered questions. These unanswered questions are precisely what makes CIPCA still an organisation made up of people, of human beings with their doubts, joy and sadness, despair and hopes, and political and social commitments.

CHAPTER 6
SOME RECURRENT THEMES

In previous chapters we have presented the chronological history of CIPCA, both in its external relations with other actors in Bolivian society, and in relation to its own organisational development. This history clearly shows how its development proposals adapt to historical contexts that always bring new elements and oblige it to redefine its role in the processes of change. On the other hand there is no doubt that an institution like CIPCA, and many other people and institutions along with it, influence the course of historical events. CIPCA has known three periods that concur with fundamental changes in Bolivian history: in the first period the main objective of the institution was establish a democratic State, overthrowing military regimes. The second period is characterised still by a disposition to simply do without the State and to concentrate on working above all from civil society. In the third period, the institution has adopted a role of critical collaboration with the State, firstly with the municipalities and then also through political lobbying at higher levels. We also can distinguish three periods in the institution's relationship with peasant and indigenous organisations: in the first period CIPCA was the driving force of these organisations, in the second period a kind of companion. In the third period the institution and the grassroots organisations became autonomous actors in civil society, each with its own objectives, agendas and alliances.

At a most concrete and everyday level, development proposals often resemble the swings of a pendulum. New generations propose development alternatives with new enthusiasm, which, with greater or lesser success, at times have already been experienced in the past. In their desire to be innovative they sometimes fall into the same traps. This is inevitable and to a certain extent healthy. It is true that new ideas always challenge elements of previous proposals, but it would be healthy not to present the questioning of old practices in too categorical a way, as if there were nothing correct about them and as if no positive results had come from those practices in the past.

Without wanting to insinuate that the results of development are a direct consequence of CIPCA's actions, there can be no doubt that the economic, social, political and cultural situation in which the rural population found itself in 1970 has become better in all aspects. The productive infrastructure has improved, there is greater food security for peasant families, there are more children going to school (although there is still a gap between boys and girls, in favour of the boys). Life expectancy in rural areas has increased, which means that basic needs such as health, housing and water are better satisfied and, without doubt, there are important advances in the emancipation and political inclusion of the peasant and indigenous population.

Let's not forget that 35 years ago the State was almost totally absent from rural areas. Neither were there private institutions and the few that existed – like CIPCA and ACLO – acted as substitutes for the State. Let's not forget that there were no roads to San Julián and Santa Rosa del Chore; that soya cultivation began in the 80s and now it is one of the most important export products. The journey from Santa Cruz to Camiri, which now takes 3½ hours, used to take 12 hours (in the rainy season, as much as 3 days). Until 1952, in some Bolivian cities Indians were forbidden to go into the main square. Let's not forget that, in the department of Cochabamba, the Quechua-speaking peasants have only had access to local power for the last 15 years. The open discrimination with which the Beni elite speaks about Indians is no longer echoed at national level. The peasants and indigenous people in the Amazonian north are breaking ties of dependency on the *habilito* to become modern agricultural workers and even producers in their own right. Peasant families on the Altiplano, the country's most wildest agro-ecological zone, are finding development solutions that combine agricultural production with migration, in a more humanly acceptable way than before. The Guaraní now play a role in national political life. The indigenous and peasant population has become a national political force. All of this was unthinkable 35 years ago.

One convincing result of 35 years' effort is that CIPCA has achieved legitimate institutional leadership in Bolivian society. But perhaps even more important is that it has fomented personal leaderships; a result that was not looked for, not worked consciously and that has never been formulated in any measurement indicator. CIPCA is an informal school of formation of leaders that now play an important role in national life. But also an informal school of formation of researchers, of promoters, sociologists, economists, broadcasters, agronomists, veterinarians, forest engineers, and still others with a social and political commitment to support the more disadvantaged sectors, contributing to a democratic, intercultural, equitable and economically sustainable Bolivia.

The following sections will look at some debates that have been present throughout the history of CIPCA and that may serve for future reflection:
1 Relations with the peasant and indigenous organisations.
2 Democracy and intercultural citizenship.
3 Sustainable rural development.
4 Role of research.
5 Public impact.
6 Relation with the co-financing agencies.
7 Internal organisation.

Before dealing with each one of these themes, it would be churlish not to stress once again, that without the continued support (of the staff) of the co-financing agencies, CIPCA would never have achieved so many positive results. Above all thanks to the institutional support of NOVIB and EED, the institution was able to develop and act in a flexible way as historical and institutional events were unfolding. There is no doubt that the people who have worked and still work in the agencies have always made a personal effort to support CIPCA, not only with financing, but also with new ideas and innovative contributions for the route the institution should take. They should all be thanked more than just once, because at times they have had to defend CIPCA against currents in their own institutions, in governmental entities and also in civil society.

As we have already mentioned in previous chapters, the most important criticisms from the agencies were that CIPCA did not reach the grassroots sufficiently; that it did not give sufficient importance to the exclusion and marginalisation of peasant and indigenous women; that it was too big an organisation and that its budgets were too high; that the CIPCA financing could be better distributed directly to the grassroots organisations; that CIPCA showed no results in relieving poverty, that its productive proposals were unrealistic; that it let itself be carried more by ideological than economic arguments; that it replaced the peasant and indigenous organisations in its protest struggles and that it replaced the municipalities; finally, that it was not sufficiently concerned with the activities of lobbying and advocacy. We will see how CIPCA has responded to these and other criticisms over the years.

RELATIONS WITH PEASANT AND INDIGENOUS ORGANISATIONS

CIPCA's three legs – organisational, educational and economic – have always been present in its working strategy, but also in the three priority themes: strengthening the grassroots organisations; democracy and intercultural citizenship; and sustainable rural development. Depending on the historical moment, each one of these three axes has had more or less priority. So, in the 1970s the strengthening of the peasant organisations through educational work and formation of leaders was the priority, while after the dark years of the dictatorship of García Meza, the economic dimension began to have more importance. Similarly, the organisational aspect has also seen numerous different moments: from an emphasis on protest to an accent on co-responsibility, from anti-state and anti-governmental postures to support to municipalities and even the national governmental.

It is no exaggeration to conclude that the history of CIPCA is, in part, the history of some grassroots organisations and vice versa. The relationship with (the leaders of) these organisations has known various different moments. At the start it was a relationship that was perhaps not paternalist, but rather one of teacher-pupil, which quickly turned into a bond of comrades-in-arms. The active role that CIPCA played at the start in the strengthening of peasant organisations has not always been the most appropriate. The institution was very activist and at times, instead of keeping step with the grasroots, it strode ahead. CIPCA paid for fares, lunches and accommodation for peasant meetings, even acting as secretary of these grassroots organisations.

CIPCA and many other NGOs have supported the grassroots organisations financially, provided services in the fields of social and technical training, offered legal and economic assistance, have given administrative assistance, have acted as intermediaries in the commercialisation, etc. Besides, many institutions played the role of protector against political repression.

Over the years CIPCA has trained many peasant and indigenous leaders who have become national leaders or have been elected as mayors, councillors, members of vigilance committees, national representatives, senators, etc. Within this range of people with local, regional and national influence there are, of course, people who after having followed the training courses of CIPCA, have taken up a position against the institution itself. This must not be considered as a failure, but rather as a positive result.

A young economist who had only entered in 2004 remembers that the image that CIPCA had in his school was of a political institution that turned out rebellious leaders. Indeed a Santa Cruz leader, asked why they were so pugnacious, replied: "we are pupils of CIPCA; they have taught us to defend our rights". This relationship between "comrades-in-arms" has at times been very agreeable for CIPCA staff. Francisco Matzusaki remembers, for example, that he came up against a roadblock when on his way back to Santa Cruz, but "...I was waved through as if I were the President of the Republic because they recognised me as the former director of CIPCA."

On the other hand it is opportune to mention that peasant and indigenous women were late to perceive CIPCA as a "comrade-in-arms". The institution has not been in the vanguard in fomenting women's organisations, nor mixed organisations with equal representation of men and women. Pressure from women of all kinds (peasant and indigenous leaders, CIPCA staff, professionals from other spheres, female staff of the co-financing agencies) has helped the institution to accept (although tardily) the need to prepare, and put into practice, training and organisational strengthening policies that take the position of peasant and indigenous women into account. It should be mentioned that, in any development cooperation entity, whether bilateral, multilateral or private, it has always been a seemingly endless struggle for women (and some men) to have the gender topic put on the development policy agenda.

Since the years of democracy, the CIPCA – grassroots relationship changed, with CIPCA seen first as comrades-in-arms and then as a kind of escort. The institution became more of an accompanist in the process of strengthening the peasant and indigenous organisations. In some places there was also distancing due to by distrust of leaders, for example of the CSUTCB, when CIPCA decided to support municipalisation. Besides, several grassroots organisations experienced some internal conflicts, which made it almost impossible to keep working with them.

NGOs have had very great and mistaken expectations in the attitude of the members of grassroots organisations. These expectations were ideologically-tinged and were based on the notion that the popular sectors, in a fairly short space of time, would create an alternative society, characterised by principles of solidarity and auto-government. Conflicts between members of the organisations, unsatisfied expectations, led to serious problems in the handling of resources. Finally, the authoritarianism of some leaders and sometimes even racist attitudes under the supposed banner of *indigenismo*, are internal factors that have caused divisions within peasant and indigenous organisations. It was difficult, for NGOs, to criticise these weaknesses within grassroots organisations, because such criticism meant, among other things, opened conflicts with some leaders, their former allies and comrades-in-arms.

An additional problem remained in the question of whether development cooperation agencies should finance grassroots organisations directly or if they would have to do so through NGOs. It is evident that, in principle, there is no problem in the grassroots organisations having direct access to the financial resources of the agencies. However, in the past this discussion was distorted by the mistaken idea that the NGO would have to eliminate itself so as to transfer all its functions and activities to the grassroots organisations. In this sense, there was a total negation of the specific functions of an NGO on one side and of that of a grassroots organisation on the other. After years of discussions, above all ideological, a kind of consensus has been reached in which the two types of organisation have their *raisons d'être* in society. This implies a relationship of interdependency, which the same grassroots organisations and NGOs will define according to their respective objectives. Here, there is no role for the agencies[161].

Another factor that implied that NGOs and the grassroots had to redefine the characteristics of its interdependency, was the fact that after the 1990s the number of NGOs increased considerably, as well as the number of consultancy agencies. The grassroots organisations were in a position to be able to choose among several "offers" of institutions and companies. In the words of Hugo Fernández: "these organisations have to be compared with a football team; in the past CIPCA was the only coach available. Now the peasant and indigenous organisations can choose between various coaches."

In the 1990s after having received a lot of criticism that it had a too active and leading a position in relation to the grassroots organisations, CIPCA changed its working strategy and defined its role as facilitator, catalyst or mediator. It began to see itself as a subsidiary, with the true protagonists being the peasants and indigenous peoples. However, all the support institutions were beginning to 'facilitate', which meant it was no longer clear who was facilitating whom and what process of change was supposedly being facilitated. This was also a rather politically unclear position as well as being easy, since it was always possible to hide behind the grassroots organisations.

Within CIPCA it was realised that there was a certain contradiction between this passive attitude and the numerous roles that, in practice, CIPCA performed. Indeed, it has never been possible to allege that CIPCA was a passive actor in Bolivian society. It is, and has always been, very much present, since it has an institutional structure that allows autonomous discussion and deliberation of its objectives, strategies and alliances. It draws up and executes plans and development projects; it develops processes of political impact at several levels; it disseminates its work publicly, etc. All this means that it can indeed be said that CIPCA is an actor in its own right in Bolivian society.

Not having abandoned its commitment to strengthening the political and economic development of the indigenous and peasant population is, without any doubt, the most profound reason for its existence. But this commitment does not mean automatically to have to take the role of follower; on the contrary, this commitment obliges CIPCA to take on an autonomous role, different from that of the grassroots. Then, in its interrelation and interdependency with these organisations, CIPCA rightly defines itself as a political actor and protagonist of the process of building a democratic and intercultural society. The most substantial consequence of this attitude has been that of acknowledging, not only in practice but also in discourse and strategy, that the tasks of democratic construction in Bolivia transcend the political and organisational strengthening of the peasant and indigenous sector. They also require that CIPCA takes a leading role in the democratic construction of the country as a whole, in matters such as gender relations, intercultural democracy, the rights and duties of citizens, the strengthening of municipal governments and political impact.

This new attitude of assuming the role of autonomous political actor has the additional advantage of clearly delineating the relationship of respect and autonomy with the peasant and indigenous organisations.

DEMOCRACY AND INTERCULTURAL CITIZENSHIP

When CIPCA decided to support the municipalities, after the promulgation of the Law of Popular Participation, it was heavily criticised by other NGOs, by the grassroots organisations and by academics. There was also considerable internal debate over the role of CIPCA in relation to municipal management. It was said that CIPCA had become too much an arm of municipal government, taking on the preparation of Municipal Development Plans (PDM) as if it were a kind of consultancy company contracted by the municipality. However, in the long run CIPCA's position has proved beneficial to everyone: municipal governments, indigenous and peasant organisations and the CIPCA staff.

The organisational solution within CIPCA was to create a peasant support unit, so as to continue working directly with the communities and their organisations, and a municipal support unit, so as to ensure that the new municipal governments would provide an efficient and supportive service, within the broader framework of rural development. Greater emphasis was given to support for those peasants and indigenous people who wanted access, and/or indeed acceded, to the municipal decsion making bodies. The communities have not always understood it thus, and in some cases they complained that CIPCA was not what it used to be, since it was dedicated mostly to helping the mayors' offices, at that time considered to be bastions of the elite. In 1994 the population was still disconcerted with the laws, whilst in 1996 people were already saying: "that law, that we considered a damn law has given us access to local power. It turned out to be a blessed law".

CIPCA has held many training activities (workshops, seminars, courses, etc.) so that all those rural men and women who aspired to an active role in the process of popular participation, might fulfil their new duties as mayors, councillors, members of vigilance committees or national representatives[162].

It is always difficult to give direct, concrete results for these ant-like tasks, achieving democracy in all aspects and at all levels. Much as the cooperation agencies would like to see these results, it is not possible to quantify them. the processes of formation cannot be evaluated in terms of direct cause and effect, let alone in the short term. However, the most important result is that the challenge itself has changed: the goal is no longer local power, but also local governability and internal democratisation of the social organisations themselves.

(see Bazoberry, Soliz and Rojas, 2006).

Municipal decentralisation brought with it an enormous process of social mobilisation which twelve years later, in many regions of the country, maintains the same level of enthusiasm as when it began. This is visible in the way in which General Treasury resources have been distributed to the municipalities, demonstrating that it is possible to have financial resources throughout the national territory. There has been greater investment in localities remote from the political centres and service institutions have multiplied in rural municipalities. Many social organisations (peasant, indigenous and neighbourhood) have been strengthened with the proliferation of meetings and debates to present demands to the municipal government. With the necessary caution, it can also be affirmed that the presence of the indigenous and peasant organisations in the municipal governments has allowed them to be projected, beyond local government, towards the national political sphere (Bazoberry, Soliz and Rojas, 2006: 17-19).

However, once these formal spaces of municipal government were won, the peasants and indigenous people, and especially the women, prove extremely vulnerable to the impositions of the administrative formal structure and/or political powers; many ended up being obliged to obey vertically-imposed policies or abandoned the posts to which they were elected (ibid: 21). For example, opportune advice was not available for women who were unable to combine their domestic tasks with their obligations as councillors, mayors or members of vigilance committees. Neither was there support to lighten their domestic workloads or to have their husbands stand in for them at home.

The events of the last years have shown that CIPCA again faces a historical moment in which it is necessary to reconsideration the analysis of the social and political forces in Bolivian society. The arrival of indigenous people and peasants to the power, both at local level and nationally, might be seen as "the salvation" or "the final point". However, it is inevitable that in many cases old leadership errors will be reproduced and other new ones will be generated.

Some paragraphs before we concluded that the theme is not simply local power but also local governability. Now we can conclude that the issue is not simply efficiency, but also democracy; in other words, that groups of citizens that have been historically excluded and marginalised have the opportunity to govern, but that they should do so within established democratic norms of mutual respect. This meant a new challenge: strengthening the State, something previously unthinkable for an NGO like CIPCA. The insertion of social movements into the political system (whether party-political or not) has called the whole division between State and civil society into question.

The result of the general elections of the 18th December 2005 is unparalleled in Bolivian history, not only because of the result in itself (53.7% in favour of Evo Morales and his party MAS), but also because it represents a clear electoral majority for a leader who represents, principally though not exclusively, the peasants and indigenous people, social sectors traditionally absent from decision-making.

It is a pity that in the same elections the women have lost ground in terms of their percentage of representation. Despite the broad nature of the social and political movement of recent years, women constitute a sector that has resigned its own demands and has lost spaces. The reduced presence of women as candidates in the elections has affected the entirety of feminine representation at national level. In conclusion, the empowerment of women is and remains a priority challenge for CIPCA.

Reflecting on the election results in January 2006, Oscar Bazoberry – by then general director of CIPCA – pointed out that most people in Bolivian and international society concurred in seeing the victorious government as an indigenous government, principally because of the origin of MAS and the leadership of Evo Morales[163]. He concludes, then, that "the achievements and errors of this government will basically be attributed to its perception as indigenous."

The main challenge will be to build a stronger State, one that responds to a dynamic society, strengthened, diverse and sustained by values of solidarity, democracy and inclusion. To speak of *economic* citizenship is to refer to the right to have a stable income; to talk of *political* citizenship is to refer to the democratic right to choose and be chosen. *Social* citizenship refers to the right to have a dignified and secure human life. These three citizenships achieve and ensure equality, inclusion and participation.

But cultural citizenship goes beyond participation and inclusion. Cultural citizenship refers to dignity, the right to be different. It refers to *co-authorship* in the construction of a multicultural and intercultural national identity. Co-authorship means not only participating in contexts already established by someone else. Co-authorship means giving content and direction to these contexts.

A new content must be given to the challenge of a pluricultural and intercultural society. A multicultural society cannot be allowed to turn into a conservative society in which everyone retreats into his or her own culture and identity. This problem is not only typical of a society as multicultural as Bolivia's, but also exists in all the other countries where there is a strong migratory tendency. Globalisation has meant that multicultural societies are considered problematic. Amartya Sen shows in his book *Identity and Violence. The Illusion of Destiny* (2006) that it is incorrect to consider societies as a sum of their own cultures. This means that individuals are considered as prisoners of their belonging and prohibits them from interchange between different ideas and lifestyles. Multiculturalism and diversity are not necessarily positive values *per se*. Only when the interrelation between cultures and lifestyles generates new knowledge and serves to so that there might be greater freedom of thought, can we speak of the positive aspects of multiculturalism. It is, then, correct for CIPCA to have changed its mission in 2005, emphasising the "moral obligation" of "…participating in the construction of a democratic, intercultural, equitable and economically sustainable Bolivia."

SUSTAINABLE RURAL DEVELOPMENT

In all the discussions over rural development and the contributions of NGOs in Bolivia, it is often forgotten that "the rural geographical environment is probably one of the most adverse in terms of climatic risk: frequents frosts, droughts, inundations and marked deterioration of renewable natural resources. Added to this are the low population density, a deficient productive and social infrastructure, problems of commercialisation, under-education of the population, the limited market, a economic policy hardly favourable to small peasant farmers, high interest rates, irregularities and corruption, etc." (Van Niekerk, 1994: 296).

CIPCA has had successes and failures in its agricultural development proposals. But no proposal can be catalogued as a total failure or an unqualified success. For example the first experiences of rotating funds were mistaken proposals in terms of the rules of the credit game, but they turned out to be the first credit offers in a rural world where the monetary economy was barely developed.

Since the Bolivian State had almost no presence in the rural zones, and considering the absence of an entity of agrarian extension, CIPCA and several other NGOs have played an important role in at least halting the de-capitalisation of the peasant economy. The question of what would have happened without the presence of CIPCA may be answered clearly in this case: without credit from FONDECO (or ANED or FADES) many peasant and indigenous families would have had no access whatsoever to financial resources and, as such, they would have had no possibility even of reproducing.

The Work Community model (CDT) has been the object of many internal and external analyses. In Chapter IV we dealt in detail with criticisms of the model. It also has to be underlined that the model, in its time, was indeed an interesting response for the Guaraní region where it managed to break the situation of self-annihilation in which practically all the communities belonging to the Guaraní people found themselves. This aspect is often forgotten when the model is criticised as not being an economic response with an eye to the future (see Soliz, 1995 for an exhaustive analysis of the Guaraní project).

The fundamental criticism of the CDT – a collective model that does not correspond to the family organisation of production– has been fully recognised by CIPCA. On the other hand, it is necessary to stress that some proposals that failed in the 1990s have been resumed in the 21st century.

A clear example is the impact of the greenhouses. It is true that the first experiences of greenhouses did not have positive results; that technological innovation has its highs and lows – which is normal in the case of innovations – and that, when the technology was perfected, the construction of greenhouses required a lot of investment. However, after several years of functioning on the Altiplano, the greenhouses have justified their existence with the production and commercialisation of vegetables. If we compare the time and investments dedicated to obtaining a greenhouse model that was technologically acceptable, with the time and investment that centres of research and development need in the USA or Europe to present a technological innovation, what was invested on the Altiplano would probably not amount to one tenth of what these latter require. On the other hand, the quantity of criticisms that the greenhouses have received is probably ten times greater than what an inapplicable technological innovation would receive in Europe or the USA. The cost of an innovation only seems problematic in the Southern countries, while in those of the North it is taken as normal.

Another fallacy always heard from people who have studied or evaluated the impact of the greenhouses is that CIPCA supposedly supported most to the farmers already "comfortable". The same people who criticised CIPCA for having 'imposed' a form of communal organisation, later criticise CIPCA, for changing the form of communal organisation into private property, and by support to those better-off families that could invest in the greenhouses. In other words, when CIPCA tries to support the poorest, it is criticised for investing in 'lost cases'; when CIPCA supports the better-off, it is criticised because it reinforces internal differentiation in the communities.

It is opportune also to mention that the impact of the greenhouses is not necessarily to be found in places where CIPCA has worked. If one takes a local look at a number of greenhouses, the experience can prove neutral or without impact. However, because of the dynamic characteristics of the market – whether by distance or costs – the experience was welcomed in other spaces, where the number of greenhouses has grown and where the technological innovation was fully adopted[164].

Since 1997 CIPCA has adapted its interventions to the characteristics of the peasant economy and has ceased to propose forms of collective organisation. The new proposals reflect a deeper knowledge of the peasant economy, taking into account the sustainable use of renewable natural resources, the family plot, the family model of production organisation, associative models of production and commercialisation, etc. Food security is no longer considered synonymous with production for self-consumption: rather, production for self-consumption, like production for the market are both considered adequate to achieve food security. Produce for market (national and eventually international) is considered an adequate means of achieving growth in income, and as such, of food security.

Since the promulgation of the INRA Law in 1996, CIPCA has been advising indigenous organisations in the reorganisation of the Indigenous Communitarian Land (TCOs). It is opportune to mention that the history of agrarian reforms has shown that the mere redistribution of land is not sufficient for raise productivity in the peasant economy. Land is only one of the resources. Without the security of having access to other resources such as sufficient manpower, financial resources and access to markets, land ownership will not resolve poverty.

The theme of gender has been incorporated in economic proposals for sustainable rural development. In the early years, women barely existed for CIPCA; they were considered as mere housewives and mothers, receivers of food. Only after the insistence of some professional women did CIPCA accept the need to consider peasant women as economic, political and social actors on the same level as men. It should be stressed that CIPCA is one of the few organisations not specialised in the gender theme which nonetheless participates actively in women's groups, such as the women's coordinating committee and the Latin American Women Transforming the Economy Network.

We all know that there is still poverty in the countryside after 35 years of CIPCA activity. In recent years people are increasingly heard blaming NGOs for the modest results they have achieved in the struggle against poverty. Although it is true that poverty persists, it is less true that NGOs like CIPCA have not had good results. What is undeniable is that NGOs have overly high and unrealistic expectations, which makes the results appear disappointing.

NGOs are not the State and, without public policies that are favourable to rural development and the peasant economy, it will be impossible for NGOs to achieve better results than simply temporary relief in the precarious situation in which the rural population finds itself. The co-financing agencies demand and expect too much from NGOs. The forms that have to be filled in order to obtain financing oblige NGOs to show unreachable results. On the other hand, NGOs also deceive themselves just as they offer too much: it is common, and CIPCA has been no exception, to exaggerate growths in production and productivity, the quantity of tonnes of harvest for commercialisation, and the speed with which the population accepts technological innovations. (Bebbington, 2001: 139).

Another unresolved problem has to do with the emphasis that CIPCA places on the agricultural component within the peasant economy. Agriculture, stockbreeding and fishing still occupy a central place because CIPCA quite rightly considers the rural population as one whose main profession is that of farmer and/or stockbreeder, however much it also dedicates itself to craftwork, commercialisation, transformation, etc. It is known that there are many peasant families whose income depends on family members who work in the city as traders, artisans, primary school teachers, domestic employees or public employees. For decades people have yearned for their children to have access to secondary and even higher education. Migration, principally to Argentina, Spain and the USA, is another highly important source of family income.

In the current debate on rural development there is a marked absence of historical knowledge. When some studies of the Latin American farming sector sustain that rural development is more than just agricultural development there are totally correct, but they forget that this is a well-known and age-old affirmation. In the 19th century peasants living in the Andes migrated to the Peruvian coast and/or the Bolivian lowlands for the cotton or sugar harvest. Likewise, since the 19th century there has been temporary migration of peasants to the intermediate cities to work in occupations such as construction workers, porters or maids. In these same intermediate cities there were artisans providing services to agricultural work, people dedicated to product transformation, and others. The urban population sent money to the countryside and received its value in kind. Military service was (and still is) another important component in lessening the family's monetary expenses and receive some form of training[165]. Research done in the 1980s has already clearly indicated the diversity of sources of income in the peasant economy and the important role played by migration in this whole system (see Figueroa, 1981; Plaza, 1979; Caballero, 1981; Gonzales de Olarte, 1984). What is new is not so much the diversity of income sources, but rather the openness to new sources, such as migration to Argentina, the USA and Europe.

Those who recommend that the work of NGOs should incorporate activities aimed at urban micro-enterprises, or formal education, confuse analysis with direct intervention. This analysis may be correct, in the sense that peasant economy income derives from very diverse sources. However, an NGO like CIPCA, which has specialised in agricultural development, should not dedicate itself to activities in which it has no expertise (e.g.. ethno-tourism or secondary education). It would be rather arrogant on CIPCA's part to think that it can intervene in any sector. Besides, to think that interventions in agriculture are no longer necessary is "… to see the peasants as being ready for conversion into magnificent artisans, eco-tourism guides, transformers, traders, etc." (Carlos Hugo Laruta, director CIPCA-La Paz 2002-2006). They also forget that, despite the importance of migration, the great majority do not migrate permanently, but keep one foot in the countryside, sowing and harvesting their crops. Finally, the peasant economy still has an important role in providing foodstuffs for the urban population.

The CIPCA approach is to accept – at the level of analysis- the existence of people who often have dual occupations and dual residences, and to support them – at the level of activity – from a rural perspective. This is a valid approach: it is in accordance with the situation in which peasant families find themselves and, besides, is in accordance with history and the specialty of the institution itself.

Some of the factors that impede the economic growth of peasant units have already been mentioned; lack of education, infrastructure and communication, poor development of markets and cultural factors. Another problem is that the peasant economy is too poor to generate savings to invest and become self-financing. According to Figueroa (2001: 125), the lack of financing is produced by two failings: that of the market and that of the State. If the primary and financial markets do not develop, neither will innovation. Thus rural development is faced with the vicious circle of underdevelopment. The peasant economy is poor because the markets are barely developed, and the markets are undeveloped because the peasant economy is poor. Given the flaws in the market, the agent that could assure initial financing would be the State. Public investment would have to be the fundamental instrument for rural development (ibid: 127).

This need to invest in the peasant economy seems even more urgent if one considers the new rules existing in international business. The Free Trade Agreements (FTAs) – for example the Free Trade Area of the Americas (FTAA) – mean that not even peasant economies can afford to be reclusive. They must open up to external markets and look for new ways of relating to the world. Since 1985, when the structural adjustment policy was introduced in Bolivia, the Bolivian economy has been immersed in the world economy. Thus, the peasant economy was never functioning in isolation from the other national and international economic sectors. In 2001 CIPCA made the decision of studying more closely the problematic of international commerce and the consequences for peasant families it is working with. Another theme that is being considered more closely is fair trade, not from a romantic angle but as a serious commercial alternative. Thus, not only are alternative commercial channels sought within the solidarity network but also, and above all, traditional channels such as supermarket chains.

Although CIPCA has adopted the position that peasant families must be full actors in the national and international commerce, one of the great problems of the peasant economy is still that the State considers this sector as a simple receiver of services and not as an indispensable actor within the national economy; in consequence the conditions under which the Bolivian small producer accedes to the market and to public services for production are much more difficult in comparison with large-scale farmers, stockbreeders and agro-export companies (Soliz and Aguilar, 2005: 25). These sectors have always benefited from favourable public policies, including subsidies and investments that are highly beneficial to them. It is notable, then, that subsidies to the indigenous peasant sector are criticised for not being sustainable, despite their being much less than subsidies to the business sector. Above all, within the agencies of co-financing there has been a period of opposition to any proposal of subsidy, arguing that subsidy is paternalist.[166] It will be clear that these arguments are based on analyses that are not economic but merely ideological.

Hopefully Bolivia will change its policies of rural development and show a pro-peasant State or, at least a State in favour of pro-poor growth. In other words: a policy of economic growth with social distribution and with priority but also particular attention to the sector of small agricultural producers.

ROLE OF RESEARCH

This section cannot be written without first mentioning the fundamental role that Xavier Albó has played in research. Since its foundation Xavier Albó has been the great defender and promoter of research in CIPCA. He has contributed enormously to the generation of knowledge of rural and intercultural Bolivia[167]. Not only through his own research, of a high academic level (see among other items appendix 2), but also through the enthusiasm with which he has trained new generations of social researchers and by having been the library's main stimulus and donor.

Without exaggeration, it can be affirmed that one of the best social sciences libraries in all Bolivia is the *CIPCA Library*, whose database contained 35.000 volumes in 2005. There is also the institutional memoir for CIPCA's own staff, students, researchers and future generations. In the whole history of CIPCA, the library was never affected when financial crises arose: all the executive directors and members of the board have defended –against all odds – the need for a specialised library.

From day of the CIPCA's foundation and even before that, there was concern about archiving all the didactic material and books that founders had donated personally. In 1970 the archives were installed in the small La Paz office and towards the end of 1975 the library already had some 7.000 volumes. Unfortunately, during the dictatorship of García Meza (1980-1982) the library's material had to be hidden and a lot of material that nevertheless was found was destroyed by the military. In 1987 a librarian was hired for two months to order the stored documents. This librarian, Lola Paredes, never stopped working in the library and later she had the support of Monserrat Pescador.

It should be mentioned that the library is also the depositary of the archives of some peasant organisations. Besides, it is a centre of documentation for the so-called grey literature. Fortunately the regional offices send their documents to the central library. Thanks to this it has been possible to recover almost all the documents from the CIPCA office in Beni, after it was totally ransacked in December 2003.

The most important donors are (networks of) NGOs, international organisms, State institutions, universities and individuals. We could mention, for example, the donation of 4,000 titles by UNITAS, donations of the Universidad Cordillera, of the BID, of two universities of USA, and many others. It is also customary for the CIPCA staff to make donations to the library. But the most important provider and individual donor is definitely Xavier Albó.

CIPCA has carried out the formation of young researchers in different ways: thematically, by having always suggested themes of national interest; and methodologically, through having insisted that there should be a permanent relation in CIPCA between research and action. Besides, the Grants Programme has provided support so that advanced students could write their theses on themes of interest to CIPCA, with the possibility of later being incorporated into the institution or to other similar institutions. The results of this programme – young people, academically and socially prepared for work in NGOs – are never taken into account in the evaluation models of the financing agencies, but should be considered as results that are not sought but are great importance for Bolivian society as a whole and particularly for the development of the social sciences.

If it is true that the close relation between research and action has seen different expressions, CIPCA has never has ceased to have one foot in the countryside, and another in the academic auditorium. This is not to insinuate that centres of pure research should not exist or that institutions dedicated only to (agricultural) extension should not exist. This type of institutions are also necessary and have their *raison d'être*. However, CIPCA's strength has always been the combination between theory and practice, research and action, reflection and promotion. It has not been easy to combine promotion and research, and the emphasis that has been given to one or the other has varied according to the historical context.

In the 1970s research played an important role in guiding the first proposals of education and training. The first economic and anthropological studies served to facilitate better understanding of the rural world and to give contextualised content to the short training courses. Later, during the dictatorship of García Meza, there was no other alternative for CIPCA than to concentrate its work on agricultural extension. Faithful to its vocation as a research centre, it resumed research after 1982, concentrating firstly on agricultural studies and then on micro-regional and multidisciplinary base-line studies. The great project of participative research – the popular historical project – is a product of this era and shows the importance that CIPCA has always given to research. During the second half of the 1990s various studies were carried out, concentrating more on the systematisation of experiences than on research. Besides, those years saw some research published on themes of national importance, but which had no direct bearing on CIPCA's actions in the field. This relative distancing between research and action has been overcome since the beginning of the 21st century, when there has been new incentive for staff not only to act but also to reflect and, besides, to investigate.

Another constant dilemma has been whether to do research whose results are applicable immediately or whether CIPCA, being a traing and promotion institution, could also produce research whose results have only long-term impact and influence. Without turning into a purely academic institution, CIPCA's research themes have attained national importance, beyond the particular moment in which it was carried out. It has not been easy to adopt this institutional posture, because the development cooperation agencies have not always been prepared to invest in research whose results are not immediately useful, much less if they took into account the fact that the institution was not an academic centre. On several occasions CIPCA has made internal financial arrangements in order to be able to carry out this research.

Finally CIPCA was not exempt from a problem faced by almost all NGOs: the relation between those who work in the field and those who do office work; between extensionists and researchers, the doers and the thinkers. Probably the fact that internally there is no longer a distinction between these two categories and that everyone participates in institutional research, has helped in overcoming this problem satisfactorily.

An additional problem should be mentioned of finding good researchers: the formation of researchers in Bolivian universities is deficient. Public opinion regarding universities is not entirely all positive and there is frequent criticism of the politicisation of university administrations, the lack of funds for research and administrative bureaucracy. Unfortunately the Bolivian university cannot be considered a meritocracy. It is important to stress the coordinated effort between CIPCA and the Programme of Strategic Research in Bolivia (PIEB) for the diploma in social research methodology, a course which 20 employees have attended.

It is unusual for co-financing agencies to adopt a pro-research position. Generally the employees (fortunately there are also happy exceptions) manifest a certain distrust of academic researchers. They question the usefulness of more conceptual or theoretical work. On the other hand, many people in Latin American NGOs have the necessary qualifications and sufficient inclination to work in the university. However, they end up working in NGOs as a consequence of the political repression of previous years and the recent economic strangulation of universities. For this reason, "members of Latin American NGOs are generally better trained academically than their colleagues in the North" (Bebbington, 2001: 6, referring to Lehmann, 1990).

PUBLIC IMPACT

Have a bearing in the public policies and public debate in favour of rural development is not an easy task. Since the evaluation of 1991 (Schwember et al.) there is a more emphatic need for CIPCA to act in the public sphere.

Over many years CIPCA has developed activities of lobbying and advocacy, though with a different emphasis and methodologies. In its first years CIPCA's relationship with the peasant and indigenous organisations had in itself an impact nature, not so much as a direct influence on public policies, but rather as an ideologically sustained work in direct support of them. Then, in the 1980s-90s, CIPCA's work in NGO networks and coordination at national and Latin American levels, the role of the institution in work panels and the position of CIPCA on national and international platforms have all had a positive influence on the process of emancipation and inclusion of the indigenous andpeasant population (both men and women). It is worthwhile to say that it was precisely the coordination with other NGOs that gave strength and importance to the networks and platforms. The third phase of impact accords CIPCA an autonomous role as an organisation of civil society. Now it is not only an accompaniment of the grassroots organiations, no longer defines its lobby and advocacy agenda in close coordination with the peasant and indgenous organisations or participate only in mobilisations, protests and pressure activities, but also in forms of relationship with the State with its own proposals so as to have a bearing on public policies.

Despite it being difficult to find direct impact of lobby and advocacy activities, we can mention some historical landmarks in which CIPCA, in coordination with the grassroots organisations and other institutions, has played a role which has been, to some degree, important. To give some examples: in breaking the Military-Peasant Pact; in the creation of the CSUTCB; breaking the chain of dependency of the Guaraní in the sugar harvest; the foundation of the APG; the publication of the popular historical project; the emergence of the indigenous peoples of Moxos; the ant-like productive and organisational work at municipal level; the alliance between indigenous peoples and peasants in the lowlands, etc.

The issues in which CIPCA could be regarded as expert – sustainable rural development, strengthening of grassroots organisations, decentralisation and intercultural citizenship – are themes of great importance to go out to the public with its own voice. The current disjunctive with interregional conflicts is that the nation must conceive a vision of region, and vice-versa. This is why themes of national interest are equally important as themes of regional interest. Moreover, when one works at micro level it is easy to forget that at times there are macro influences that cannot be worked on at micro level. This is where CIPCA must also propose international themes like Bolivia's place in Latin America and in the world.

In order to carry out lobby and advocacy activities, it is essential to have a good communication and dissemination policy. Radio was a very important and almost unique medium of communication in the 1970s and 80s; between 1990 and 2000 the *Internet* steadily increased in importance. CIPCA has always utilised the communications media, whether through its own radio programmes, the edition of bulletins and television programmes, its excellent webpage or the network of electronic communication used to distribute *Cipca Notes*.

As with lobby and advocacy, CIPCA's communication and dissemination role has also changed. Previously it acted as a channel, giving space to the grassroots so that they could distribute their own information. However, since the start of the 21st century it is no longer simply a conduit for the information of others, but CIPCA uses the media to present its own agenda. It goes out to the public with its own opinion. The same is true of the grassroots organisations, which no longer need a facilitating entity like CIPCA to emit their opinions.

This new orientation is not without its problems, since greater visibility brings more criticism. Bazoberry responds to this dilemma: "it is not a question of hiding in the shadows, waiting for time to pass. One has to be more rigorous in reducing the negative cost of visibility."

It is difficult to know if the activities of CIPCA and the results of its research have influenced the process of decision-making as regards public policies. Generally, the issues are suitable for impact, but one can never know for certain if the political doers let themselves be inspired by the opinions of CIPCA. Other factors are influential, like power relations and interest groups. Moreover, distributing the results of the work is no guarantee that they will be utilised in the formulation of policies. However, dissemination and communication do create a base for later use of some kind. Impact means influence not only on public policies; it also includes influence on public opinion and the agenda for debate.

RELATION WITH CO-FINANCING AGENCIES

CIPCA emerged – like other organisations – because of a desire to do something proactive in the struggle against dictatorship and in favour of the inclusion of peasants and indigenous peoples in national life. The relations in the 1970s and 80 were characterised by international solidarity against Latin America dictatorships. In which era, cooperation with Latin American NGOs became a relationship of mutual respect and learning. They were difficult years in political terms, but at the same time years in which the sky was the limit in terms of financing.

Kees van Dongen, responsible of Bolivia for NOVIB between 1983 and 1989:

Nobody in NOVIB knew what organisations like CIPCA, INEDER and IPTK were doing. Before 1983 there were not even visits to the organisations. The first time anyone other than Sjef Theunis visited CIPCA was as late as 1983. In those years one could talk of a circle of friends in which Lucho Alegre had become the most important person. Neither should it be forgotten that inside NOVIB, the Latin

American department was the most important: we had a Chilean head, Sjef Theunis was pro Latin America, and Latin America solidarity committees had an important voice in Dutch public opinion.

In the 1970s and 80s, relationships with private agencies in Europe and Canada began as an informal relationship between friends of the South and North, often based on sympathies of a political or ideological nature. After the 1990s, multilateral organisations like the World Bank and organisations of the United Nations discovered NGOs and considered them the new "*prima donnas*" of development cooperation. The advantage of this was that NGOs could have access to more financial resources. The disadvantage was the obligation to satisfy the political will of these finance agencies, with the consequent risk that the finance agencies, rather than the NGO, would define the latter's agenda[168].

For NGOs cooperation had both positive and negative effects. If in many cases it allowed NGOs to be created and to survive, it also generated financial dependency, due among other things to constant changes in financing policies, with a negative effect on efforts towards continuity and sustainability of actions. Cooperation resources are currently shrinking: the demand is for more and bigger results, for direct impact, without having defined what is understood by impact and what type of impact is being sought. On the other hand, the growing trend of wanting to dispense with NGOs seems contradictory at a juncture at which they are "required" as facilitators of political alliances, providers of technical assistance and training programmes, and business managers. In general, over the course of all these years, the agencies have conceived NGOs as "an instrument for the implementation of their projects and not as a social phenomenon" (Bebbington, 2001: 8).

In the year 2000 other type of organisations appeared in Europe and USA: many thousands of small foundations, associations, clubs and other groupings of volunteers who want to 'do something' for poor people, but prefer not to channel their money through established development cooperation agencies. Neither do they want local NGOs to execute the projects; they prefer to do it themselves, whether through sending volunteers or use friends in the countries targeted, under the (mistaken) impression that this is more efficient and inexpensive. It is a return to the 1950s, when people from rich countries went to poor countries to help local people with projects and assistance programmes, under financial control from the North[169].

CIPCA has always managed to maintain its autonomy despite (or thanks to) the great range of co-financing agencies thathave supported it. There have also been various moments in its history when it could have become a sort of consultancy[170], but it has always maintained the decision to remain a development NGO at the service of the peasant and indigenous population. Thus, in 2000, when CIPCA went through an acute financial crisis, it did not let itself be carried by fashion and decided to consolidate its historical relationship with the well-known development cooperation agencies.

Despite relations between CIPCA and these agencies always having been cordial, it must be accepted that these relations are not 100% horizontal. It is a fallacy to think that the agency and the NGO have the same power in decision-making processes. An open relationship, cordial and respectful, does not resolve the fact that the agencies will always have the last word. If an agency decides not to finance CIPCA or to cut its financing, CIPCA has to accept the decision. And it has had to accept such decisions several times over the course of 35 years[171]. On the other hand, however much agencies deny it, they also depend on NGOs. The results achieved by co-financing agencies in great measure depend on the results achieved by NGOs. It is, then, correct to speak of mutual dependency or interdependency.

Never has there been a relation of beneficence between CIPCA and the agencies. Rather, there have been several agencies that have consciously sought out the institution because to finance it meant to create a positive image of the agency itself. Here are the views of three people:

Nico van Niekerk:

"I had a kind of voluntary work experience in NOVIB instead of doing my obligatory military service. Then I worked for a while in La Paz, and was there when Sjef Theunis – ex-priest and recently-appointed director of NOVIB – did a tour of Latin America in search of new organisations. I presented him to Xavier Albó and the two got on immediately."

So it was not CEBEMO, the then Catholic Dutch cooperation agency, but NOVIB, the laic agency with strong if informal relations with social-democracy, which began to finance CIPCA. In Holland NOVIB was considered a privileged agency because "it had CIPCA in its portfolio".

Hilda Carrera of *Secours Catholique* (Caritas-France):

"I was educated in the spirit of Liberation theology. I read Xavier Albó's books at university. In 1988 I began working in Secours Catholique and when, in 1990, we formulated a new strategy for Latin America, I wanted CIPCA to come in as a counterpart. I made contact with Hugo Fernández and in this way we established relations between CIPCA and Secours Catholique."

Marcos Devisscher of FOS-Belgium:

"FOS works only with grassroots organisations and not with intermediary organisations. But in the late 80s FOS decided that was necessary also to establish relations with an NGO so that FOS might learn about debates with the staff of that NGO. FOS did not learn enough by working only with grassroots organisations. It is for this reason that FOS decided to finance CIPCA."

Not only FOS has been able to make the most of debates with CIPCA people. There are other representatives that say explicitly that they have learned from CIPCA:

Koos Michel of NOVIB:

"With CIPCA you have to have high-level debates, but NOVIB staff do not always attain the CIPCA level. When there is asymmetry in a relationship due to lack of knowledge, the risk is that financial dependency in the relationship may have an undesirable influence."

Andrés Croggon of Christian Aid:

"In order to present projects to the European Union we needed an NGO with an established management capacity. CIPCA was one of the few organisations that could respond adequately to so many requisites. It has great managerial capacity and has been a huge support for Christian Aid in the presentation and approval of projects."

Yvonne Buschor of *Fastenopfer*:

"CIPCA is a institution from which we can learn. We do not feel ourselves to be just a financing agency, we have learned a lot from CIPCA. CIPCA is an important referent for cooperation in Switzerland."

After 1985, relations between the agencies and CIPCA became more formal. Both the agencies and the NGOs had grown considerably. They had more money and more staff. The most business-oriented phase began, in which Planning, Monitoring and Evaluation (PME) were seen as the salvation. However, neither NGOs nor the development cooperation took this to be an instrument of learning. It appears that, from the agencies' point of view, the fundamental reason was the need to generate data with which they could defend their budgets. The PME became a mechanism to quantify results. Despite the great majority of NGO and development cooperation representatives reaching the conclusion that trying to capture reality in quantitative data is an illusion. Nevertheless, they all go on in the same dance because the higher links in the chain demand it. It should not be forgotten that many cofinancing agencies have to answer to their respective governments and/or parliaments.

In April 2006 came the publication in Holland of the report of a high level commission (Commissie Dijkstal, 2006)[172] which had reached the conclusion that there are considerable limitations in the evaluation of results, due to both methodological problems and imperfections in the way the gathered information is used. This means the creation of a 'paper reality'. It concluded that the measurement of results is not an adequate instrument with which to judge the effectiveness of NGOs, and not even for being accountable. For being accountable it is better to bear three criteria in mind: internal governability, quality of management and transparency (ibid: 28).

FINAL REFLECTION

CIPCA has shown that it is an institution with internal debate and readiness to reformulate its ideas and opinions. Is this because it has never been subject to political parties, or rather because being under the Company of Jesus umbrella obliged it always to call its ideological positions into question?

At least one of the Jesuits' principles has been favourable to CIPCA: you cannot live in this world without being familiar with it, you have to do research. It must also be acknowledged that, without the Company, CIPCA would have had many more problems during the years of dictatorship. At times of crisis this help has always existed, the last time was in 2002 when the office in San Ignacio de Moxos was ransacked. Another important characteristic, and one which CIPCA has always defended throughout its history, is that it respects the party political opinions of the institution's employees, but also demands that the institution not be used as an instrument for party ends.

The history of CIPCA does not end with an institution that no longer has problems or doubts, that has given up trying to improve its performance. CIPCA is an institution with a long history behind it and, nonetheless, has many unanswered questions. Much as it has learned from its own past; much as its daily business was always adapted to the political, economic, social and cultural environment, all these "lessons learned" never end. CIPCA will always make some decisions that are right and others that are wrong, sometimes responding correctly and at other times mistakenly, will always have certainties and doubts. It is precisely this attitude of non-arrogance, this spirit of continuing to question its own successes and results, which makes it a human institution, innovative and creative.

In order to work at CIPCA (and to write its history) one has to believe in its project, have a certain mystique and always be looking for alternatives and proposing new ideas. Whether this attitude was influenced by the Jesuits, only history will tell.

I would like to conclude this history of 35 years of institutional commitment to rural development with the following parable:

At nightfall an old man was walking along a sandy beach, when he saw a girl who was picking up starfish and putting them back in the water. He went up to her and asked what she was doing. She replied that the starfish would die in the sand under such strong sunlight. "But the beach stretches out for many kilometres and there are many thousands of starfish", said the old man, "how can your effort make any difference?" The girl looked at the starfish she had in her hand and then threw it far into the safety of the ocean. "At least it made all the difference for that one", she replied.

BIBLIOGRAPHY

Albó, Xavier (1978) *El enfoque de CIPCA en Bolivia* (CIPCA's focus in Bolivia), Paper presented at the Technical Meeting on Inter-American *Indigenista* Action, Pátzcuaro, México.

Albó, Xavier (1985) "De MNRistas a kataristas: campesinado, estado y partidos (1953-1983)" (From MNR to Katarism: peasantry, State and parties (1953-1983)", in: *Historia Boliviana*, V 1-2: 87-127, Cochabamba.

Albó, Xavier (1990) *La comunidad hoy* (The community today), CIPCA, Research Notebooks No. 32, La Paz.

Albó, Xavier (1993) *¿...y de Kataristas a MNRistas?* (¿...and from Katarism to the MNR?) CEDIN-UNITAS.

Albó, Xavier (1999) "Etnías y pueblos originarios: diversidad étnica, cultural y lingüística" (Ethnicity and native peoples: ethnic, cultural and linguistic diversity) in: Campero Prudencio (ed.) 1999, pp. 451-482.

Albó, Xavier (1999) *Ojotas en el poder local, cuatro años después* (Sandals and local power, four years on), CIPCA-PADEM, Research Notebooks No. 53, La Paz.

Albó, Xavier (2002) *Una casa común para todos. Iglesia, ecumenismo y desarrollo en Bolivia* (A common home for all. Church, ecumenism and development in Bolivia), Clave Consultants, EED, CIPCA, Research Notebook No. 57, La Paz.

Albó, Xavier and Josep M. Barnadas (1990) *La cara india y campesina de nuestra historia.* (The Indian and peasant face of our history), UNITAS and CIPCA, 3rd ed., La Paz.

Albó, Xavier and Víctor Quispe (2004) *Quiénes son indígenas en los gobiernos municipales* (Who is indigenous in municipal government?), CIPCA, Research Notebooks No. 59, La Paz.

Albo, Xavier, Thomas Greaves and Godofredo Sandóval (1981-83) *Chukiyawu, la cara aymara de La Paz* (Chuquiyawu, the Aymara face of La Paz), CIPCA, Research Notebooks Nos. 20, 22 and 24, La Paz.

Alcorez, Carmen and Xavier Albó (1979) *1978: el nuevo campesinado ante el fraude* (1978: the new peasantry faced with fraud), CIPCA, La Paz.

Archetti, E. et al. (1979) *Economía Campesina* (Peasant Economy), DESCO, Lima.

Arze Aguirre, René D. (1999) "Visión histórica: notas para una Historia del Siglo XX en Bolivia" (Historical vision: notes for a 20th-century history of Bolivia), in: Campero Prudencio (ed.) 1999, pp. 47-66.

Banfield, 1958 *The Moral Basis of a Backward Society*, Free Press, Glencoe.

Bazoberry, Oscar (2003) "Iniciativas empresariales: su necesidad y forma administrativa", (Business initiatives: their needs and administrative form) in: *Seminar on shared-risk business modalities*, SNV, La Paz, pp. 33-40.

Bazoberry, Oscar, Lorenzo Soliz and Juan Carlos Rojas (2006) *Vivencias y miradas sobre la participación popular* (Experiences and visions of popular participation), CIPCA, Research Notebook No. 65, La Paz.

Bebbington, Anthony (2001) "Reflections on the North-South relationship in the construction of knowledge of NGOs in Latin America", Paper prepared for the Seminar *"Studies on Non-Governmental Organisations in Latin America: situation and perspectives*, São Paulo (mimeo).

Bebbington, Anthony et al. (2001) *Contributions of the Dutch Co-Financing Program to Rural Development and Rural Livelihoods in the Highlands of Peru and Bolivia.* Synthesis Report, Boulder, Colorado (mimeo).

Bengoa, José (1988) "Education for social movements", in: Anke van Dam, Jan Ooijens and Gerhard Peter (eds.) *Popular Education in Latin America*, CESO Paperback No. 4, The Hague.

Berreta, Horacio (1992) "Algunos aspectos de la identidad de las organizaciones no-gubernamentales" ("Some aspects of the identity of non-governmental organisations"), in: *Pobreza Urbana y Desarrollo [Urban Poverty and Development]*, Year 1, No 2, pp. 36-44.

Biekart, Kees (2002) *Medefinancieringsorganisaties in maatschapijopbouw (Co-financing agencies and the construction of civil society)* Stuurgroep Evaluatie Nederlands Medefinancieringsprogramma (mimeo).

Bombarolo, Felix et al. (1992) *El rol de las organizaciones no-gubernamentales en el desarrollo de América Latina* (The role of non-governmental organisations in Latin American development) Ed. FICONG, Buenos Aires.

Breytenbach, Breyten "Making Being on Arts and Culture", in: Hivos Culture Fund *Moving Cultures*, 2005, pp. 8-29

Caballero, Armengol José (2005) *Resumen Historia Nacional* (National History Summary) (mimeo, PowerPoint presentation).

Caballero, José María (1981) *Economía agraria de la Sierra* (Agrarian economy of the Sierra), IEP, Lima.

Calderón Gutiérrez, Fernando (1999) "Actores sociales: un siglo de luchas sociales", (Social actors: a century of social struggles) in: Campero Prudencio (ed.) 1999, pp. 427-450.

Calderón, Fernando and Jorge Dandler (eds) (1986) *Bolivia: la fuerza histórica del campesinado*, (Bolivia: the historical strength of the peasantry) UNRISD, Geneva.

Campero Prudencio, Fernando (ed.) (1999) *Bolivia en el Siglo XX* (Bolivia in the 20th century), Harvard Club of Bolivia, La Paz.

Chayanov, A.V. (1979) "La organización de la unidad económica campesina" (The organisation of the peasant economic unit) in Plaza (ed.), pp. 85-104.

CIPCA (1991) *Por una Bolivia diferente, aportes para un proyecto histórico popular* (For a different Bolivia, contributions to a popular historical project) Research Notebooks No. 34, La Paz.

CIPCA (2005) www.cipca.org.bo

CIPCA and CRS (2005) *De la Movilización al Impacto. Índice CIVICUS de la Sociedad Civil en Bolivia* (From Mobilisation to Impact. CIVICUS Index of civil society in Bolivia), Research Notebooks No. 64, La Paz.

CIPCA-CORDECRUZ (1986) *Plan de desarrollo rural de Cordillera. Diagnóstico-Estrategia* (Cordillera rural development plan. Survey-strategy) (7 vols).

CIPCA-CORDECRUZ (1987) *Programa de Desarrollo Campesino de Cordillera- PDCC* (Programme of Peasant Development in Cordillera) (9 vols).

CIPCA-NOVIB (1998) *Desarrollo sostenible desde los Andes* (Sustainable development from the Andes), CIPCA, NOVIB, Clave Consultants, La Paz.

Commissie Dijkstal (2006) *Vertrouwen in een kwetsbare sector? Rapport van de Commissie Draagvlak en Effectiviteit Ontwikkelingssamenwerking* [Trust in a vulnerable sector. Report by the Commission for Support and Effectiveness of Development Cooperation], ICCO- KIT- SNV.

Comission of Development and Environment of Latina America and the Caribbean (1990) *Nuestra agenda propia* (Our own agenda), IBD-UNDP, Santiago.

Cortez, Leila and Eduardo Mendoza (eds.) (2004) *Apuntes del Mundo Rural Boliviano* (Notes on the Bolivian Rural World), CIPCA, Research Notebook No. 60, La Paz.

Cottle, Patricia and Carmen Beatriz Ruíz (1993) *Comentarios al documento "Estrategias y lineamientos metodológicos generales par el trabajo con mujeres en CIPCA* (Comments on the document "Strategies and general methodological guidelines for work with women in CIPCA"), La Paz.

Crespo, Mónica (1993) "Experiencias, esfuerzos actuales, limitaciones y perspectivas de CIPCA en el trabajo de género" (CIPCA's experiences, current efforts, limitations and perspectives in gender work), in: *RURALTER, Revista de Desarrollo Rural Alternativo*, Special Numbers 11 and 12, La Paz (pp. 251-266).

Degregrori, Carlos Iván (2000) *No hay país más diverso. Compendio de antropología peruana* (There is no country more diverse). Compendium of Peruvian anthropology, Series "Perú Problema", IEP, Lima.

De Janvry, Alain (1981) *The Agrarian Question and Reformism in Latin America*, John Hopkins, Baltimore-London.

Durán, J. (1990) *Las nuevas instituciones de la sociedad civil, impacto y tendencias de la cooperación internacional y ONGs del rural area de Bolivia* (The new institutions of civil society: impact and tendencies of international cooperation and NGOs in rural areas of Bolivia), La Paz (mimeo).

Elias, Bishelly and Germán Huanca (2005) *Compro Boliviano: los primeros pasos* (I Buy Bolivian: the first steps), CIPCA, Research Notebooks No. 61, La Paz.

Erasmus, C.J. (1968) "Community Development and the Encogido Syndrome", in: *Human Organisation*, Vol. 27, No. 1, pp. 65-74.

Eyben Rosalind (2003) *Donors as political actors: fighting the Thirty Years War in Bolivia*, Institute of Development Studies, Brighton, Sussex (mimeo).

Eyzaguirre, José Luis (2005) *Composición de los ingresos familiares de campesinos indígenas. Un estudio en seis regiones de Bolivia* (Composition of the family income of indigenous peasants. A study in six regions of Bolivia), CIPCA-PLURAL, La Paz.

Fals Borda, 0. (1978) "Por la praxis: el problema de cómo investigar la realidad para transformarla", (Through praxis: the problem of how research reality so as to transform it), in: Cartagena World Symposium *Crítica y política en ciencias sociales. El debate: teoría y práctica*

(Criticism and politics in the social sciences. Debate: theory and practice) volumes I and II, Ed. Punta de Lanza, Bogotá, pp. 209-249.

Feder, E. (1976) "The World Bank programme for the self-liquidation of Third World peasantry", in: *The Journal of Peasant Studies*, vol. 3, pp. 343-354.

Figueroa, Adolfo (1981) *La economía campesina de la Sierra del Perú* (The peasant economy of the Peruvian Sierra), Pontificia Universidad Católica, Lima.

Figueroa, Adolfo (2001) *Reformas en sociedades desiguales. La experiencia peruana* (Reforms in unequal societies. The Peruvian experience), Pontificia Universidad Católica, Lima.

Foster, G.M. (1965) "Peasant Society and the Image of the Limited Good", in: *American Anthropologist*, Vol. 67, No. 2, pp. 293-316)

Frank, André Gunder (1976) *Capitalismo y subdesarrollo en América Latina* (Capitalism and underdevelopment in Latin America), Siglo XXI, Mexico.

Freire, P. (1968) *Pedagogía del oprimido* (Pedagogy of the oppressed), Siglo XXI, Buenos Aires.

García Linera, Alvaro, Marxa Chávez León and Patricia Costas Monje (2004) *Sociología de los movimientos sociales en Bolivia* (Sociology of social movements in Bolivia), DIAKONIA and OXFAM, La Paz.

Gianotten, Vera et al. (1994) *Assessing the gender impact of development projects. Case studies from Bolivia, Burkina Faso and India*, KIT Press, Amsterdam.

Gianotten, Vera and Ton de Wit (1986) *Organización campesina: el objetivo político de la educación popular y la investigación participativa* (Peasant organisation: the political objective of popular education and participative research) CEDLA, Amsterdam.

Golte, Jürgen (2000) "Economía, Ecología, Redes. Campo y ciudad en los análisis antropológicos" (Economy, Ecology, Networks. Countryside and city in anthropological analysis), in: Carlos Iván Degregori, 2000, pp. 204-234.

Gonzales de Olarte, E. (1984) *Economía de la comunidad campesina* (Economy of the peasant community), IEP, Lima.

Gutiérrez, Gustavo (1977) "Praxis de liberación y fe cristiana" (Praxis of liberation and Christian faith) in: R. Gibellini (ed.) *La nueva frontera de la Theología en América Latina* (The new frontier of Theology in Latin America), Ed Sígueme, Salamanca.

Hall, B. (1982) "Breaking the Monopoly of Knowledge: Research Methods, Participation and Development", in: B. Hall et al. *Creating Knowledge: a Monopoly? Participatory Research in Development*, New Delhi.

Harris, O (1985) "Una visión andina del hombre y de la mujer" (An Andean vision of man and woman) in: *Allpanchis*, Vol. 21, No. 25, Cusco, pp. 17-41.

Holmberg, A.R. (1966) *Vicos: método y práctica de la antropología aplicada* (Vicos: method and practice of applied anthropology), Ed. Estudios Andinos, Lima.

Huacani, C. et al. (1979) "Estudio de caso: Warisata-escuela-ayllu" (Case study: Warisata-school-ayllu), in: *Perspectivas de la educación en América Latina* (Perspectives on education in Latin America), CEE, Mexico, pp. 179-209

Huizer, G. (1976) *El potencial revolucionario del campesinado en América Latina* (The revolutionary potential of peasants in Latin America), Siglo XXI, Mexico.

Huizer, G. (1979) "Anthropology and politics: from naïveté toward liberation", in: G. Huizer and B. Mannheim (eds) *The politics of anthropology. From colonialism and sexism toward a view from below*, Mouton, The Hague-Paris, pp. 3-41.

Hurtado, Javier (1986) *El Katarismo (*Katarism*)*, Hisbol, La Paz.

Jara, O. (1981) *Educación popular: la dimensión educativa de la acción política* (Popular Education: the educational dimension of political action), Alforja, San José.

Kay, Cristóbal and Miguel Urioste (2005) *Land Reform Policies, Rural Poverty and Development Strategies in Bolivia,* Paper presented in the of ISS-UNDP workshop on Land Policies, Poverty Reduction and Public Action, The Hague, 2005 (mimeo).

Klein, Herbert (2001) *General History of Bolivia*, Cambridge University Press.

Landim, Leilah (1987) Non-governmental Organisations in Latin America, in: World Development, Vol. 15, Supplement, pp. 29-38

Langer, Erick D. (1999) "Una mirada desde afuera: una visión histórica de Bolivia en el Siglo XX" (From the outside looking in: a historical vision of Bolivia in the 20th century), in: Campero Prudencio (ed.) 1999, pp. 67-88.

Lehmann, David (1990) *Democracy and Development in Latin America. Politics, economics and religion in the post-war period*, Polity Press, Cambridge.

León, Rosario (1990) "Bartolina Sisa: The Peasant Women's Organisation in Bolivia", in: Elizabeth

Jelin (ed) *Women and Social Change in Latin America*, UNRISD, London, pp. 135-150.

Mesa, José de, Teresa Gisbert and Carlos D. Mesa Gisbert (2003) *Historia de Bolivia* (History of Bolivia), 5th edition, updated and augmented, La Paz.

Molano, A. (1978) "Anotaciones acerca del papel de la política en la investigación social" (Notes concerning the role of politics in social research), in: World Symposium of Cartagena *Criticism and politics in the social sciences. The debate: theory and practice*, volumes I and II, Ed. Punta de Lanza, Bogotá, pp. 319-360.

Niekerk, Nico van (1994) *Desarrollo rural en los Andes. Un estudio sobre los programas de desarrollo de las Organizaciones no Gubernamentales* (Rural development in the Andes. A study of development programmes of Non-Governmental Organisations), Leiden Development Studies No. 13, Leiden.

Niekerk, Nico van (2003) "Social scientists as social activists: a short history of the recent evolution of 'Lo Andino' in Peru and Bolivia", in: Ton Salman and A. Zoomers (eds) *Shifting margins of a marginal world*, CEDLA Latin American Studies No. 91, Amsterdam, pp. 99-120).

PADER-COSUDE (coord.) (1999) *Municipio Productivo: Promoción Económica Rural* (Productive Municipality: Rural Economic Promotion), Ministry of Agriculture, Cattle-Rearing and Rural Development, La Paz.

Pajuelo, Ramón (2000) "Imágenes de la comunidad. Indígenas, campesinos y antropólogos en el Perú" (Images of the community. Indigenous people, peasants and anthropologists in Peru), in: Carlos Iván Degregori 2000, pp.123-179.

Parmentier, Denise (1988) *Transcription of interviews and first draft of the history of CIPCA from 1971 to 1985* (not published).

Pifarré, Francisco and Xavier Albó (comp.) (1986) *El Espino, una semilla en el turbión* (El Espino, a seed in the squall), CIPCA, La Paz.

Plaza, O (ed.) (1979) *Economía campesina* (Peasant economy), DESCO, Lima.

Prudencio, J. (1991) *Políticas agrarias y seguridad alimentaria en Bolivia* (Agrarian policies and food security in Bolivia), CEP-UNITAS, La Paz.

Puente, Rafael *Arakuarenda. Un centro intercultural de capacitación para el desarrollo Guaraní* (Arakuarenda. an intercultural training centre for Guaraní development), FIS/Arakuarenda, Camiri, 1994.

Rojas Ortuste, Gonzalo, Luís Tapia Mealla and Oscar Bazoberry Chali (2000) *Elites a la vuelta del siglo. Cultura política en el Beni* (Elites at the turn of the century. Political culture in Beni), PIEB, La Paz.

Salmen, Lawrence and A. Paige Eaves (1989) *World Bank Work with Nongovernmental Organisations*, Policy, Planning and Research Working Paper No. 305, Washington.

Saucedo Tapia, Luis (s.f.) "El municipio como protagonista" (The municipality as protagonist), in: UNITAS (s.f.) *Escenarios actuales y futuros en el desarrollo rural* (Current and future scenarios in rural development), La Paz (pp. 97-104).

Rural Secretariat (2004) *ONGs y desarrollo rural. Un ensayo para la discusión* (NGOs and rural development. A discussion essay). Internal work document, La Paz-Lima (mimeo).

Sen, Amartya (2006) *Identity and Violence. The Illusion of Destiny*, W.W. Norton, Cambridge.

Solari, A. et al (1976) *Teoría, acción social y desarrollo en América Latina* (Theory, social action and development in Latin America), ILPES, Siglo XXI, México.

Soliz, Lorenzo (1995) *Elementos modernos y postmodernos en la explicitación del proyecto Guaraní-Chiriguano* (Modern and postmodern elements in the explicitation of the Guaraní-Chiriguano project), Universidad Católica Boliviana, Cochabamba (mimeo).

Soliz, Lorenzo and Silvia Aguilar (2005) *Producción y economía campesina-indígena. Experiencias en seis ecoregiones de Bolivia 2001-2003* (Production and peasant-indigenous economy. Experiences in six eco-regions of Bolivia, 2001-2003), CIPCA, Research Notebooks No. 62, La Paz.

Souza, Herbert de (1992) "ONGs en la década del 90" (NGOs in the 1990s), in: DESCO-ISS *Construyendo juntos el futuro* (Building the future together), Lima-The Hague, pp. 183-191.

Stavenhagen, R. (1971) "Descolonizando las ciencias sociales aplicadas" (Decolonising the applied social sciences), in: *Organización Humana*, vol XXX, no. 4

Stavenhagen, R. (1979) *Las clases sociales en las sociedades agrarias* (Social classes in agrarian societies), Siglo XXI, Mexico.

Ticona Alejo, Esteban and Xavier Albó (1997) *Jesús de Machaqa: la marka rebelde* (Jesús de Machaqa: the rebel town). Volume 3: *La lucha por el poder comunal* (The struggle for communal power), CEDOIN and CIPCA, Research Notebook No. 47, La Paz.

Toranzo Roca, Carlos (1999) "Introducción del libro *Bolivia en el Siglo XX*" (Introduction to the book *Bolivia in the 20th century*) in Camero Prudencio (ed) 1999, pp. 1-19.

UDAPE (2003) *Estrategia Boliviana de Reducción de la Pobreza: Informe de Avances y Perspectivas* (Bolivian Poverty Reduction Strategy: Report on Advances and Perspectives), La Paz.

Urioste, Miguel (1992) "Comunidades Campesinas y Desarrollo Rural" (Peasant Communities and Rural Development), in: *Futuro de la Comunidad Campesina* (Future of the Peasant Community), Research Notebooks No. 35, CIPCA, La Paz, pp. 101-116.

Urioste, Miguel (2002) *Desarrollo Rural con Participación Popular* (Rural Development with Popular Participation), Fundación Tierra, La Paz.

Urioste, Miguel (2003) *La reforma agraria abandonada: Valles y Altiplano* (The abandoned Agrarian Reform: Valleys and Altiplano), Fundación Tierra, La Paz.

Vío Grossi, Francisco, Ton de Wit and Vera Gianotten (eds) *Investigación Participativa y Praxis Rural* (Participative Research and Rural Praxis), Mosca Azul Eds, Lima, 1981.

World Bank (1989) *Operational Directive 14.70: Involving Nongovernmental Organisations in Bank-Supported Activities*, Washington.

World Bank (1990) *Bolivia, Poverty Report*, Washington.

World Commission on Environment and Development (1987) *Our Common Future* or *Brundtland Report*, United Nations, New York.

Internal documents

1976 *Five years with the Bolivian peasant.*
1978 *Survey of society and peasantry in Bolivia.*
1984-1991 *Policies of CIPCA.*
1986 *Performance evaluation of CIPCA La Paz.*
1986 *The 'work community' model (The CDT model).*
1988 *CONAP Report on annual evaluations 1987.*
1987 to 2004: *Annual Reports on activities.*
1987 *Decennial Plan and Triennial Plan 1988-1990.*
1989 *Bases for a legal and functional structure of the CDT.*
1990 *Triennial plan 1991-1993.*
1990 *Appendix 8 "The feminine and gender perspective" from the Triennial plan 1991-1993.*
1991 *The problematic of women in CIPCA's work.*
1993 *Triennial plan 1994-1996.*
1995 *Work Document No. 3 for Quinquennial Planning (Recommendations).*

1995 *Act of Foundation, Statute and Rules for the Centre for Research and Promotion of the Peasantry, CIPCA.*
1996 *Strategic plan 1997-2001.*
1996 *Performance evaluation of CIPCA La Paz.*
1999 *Opinion of CIPCA on the Evaluation Report of the Strategic Plan 1997-2001.*
2000 *Strategic Plan 2001-2005.*
2001 *Internal policies.*
2003 *Study of the gross value of production and composition of peasant family income.*
2004 *Strategic plan 2005-2010.*
2005 *Systematisation: technological and organisational innovation in the production and commercialisation of vegetables on the Bolivian Altiplano.*

Evaluations

Albó, Xavier, Rafael García Mora and Freddy Salazar (1999) *An eight-year decennial.*

Alemán, Silvia et al. (1999) *Mid-term Evaluation Report of the Strategic Plan 1997-2001*, La Paz.

Alvarado, José, Enrique Tinoco Gómez and Néstor Sainz (1985) *Triennial Programme Evaluation, 1982-1985*, La Paz.

Armani, Domingos (2004) *Mid-term Evaluation Report of the Strategic Plan 2001-2005*, La Paz.

Mejía, Cristina et al. (1995) *Evaluation-Valuation of CIPCA Bolivia 1991-1995*, La Paz.

Schwember, Hermán et al. (1991) *External evaluation of the CIPCA institutional programme, 1988-1991*, NOVIB, The Hague.

APPENDICES

APPENDIX 1
PEOPLE INTERVIEWED

Name	Function
Abraham Mamani	President of Animal Health Promoters – Guaqui
Adolfo Yónima	President Sub-Central TIM
Adrían Cruz	Agronomist CIPCA Santa Cruz
Andrés Croggon	Latin American Head Christian Aid (2003-2006)
	Responsible for Peru-Bolivia Christian Aid (1995-2003)
Antonio Copa	Veterinary CIPCA La Paz
Aurelio Huallpa	Member Peasant Sub-Federation, Ancoraimes
Benigno Urapuca	(ex) Leader CPESC (Guarayos)
Benigno Vargas	Executive Secretary FDUTC-SC
Bernardino Soliz	Agronomist CIPCA Cochabamba (1990-2002)
Bienvenido Zacu	Advisor CPESC and Oriental Block
Bishelly Elías	Economist UAP CIPCA National
Carlos (Lito) de la Riva	Director CIPCA Cochabamba (1989-1994)
Carmelo Aguilera	Executive Secretary CSUTCG
Carmen Beatriz Ruiz	(ex) Member UAP CIPCA National
	Coordinator "Apostamos por Bolivia" (Betting for Bolivia)
Carmiña García B.	Regional Director CIPCA Beni
Celima Torrico	Broadcaster CIPCA Cochabamba
Claudio Pinto	Communal Captain Villa Hermosa (Chuquisaca)
Claudio Pou	Responsible PME CIPCA National
Coraly Salazar	Economist UAP CIPCA National
Cristóbal Mujica	(ex) Leader Peasant Oeganisation Guaqui
Cruz Bravo	Member Communal Council
	Captain Kaaguasu
Denise Parmentier	Responsible CIPCA Oral History (1971- 1987)
	Programme Officer NOVIB's South Africa Programme
Detlef Leitner	Responsible EED's Andean Region Programme
Eduardo Acevedo	Regional Director CIPCA Cochabamba
Eduardo Arduz	Hydrologist CIPCA La Paz
Eduardo Mendoza	Regional Director CIPCA Santa Cruz
Edvan Chávez	Member Peasant Support Unit CIPCA Cordillera
Enrique Jordán	(ex) Parish priest of San Ignacio de Moxos
Erlin Malale	Executive Secretary of FSUTCRMD
Eufronio Toro	Regional Director CIPCA North
Eulogio Nuñez	Responsible Regional Support CIPCA Santa Cruz
Evaristo Laime	(ex) Member Vigilance Committee Ancoraemes
Exipión Villarroel	Irrigation Committee of Qoari – Tiraque
Fátima Zelada Callau	Responsible Technical Team CIPCA Beni
Felipe Román	(ex) Responsible Organisation Unit CIPCA Cordillera
Félix Gonzales	Mayor Toro Toro (North Potosí)
Fidel Mamani	Responsible Municipal Management CIPCA La Paz
Florencio Orcko	(ex) Vice-President MST
Francisco Matzusaki	(ex) Director CIPCA Santa Cruz

	Board member CIPCA
Fremín Encinas	(ex) Member FDUTC-SC
Gabriel Mamani	President APROLAC – Viacha
Gabriela Sabat	Accountant CIPCA National
Georg Krekeler	Responsible Misereor Bolivia (1989-1994)
	Local advisor Misereor (1995-2005)
Germán Huanca	(ex) Responsible Commercialisation Unit CIPCA National
Gloria Querejazu	(ex) Member CIPCA Santa Cruz
	Board member CIPCA
Gonzalo Rojas	(ex) Member CIPCA La Paz
	(ex) member CIPCA National (CONAP)
Guido Machaqa	Educator CIPCA Cochabamba 1988-1999
Guido Valdez	Agronomist CIPCA La Paz
Heidy Teco	Agronomist CIPCA North
Herculiano Ramos	Broadcaster CIPCA Cochabamba (1982-1997)
Hermán Schwember	CIPCA accompaniment for NOVIB (1985-1995)
Herminia Sandoval	Municipal Councillor Riberalta (Beni)
Hilda Carrera	Responsible Bolivia Programme Secours Catholique
Hugo Fernández	Secretary UNITAS(ex) Director General CIPCA
Inés Miranda	Leader FDUTC-SCMAS Representative
Ismaél Guzmán	Responsible Organisational Unit CIPCA Beni
Iván San Miguel	Economist CIPCA North
Jorge Lozano	Sociologist CIPCA Cochabamba 1986-1990
José Avila	(ex) Responsible Micro-regions(ex) Member of UAP
José Luis Romero	(ex) Responsible Municipal Support
Juan Carlos Gutiérrez	Responsible Guarayos; CIPCA Santa Cruz
Juan Carlos Rojas	Responsible UAP; CIPCA National
Juan Poma	Patapatuni Community – Ancoraemes
Julián Chacai	Member CIPCA Cordillera (1976-2005)
Julio Urapotina	Solicitor CIPCA North
Justina Machaqa	(ex) Leader Sub-Federation Bartolina Sisa(ex) Vigilance Committee
	Member Councillor Ancoraemes
Kees van Dongen	(ex) Responsible NOVIB's Bolivia Programme
Koos Michel	Responsible NOVIB's Bolivia Programme
Leila Cortéz	Responsible Communication CIPCA Santa Cruz
Lola Paredes	Librarian
Lorenzo Soliz	(ex) Regional Director CIPCA Cochabamba
	Responsible Support Team General Director
Luz Gina Taboada	Sociologist CIPCA North
Malvina Poma	Community Chusñupa – Viacha
Manuel Cuadiy	Executive Secretary FSUTCRVD
Marcelo Arandia	Regional Director CIPCA Cordillera
Marcelo Yujra	Delegate APROLAC – Mamani Community
Marcos Devisscher	Coordinator FOS Bolivia
María de los Angeles Carvajal	Agronomist CIPCA La Paz
María Eugenia Moscoso	(ex) Regional Director CIPCA Santa Cruz
	Board member FONDECO
	Board member CIPCA
Mariano Singuri	Agroforestry Promoter Santa Rosa
Mario Enríquez	Agronomist CIPCA La Paz
Martha García	(ex) Educator CIPCA Cochabamba
	(ex) Director CIPCA Cochabamba
Martha Maraz	(ex) Secretary CIPCA Cordillera

Mauro Hurtado	Educator CIPCA Cordillera
Miguel Valdéz	Responsible Regional Support CIPCA Cordillera
Milton Barba	Administrator CIPCA Cordillera
Modesto Lunda	Agroforestry Promoter Santa Rosa
Mónica Méndez	(ex) Secretary CIPCA Cochabamba
Nancy Camacho	Responsible Peasant Support Unit CIPCA Cochabamba
Nico van Niekerk	Researcher
	Employee Netherlands Ministry of Foreign Affairs
Olver Vaca Ruiz	Agronomist CIPCA Beni
Omar Quiroga	Regional Support CIPCA Santa Cruz
Oscar Bazoberry	Director General CIPCA (1999-2005)
	(ex) Regional Director CIPCA Beni
	(ex) Member, CIPCA Cordillera
Osmán Medina	(ex) Broadcaster CIPCA Santa Cruz
Pablo Romero Yaguaru	Technical Suppor, APG Captain Kaami zone
Paola Borda	Municipal Management CIPCA La Paz
Pascuala Parra	Broadcaster CIPCA La Paz
Pelagio Pati	Sociologist CIPCA La Paz
Rafael García Mora	Director ACLO
	(ex) Director CIPCA Camiri and CIPCA La Paz
Rafael García de la Bridge	(ex) Regional Director CIPCA Santa Cruz
Ramón Gómez	Captain Kaami zone
Rodrigo Medina	Municipal Councillor Gonzalo Moreno (Pando)
Román Loayza	Senator MAS(ex) Executive Secretary CSUTCB
Rómulo Matareco	Forestry Technician CIPCA Beni
Roxana Liendo	(ex) Regional Director CIPCA La Paz
Ruth Yarigua	Gender Secretary APG
Salustino Flores	General Secretary Peasants Organisation Andrés Ibáñez Province
Santiago Puerta	Responsible Municipal Support CIPCA Cordillera
Seferino Saravia	Former leader Pomasara Community – Ayo Ayo
Segundina Flores	Executive Secretary FDMCSC-BS
Silvia Escóbar	Board member CIPCA
Sobeida Ruíz	Municipal Councillor San Ignacio de Mojos
Susana Mejillones	Municipal Management CIPCA La Paz
Tomás Coaquira	(ex) Leader Peasant Organisation Santa Rosa
	(ex) Councillor Santa Rosa
Tomasa Aramayo	Vice-President APG
	Captain Iupaguasu
Ulises Medina	(ex) Economist CIPCA Cordillera
Valentín Pérez	Municipal Management CIPCA La Paz
Víctor Hugo Cárdenas	(ex) Member CIPCA La Paz
	Member CIPCA Assembly
	(ex) Vice-President of the Republic
Wilson Changaray	Secretary Land & Territory Captaincy Kaaguasu
Xavier Albó	Founder CIPCA
	Researcher CIPCA
Yvonne Buschor	Responsible Bolivia Programme Fastenopfer (1992-2000)
	Responsible Southern Sector Projects Fastenopfer (2000-2005)

APPENDIX 2
RESEARCH NOTEBOOKS AND OTHER SIGNIFICANT PUBLICATIONS

1973 Albó, Xavier; Mamani, Mauricio. "Esposos, suegros y padrinos entre aymaras". Cuadernos de Investigación, N° 1. La Paz, 1976. 71 p. (2ª. Ed. 1976).

1974 Albó, Xavier. "El futuro de los idiomas oprimidos". Cuadernos de Investigación, N° 2. La Paz, 1974. 22 p. (2ª ed. 1977).

1974 Albó, Xavier. "Idiomas, escuelas y radios en Bolivia". Cuadernos de Investigación, N° 3. La Paz, 1974. 30 p. (2ª ed. 1977).

1974 Quiroga, Néstor Hugo; Albó, Xavier. "La radio: expresión libre del aymara". Cuadernos de Investigación, N° 4. La Paz, 1974. 27 p.

1974 Iriarte, Gregorio. *Sindicalismo campesino.* Cuadernos de Investigación, N°5. La Paz, 1974. 101 p. (2ª ed. 1977).

1975 Barnadas, Joseph M. *Apuntes para una historia aymara.* Cuadernos de Investigación, N° 6. La Paz, 1976. 103 p. (2ª ed. 1978).

1976 Harris, Olivia; Albó, Xavier. *Monteras y guardatojos: campesinos y mineros en el norte de Potosí.* Cuadernos de Investigación, N° 7. La Paz, 1976. 77 p.

1975 Albó, Xavier. "La paradoja Aymara: solidaridad y faccionalismo". Cuadernos de Investigación, N° 8. La Paz, 1975. 54 p.

1975 Dandler, Jorge. "Campesinado y reforma agraria en Cochabamba (1952-1953): dinámica de un movimiento campesino en Bolivia". Cuadernos de Investigación, N° 9. La Paz, 1975. 40 p.

1976 Platt, Tristan. "Espejos y maíz: temas de la estructura simbólica andina". Cuadernos de Investigación, N° 10. La Paz: CIPCA, 1976. 56 p.

1976 CIPCA. *Yungas: los otros aymaras; diagnóstico económico-socio-cultural de Sud Yungas.* Cuadernos de Investigación, N° 11. La Paz, 1976. 79 p.

1976 CIPCA. *Los aymaras dentro de la sociedad boliviana. Ciclo los Aymaras dentro de la Sociedad Boliviana.* Cuadernos de Investigación, N° 12. La Paz, 1976. 85 p.

1977 Albó, Xavier. *Khitïpxtansa? = ¿Quiénes somos?: (identidad localista, étnica y clasista en los aymaras de hoy).* Cuadernos de Investigación, N° 13. La Paz, 1977. 52 p.

1977 Cárdenas, Víctor Hugo; Albó, Xavier. *Bibliografía comentada del departamento de La Paz.* Cuadernos de Investigación, N° 14. La Paz, 1977. 258 p.

1977 CIPCA. *Coripata: tierra de angustias y cocales.* Cuadernos de Investigación, N° 15. La Paz, 1977. 191 p. 1978 Sandoval, Godofredo; Albó, Xavier. *Ojje por encima de todo: historia de un centro de residentes ex-campesinos en La Paz.* Cuadernos de Investigación, N°16. La Paz, 24 julio 1978. 114 p.

1983 Albó, Xavier. *¿Bodas de plata? O réquiem para una reforma agraria.* Cuadernos de Investigación, N° 17. La Paz, noviembre 1983.105 p.

1979 Alcoreza, Carmen; Albó, Xavier. *1978: El nuevo campesinado ante el fraude.* Cuadernos de Investigación, N° 18. La Paz: CIPCA, mayo 1979. 175 p.

1979 Albó, Xavier. *Achacachi: medio siglo de lucha campesina.* Cuadernos de Investigación, N° 19. La Paz, septiembre 1979. 171 p.

1981 Albó, Xavier; Greaves, Tomás; Sandoval, Godofredo. *Chukiyawu: la caraaymara de la Paz; I El paso a la ciudad.* Cuadernos de Investigación, N° 20.La Paz, 1981. Tomo 1, 149 p.

1980 Iriarte, Gregorio. *Sindicalismo campesino: ayer hoy y mañana.* Cuadernos de Investigación, N° 21. La Paz, abril 1980. 128 p.

1982 Albó, Xavier; Greaves, Tomás; Sandoval, Godofredo. *Chukiyawu: la cara aymara de la Paz; II Una odisea: buscar "pega".* Cuadernos de Investigación,N° 22. La Paz, 1982. Tomo 2, 203 p.

1982 Ustáriz, Germán; Mendoza, Domingo. *El fenómeno del "rescatismo" en la comercialización de la papa.* Cuadernos de Investigación, N° 23. Cochabamba, 1982. 138 p.

1983 Albó, Xavier; Greaves, Tomás; Sandoval, Godofredo. *Chukiyawu: la caraaymara de la ciudad de La Paz; III Cabalgando entre dos mundos.* Cuadernos de investigación, N° 24. La Paz, 1983. Tomo 3. 196 p.

1985 Albó, Xavier. *Desafíos de la solidaridad aymara.* Cuadernos de Investigación, N° 25. La Paz: CIPCA, 1985. 165 p.

1986 Harris, Olivia; Albó, Xavier. *Monteras y Guardatojos: campesinos y mineros en el norte de Potosí en 1974.* Cuadernos de Investigación, N° 26. La Paz, 1986. 185 p.

1986 Escobar, Filemón. *La mina vista desde el guardatojo: testimonio de Filemón Escobar.* Cuadernos de Investigación, N° 27. La Paz, 1986. 77 p.

1986 Pifarré, Francisco; Albó, Xavier (comps). *El Espino, una semilla en el turbión: vida, muerte y resurrección de una comunidad Ava – Guaraní.* Cuadernos de Investigación, N° 28. Charagua, 1986. 324 p.

1987 Sandoval, Godofredo; Albó, Xavier; Greaves, Tomás. *Chukiyawu: la cara aymara de La Paz; IV Nuevos lazos con el campo.* Cuadernos de Investigación, N° 29. La Paz, 1987. Tomo 4. 195 p.

1988 Meliá, Bartomeu. *Ñande Reko: nuestro modo de ser y bibliografía general comentada.* Cuadernos de Investigación, N° 30. La Paz, 1988. 222 p.

1989 Pifarré, Francisco. *Historia de un pueblo.* Cuadernos de Investigación, N° 31. La Paz, 1989. 542 p.

1990 Albó, Xavier. *La comunidad hoy.* Cuadernos de Investigación, N° 32. La Paz, 1990. 433 p.

1991 Farré, Luis. *Mbya iñee: el idioma guaraní-chiriguano a su alcance.* Cuadernos de Investigación, N° 33. Charagua, Camiri, 1991. 269 p.

1991 CIPCA. *Por una Bolivia diferente: aportes para un proyecto histórico popular.* Cuadernos de Investigación, N° 34. La Paz: CIPCA, 1991. 268 p.

1992 CIPCA. *Futuro de la comunidad campesina.* Cuadernos de Investigación, N°35. La Paz, 1992. 298 p.

1993 Marzal, Manuel; Albó, Xavier; Meliá, Bartomeu. *Rostros indios de Dios.* Cuadernos de Investigación, N° 36. La Paz: CIPCA, HISBOL, UCB, 1993. 191 p.

1992 Albó, Xavier; Layme, Félix. *Literatura aymara: antología. I. Prosa.* Cuadernos de Investigación, N° 37. La Paz, 1992. 232 p.

1993 Albó, Xavier; Barrios Morón, Raúl, (coords.) *Violencias encubiertas en Bolivia. Vol. I, Cultura y Política.* Cuadernos de Investigación, N° 38. La Paz: CIPCA, Aruwiyiri, 1993. v. 1, 208 p.

1993 Albó, Xavier; Barrios Morón, Raúl, (coords.) *Violencias encubiertas en: Bolivia. Vol. II, Coca, vida cotidiana y comunicación.* Cuadernos de Investigación, N°39. La Paz: CIPCA, Aruwiyiri, 1993. v. 2, 308 p.

1994 Spedding, Alison. *Wachu wachu: cultivo de coca e identidad en los Yunkas de La Paz.* Cuadernos de Investigación, N° 40. La Paz: CIPCA, COCAYAPU, Hisbol, 1994. 297 p.

1994 Rojas Ortuste, Gonzalo. *Democracia en Bolivia hoy y mañana: enraizando la democracia con las experiencias de los pueblos indígenas.* Cuadernos de Investigación, N° 41. La Paz, 1994. 152 p.

1994 Cerrón Palomino, Rodolfo. *Quechumara: estructuras paralelas de las lenguas quechua y aymara.* Cuadernos de Investigación, N° 42. La Paz, 1994. 184 p.

1995 Ticona, Esteban; Rojas Ortuste, Gonzalo; Albó, Xavier. *Votos y wiphalas: campesinos y pueblos originarios en democracia.* Temas de la Modernización. Cuadernos de Investigación, N° 43. La Paz: CIPCA, Fundación Milenio, 1995. 239 p.

1995 Albó, Xavier. *Bolivia plurilingüe: guía para planificadores y educadores.* Cuadernos de Investigación, N° 44. La Paz: CIPCA, UNICEF, 1995. 3 v.

1996 Choque, Roberto; Ticona, Esteban; Albó, Xavier, ed. *Jesús de Machaqa: la marka rebelde 2. Sublevación y masacre de 1921.* Historia y Documentos. Cuadernos de Investigación, N° 46. La Paz: CIPCA, CEDOIN, 1996. 353 p.

1997 Ticona, Esteban; Albó, Xavier. *Jesús de Machaqa: la marka rebelde 3. La lucha por el poder comunal.* Historia y Documentos. Cuadernos de Investigación, N° 47. La Paz: CIPCA, CEDOIN, 1997. 409 p.

1996 Dixhoorn, Nico van. *Manejo del agua en el Chaco guaraní.* Cuadernos de Investigación. N° 48; SNV-Bolivia, N° 15. Santa Cruz, 996. 274 p.

1996 Soria Martínez, Carlos. *Esperanzas y realidades: colonización en Santa Cruz.* Cuadernos de Investigación, N° 49. La Paz, 1996. 196 p.

1998 Penner, Irma. *Entre maíz y papeles: efectos de la escuela en la socialización de las mujeres guaraní.* Cuadernos de Investigación, N° 50. La Paz, 1998. 179 p.

1999 Fernández Juárez, Gerardo. *Médicos y yatiris: salud e interculturalidad en el altiplano aymara.* Cuadernos de Investigación, N° 51. La Paz: CIPCA, OPS/OMS, 1999. 276 p.

1999 Albó, Xavier. *Iguales aunque diferentes.* Cuadernos de Investigación, N° 52. La Paz: CIPCA, UNICEF, 1999. 134 p.

2002 Albó, Xavier y equipo CIPCA. *Ojotas en el poder local: cuatro años después.* Cuadernos de Investigación, N° 53. La Paz: CIPCA, PADER, octubre 1999. 145 p.

2000 Astvaldsson, Astvaldur; *Jesús de Machaqa: la marka rebelde 4. Las voces de los wak'a: fuentes principales del poder político aymara.* Cuadernos de Investigación, N° 54. La Paz, marzo 2000. 304 p.

2002 Albó, Xavier. *Pueblos indios en la política.* Cuadernos de Investigación, N°55. La Paz, 2002. 246 p. (2003 2ª reimpresión)

2002 Albó, Xavier. *Educando en la diferencia: hacia unas políticas interculturales y lingüísticas para el sistema educativo.* Cuadernos de Investigación, N° 56. La Paz: CIPCA, UNICEF, 2002. 264 p.

2002 Albó, Xavier. *Una casa común para todos: Iglesia, ecumenismo y desarrollo en Bolivia.* Cuadernos de Investigación, N° 57. La Paz: CIPCA, Clave, EED/EZE, 2002. 180 p.

2003 Albó, Xavier, Anaya, Amalia. *Niños alegres, libres, expresivos: la audacia de laeducación intercultural bilingüe en Bolivia.* Cuadernos de Investigación, N°58. La Paz: CIPCA, UNICEF, 2003. 280 p.

2003 Choque, Roberto. *Jesús de Machaqa: la marka rebelde 1. Cinco siglos de historia.* Cudernos de Investigación, N° 45 La Paz, 2003. 390 p.

2004 Albó, Xavier; Quispe, Víctor. *Quiénes son indígenas en los gobiernos municipales.* Cuadernos de Investigación, N° 59. La Paz, CIPCA, Plural, 2004. 192 p.

2004 Cortez, Leila; Mendoza, Eduardo (comps.). *Apuntes del mundo rural boliviano.* Cuadernos de Investigación, N° 60. Santa Cruz, 2004. 210 p.

2005 Elias, Bishelly; Huanca, Germán. *Compro boliviano: los primeros pasos.* Cuadernos de Investigación. N° 61. La Paz, 2005. 140 p.

2005 Soliz, Lorenzo; Aguilar, Silvia (comps.). *Producción y economía campesinoindígena: Experiencias en seis ecoregiones de Bolivia 2001-2003.* Cuadernos de Investigación, N° 62. La Paz, 2005. 244 p.

2005 Eyzaguirre, José Luis. *Composición de los ingresos familiares de campesinos e indígenas: Un estudio en seis regiones de Bolivia.* Cuadernos de Investigación, N° 63. La Paz, 2005. 397 p.

2005 CIPCA-CRS *De la Movilización al Impacto. Indice CIVICUS de la Sociedad Civil en Bolivia*, Cuadernos de Investigación N° 64, La Paz 2005. 190 p.

Other publications, co-editions

1973 Barnadas, Joseph M. *Charcas: orígenes históricos de una sociedad colonial.* La Paz: CIPCA, 1973. 635 p.

1979 Siquier, Gabriel; Farré, Luis. *Mbya Iñee = Idioma Guaraní.* Charagua, 1979. 123 p.

1979 Albó, Xavier. *Khitïpxtansa =¿Quiénes somos?,* La Paz: Instituto Indigenista Interamericano, 1979. 56 p.

1980 CIPCA; ACLO. *Métodos de evaluación de proyectos de producción agrícola.* Sucre: Qori Llama, 1980. 483 p.

1989 Rivas, Hugo. *Modelo económico y deuda externa: el modelo de acumulación y el endeudamiento externo en Bolivia 1972-1987.* Documentos de Análisis, N° 6. La Paz, UNITAS, CIPCA, 1989. 330 p.

1989 Albó, Xavier y otros. *Para Comprender las culturas originarias de Bolivia. Bolivia Pluricultural y Multilingüe.* La Paz: CIPCA, UNICEF, MEC, 1989. 298 p. (3ª.ed. 1995).

1990 Albó, Xavier; Barnadas, Joseph M. *La cara india y campesina de nuestra historia.* La Paz: CIPCA, UNITAS, junio 1990. 324 p. (3ª.ed. 1990).

1993 Amadio, Máximo; López, Enrique. *Educación Bilingüe intercultural en América Latina: guía bibliográfica.* La Paz: CIPCA, UNICEF, 1993. 84 p.

1993 Beaudoux, Etienne. *Guía metodológica de apoyo a proyectos y acciones para el desarrollo de la identificación a la evaluación.* La Paz: CIPCA, CEP, IEPALA, RURALTER. 1993. 197 p.

1993 Albó, Xavier. *Y de kataristas a MNRistas?: la sorprendente y audaz alianza entre aymaras y neoliberales en Bolivia.* La Paz: CEDOIN, UNITAS, 1993. 80 p.

1995 Mondain Monval, Jean-Francois. *Diagnóstico rápido para el desarrollo agrícola.* Serie Metodológica, N° 2 La Paz: CIPCA, CICDA/ RURALTER, NOGUB. 1995. 147 p.

1995 Penner, Irma, comp. *Historia de Mujeres guaraníes = kuña iñeenduka.* La Paz: CIPCA, UNICEF, 1995. 166 p.

1995 Vis, Herman; Guzman, Nimer; Zapata, Pura. CIPCA Santa Cruz. *Producción de aves.* Santa Cruz, julio 1995. 87 p.

1995 Vis, Herman; Guzman, Nimer; Zapata, Pura. CIPCA Santa Cruz. *Producciónde ovejas.* Santa

Cruz, diciembre 1995. 132 p.

1996 CIPCA; CEDOIN; BOLIVIA. Museo Nacional de Etnografía y Folklore. *Pueblosindígenas de las tierras bajas de Bolivia: catálogo etnológico*. La Paz, 1996. 316 p.

1999 Brito, Sonia, coord. *Políticas públicas con equidad de género para los pueblos indígenas de tierras bajas*: Memoria 1er. y 2º taller. La Paz, TIJARAIPA, CIPCA, 1999. 196 p.

2000 Martínez Montaño, José, ed. *Atlas territorios indígenas en Bolivia: situaciónde las tierras comunitarias de origen (TCOS) y proceso de titulación*. Santa Cruz:CIPCA, CERES, INRA, SNV, 2000. 263 p.

1999 García Mora, Rafael, coord. y otros. *Desarrollo sostenible desde Los Andes*. LaPaz: NOVIB, CIPCA, CLAVE, 1999. 227 p.

2002 CIPCA; CIOEC. *Propuestas para el sector agropecuario: elecciones generales*

2002. La Paz, 2002. 81 p.

2004 Bazoberry, Oscar; Urapotina, Julio; Taboada, Gina, (comps.) *Entre el castañoy la hormiguita: historia de la comunidad Santa María, provincia Vaca Diez, Amazonía boliviana*. La Paz, 2004. 126 p.

2004 CIPCA; APG. *Plan de gestión territorial TCO Charagua Norte: inventario de recursos naturales*. Charagua, 2004. v.1, 222 p.

2004 CIPCA; APG. *Plan de gestión territorial TCO Charagua Norte: diagnóstico socioeconómico. Estrategia de gestión territorial sobre la base del desarrollo local sostenible*. Charagua, 2004. v.2, 194 p.

2004 CIPCA; APG. *Plan de gestión territorial TCO Parapitiguasu: inventario de recursos naturales*. Charagua, 2004. v.1, 220 p.

2004 CIPCA; APG. *Plan de gestión territorial TCO Parapitiguasu: Diagnóstico socioeconómico y estrategia de gestión territorial*. Charagua, 2004. v.2., 189 p.

2004 Guzmán, Ismael. *Provincia Mojos: tierra, territorio y desarrollo*. La Paz: CIPCA, Fundación Tierra, 2004. 155 p.

2005 Lipa, Cristina; Hurtado, Mauro. *Incidencia política para el desarrollo local: una experiencia en 32 comunidades del Chaco*, La Paz, CIPCA, 2005. 79 p.

2005 Pellens, Tom; Navia, Nicómedes. *Dinámica de la economía campesina de valles: una aproximación a comunidades de Cochabamba y norte de Potosí*. La Paz, agosto 2005. 98 p.

2005 Nuñez Del Prado, José; Romay, Marco Antonio. *Tratado de libre comercioBolivia-Estados Unidos: dos miradas del impacto en el agro campesino indígena*. La Paz, 2005. 234 p.

2005 CIPCA; Capitanía de Kaaguasu. *Plan de gestión territorial indígena de la TCO Kaaguasu Gutiérrez, Santa Cruz*, 2005. 313 p

2005 Peréz, Valentín; Copa, Antonio. *Manual de veterinaria para auxiliares de sanidad animal*. Ganadería Alto Andina. La Paz, 2005.

APPENDIX 3
DEVELOPMENT COOPERATION AGENCIES

Name	Country	Type of cooperation
Arquitectos sin Frontera	Spain	Co-funding Agency
ATICA	Bolivia	Programme of the Swiss Agency for Development and the Government of Bolivia
Ayuda en Acción	Spain	Co-funding Agency
BARSA	Spain	Technical Cooperation
Broederlijk Delen	Belgium	Co-funding Agency
Brücke	Switzerland	Co-funding Agency
CAFOD	Ireland	Co-funding Agency
Caritas Boliviana	Bolivia	Institution of the Catholic Church
Caritas Española	Spain	Co-funding Agency
CECOTRET	Switzerland	Technical Cooperation
CEXECI	Spain	Technical and Cultural Cooperation
Christian Aid	United Kingdom	Co-funding Agency
COSUDE	Switzerland	Bilateral Cooperation
CRS	EU	Co-funding Agency
DDPC	Bolivia	USAID Programme
DED	Germany	Volunteer Services
EED	Germany	Co-funding Agency
Fastenopfer	Switzerland	Co-funding Agency
Fondo Contravalor Suiza	Switzerland/Bolivia	Bilateral Cooperation
FOS	Belgium	Co-funding Agency
FOSC	The Netherlands	Small Embassy Projects
Fundación Hiller	Bolivia	Private Foundation
Fundación Torre del Palau	Spain	Student Support Programme
IICD/HIVOS	The Netherlands	Co-funding Agency
Inermón	Spain	Co-funding Agency
IPADE	Spain	Co-funding Agency
Manos Unidas	Spain	Technical Cooperation
MISEREOR	Germany	Co-funding Agency
NOVIB	The Netherlands	Co-funding Agency
OXFAM América	EU	Co-funding Agency
OXFAM Inglaterra	United Kingdom	Co-funding Agency
PRODISA	Belgium	Technical Cooperation
PRORURAL	Bolivia	Programme that supports initiatives of producers and their organisations
Secours Catholique	France	Co-funding Agency
SNV	The Netherlands	Volunteer Services
Trocaire	Ireland	Co-funding Agency
UNICEF	Bolivia	Multilateral Cooperation
VETERMON	Spain	Co-funding Agency
Volens	Belgium	Volunteer Services

NOTES

1. Sjef Teunis, director of NOVIB between 1972 and 1988, died on the 24th May 1993.
2. The Spanish acronyms are used, while in the list of abbreviations an English translation is provided.
3. For explanation of the agencies' acronyms we refer to the abbreviations. The original names of the agencies no longer reflect their current activities.
4. With this definition CIPCA distinguishes itself from those institutions that execute government projects and/or those of cooperation agencies such as USAID (*United States Agency for International Development*) and the World Bank, as well as those institutions that offer (paid) services as consultant, profit-making companies.
5. *Broodschrijver* is a Dutch word meannig that the author earns his or her daily bread writing what the institution employing him or her wants to read. When I asked for a translation into Spanish, my friends could only give me a translation into Aymara that captures only half the meaning – *escritor llunk'u*.
6. Denise Parmentier has given authorisation for the use of transcriptions of interviews without the need to quote her continually. Special thanks are due to her because, when she flew from Santa Cruz to La Paz with the first transcriptions in her luggage, there was such strong turbulence that all the passengers thought the plane was going to crash. The women sitting next to her expressed her concern for her children, who would have been orphaned by the accident. Denise replied: "I'm worried because the documentos in my case are going to be lost".
7. The three authors have given permission to use the text without the need to cite them continually. The title *Un Decenal de Ocho Años* (An eight-year decennial) refers to the fact that the decennial plan (1988-1997) with which IPCA had worked since 1988 had to be interrupted in 1995, two years before its conclusion. The context had changed so much, both with the Popular Participation Law and the new municipalisation, that the focuses of the decennial plan proved obsolete.
8. The co-financing agencies (ACF) support NGOs in Latin America, Africa and Asia with private funds or with funds from their respective governments. Throughout its history CIPCA has received support from more than 35 ACF's.
9. Parts of the historical summaries with which each chapter begins are summaries of the chapter on the history of Bolivia entitled *Bolivia in the 20th Century*, edited by Fernando Campero Prudencio (1999). Another two books that have been frequently used are Herbert Klein's *A Concise History of Bolivia* (2001) and the *Republican era (1900-2000)*, a summary of the book *History of Bolivia* (2003) by José de Mesa, Teresa Gisbert and Carlos D. Mesa Gisbert. This summary is found on the webpage www.bolivia.gov.bo. With regard to the peasant-indigenous theme, also taken into account were the parts corresponding to the book *The Indian and peasant face of our history* by Xavier Albó and Josep M. Barnadas (1990). For other books and articles we refer to the bibliography.
10. In Bolivia there are several geographical regions that are divided up according to their physical characteristics: the Altiplano is a highland plain between 3500 and 5000 metres above sea level, where hardly any product can grow. It is the homeland of the potato, the lama and the alpaca. The Andean valleys are the mountains between 2500 and 3500 metres, which have a more prosperous climate. The Yungas are the sub-tropical sloping areas of the Andes descending to the Amazon region. Their altitude is between 1000 and 2500 metres. The north of Bolivia is predominantly Amazonian tropical rainforest, while the frontier with Argentina consists of dry lowlands called the Chaco. In the Santa Cruz region the former forests have been cut down and the whole region is an important agricultural (soybeans) and cattle-breeding region.
11. Economically the Bolivian rural population is divided up into 1) peasant families without land living in communities in the Altiplano and the valleys, 2) the indigenous people of the lowlands, whose economy depends on agriculture, raising cattle, timber and non-timber activities within a context of communal land ownership (TCO), colonisers: 3) peasants who have migrated from the highlands to the lowlands and are small landowners, 4) agro-industry entrepreneurs and 5) big landowners who still run the risk that their land will be expropriated as a result of current land reform law.
12. The indigenous population of Bolivia speaks different original languages. The majority speaks Aymara (in the Altiplano) and Quechua (in the valleys). The original population of the Chaco are the Guaraní, while in the low lands around Santa Cruz the Chiquitano and Guarayos Indians live. Other indigenous peoples are the Moxos people in the Beni, Esse-eja, Tacana, Ayoreo, Yaminahua,

13 Machineri, Paikoneka, Yuracaré, Chimane, etc. Of all these lowland Indians, only the Guarani and Guarayos Indians still speak their original language.

13 This indigenous Aymara movement took the name *katarismo* in homage to the 18th century hero Tupaj Katari.

14 See Xavier Albó "From MNRists to Katarists: peasantry, state and party, 1953-1983", in: *Bolivian History*, Vols. 1-2: 87-127, Cochabamba 1985 and Javier Hurtado, *El Katarismo,* Hisbol, La Paz, 1986.

15 Bartolina Sisa was born in 1753. At the age of 25 she joined the Aymara army led by Tupaj Katari, her companion. She was assassinated by the Spanish in 1782.

16 An interesting piece of information is that Xavier Albó met Dom Helder Camara when he was studying at Cornell University.

17 It is worth noting that at the end of the 1990s, the word 'client' became fashionable once again. The employees of the international development cooperation thought they were inventing something new in adhering to the *management* and *marketing* manuals used by private firms (see chapter V). Unbeknown to them, even 1950s community development manuals use the word 'client'.

18 For the history of participative research see Gianotten and de Wit, 1985.

19 According to the customs of that era we speak of "peasants" rather than "peasant families". No theory of community development (whether capitalist, culturalist or Marxist) took into account that there are also women who live in the countryside and that exercise productive and reproductive functions.

20 It must be notes that these romantic interpretations of indigenous culture and community life are still in vogue.

21 See below.

22 An interesting detail is that Monsignor Esquivel, before entering the seminar, had worked as a porter in the San Calixto Jesuit School.

23 Between 1968 and 1969 the Faculty of Social Work of the Universidad Mayor de San Andrés (UMSA) was created and the Catholic University of Bolivia was founded.

24 Then located at Calle Illampu, N° 733.

25 The author of this publication and Ton de Wit visited CIPCA in 1976 when they arrived in Bolivia as Dutch social scientists and development workers. Xavier Albó received them in his room, quickly removing books and papers from his bed, and offering them tea while they sat on his sofa-bed.

26 In Calle Socabaya N° 340.

27 See Xavier Albó and the CIPCA team (1972) "Dynamic in the inter-community structure of Jesús de Machaqa" en: *América Indígena* 32/2, pp. 773-816.

28 A previous experience in the same zone of Achacachi is the very well-known *ayllu* school of Warisata, founded in 1931. Based on the organisational model of communal property, local committees were organised for integral educational actions, literacy classes and community development. The communal lands surrounding the school were used and education imparted that was based on Aymara culture itself (Huacani et al., 1979).

29 See the Research Notebooks No. 11 *Yungas, los otros Aymaras* (Yungas, the other Aymara 1976), and No. 15 *Coripata, tierra de angustias y cocales* (*Coripata, land of anguish and coca-fields* 1977).

30 EZE was the German evangelical cooperation development agency. Towards the end of the 1990s it changed its legal status in the wake of the fusion of various protestant agencies. It is currently known as EED.

31 It should be clarified that the incumbent Provincial Superior at that time was father Antonio Menacho.

32 At this moment, Francisco Xavier Santiago had already left CIPCA.

33 In 1970 Acción Cultural Loyola (ACLO) had initiated important global research in two provinces of the department of Chuquisaca: Belisario Boeto and Hernando Siles. However, with General Banzer's military coup, the processing of already-collected data was truncated and the main researchers persecuted and forced into foreign exile. ACLO asked for help from the incipient CIPCA team. They moved for some months to Sucre and, along with local staff, successfully concluded the stagnated research.

34 For a list of all CIPCA research and publications, see Appendix 2.

35 With these ideas CIPCA implemented a kind of product chain approach *avant la lettre*.

36 Two of Xavier Albó's publications show by their very titles how politics can change. During the 1970s the Katarists opposed the old (pro-government) MNR, whilst in the 1990s the Katarists made an alliance with the MNR and in this way reached the vice-presidency: (1) "De MNRistas a kataristas: campesinado, estado y partidos (1953-1983)" (From MNR to Katarism: peasants, State and parties (1953-1983)" in: *Historia Boliviana*, V 1-2: 87-127, Cochabamba, 1985 and (2) *¿...y of Katarists to MNRistas?* (¿...and from Katarism to MNR?) CEDOIN-UNITAS, 1993.

37 The theme of this radio serial was the rebellion of

Zárate Willka in 1899.

38 The founding institutions were: Department of Cooperative Promotion of the Church's Social Action (DEFOCOOP), National Federation of Mining Cooperatives (FENCOMIN), Villa el Carmen Communal Centre, San Gabriel Foundation and CIPCA.

39 See also the closing paragraph of the present chapter.

40 Before handing the administration of Radio San Gabriel to the Brothers of La Salle, the Maryknoll fathers had offered it to CIPCA. This proposal was rejected after analysing the advantages and disadvantages of owning a communications medium. Unlike ACLO, CIPCA always discarded this possibility because of its logistical implications. The debate returned with the creation of each new office.

41 *Casimiro* (with Oxfam) on the vicissitudes of an Aymara on the Altiplano, the (big) city and the colonisation areas; and *El Camino* (*The Road*, with Novib) on the problematic of coffee production and commercialisation in Coripata.

42 Responsible for the department of diffusion at CIPCA La Paz.

43 Martha García has been also National Secretary of Rural Development in the first government of Sánchez de Lozada (one year and a half). She was invited to assume this responsibility in her capacity as militant of the Free Bolivia Movement and in recognition of the work she undertook in Mizque, as director of CEDEAGRO, the institution she founded when she left CIPCA.

44 Captive communities are communities whose members are obliged to work for the big landowner; the men on the field, the women in the house. They generally receive food, clothes and housing in return for their labours but very little cash. They have to spend the few pennies they earn in the hacienda's shop. Normally they have so many debts with the landowner that it is impossible for them to leave the hacienda. These kinds of feudal working relations are still to be found today in Bolivia.

45 A cane-cutter harvested two tonnes per day, earning 15 pesos per tonne, or 30 pesos a day. A contractor earned 2 pesos per tonne, or 4 pesos per cutter per day. He had between 50-100 cutters under contract, which meant he earned 200-400 pesos a day. These data were provided by the son of a contractor.

46 The Captaincy is a Guaraní organisational structure that conjoins several communities from the same zone. The name captaincy is due to the Spanish invaders' practice of repaying the loyalty of Guaraní informers with the title of "Capitán" (Captain) of a zone or mission (Soliz, 1995; Pifarré, 1989)

47 The villagers of El Espino were heavily subjugated by a Santa Cruz engineer who wanted to take their lands from them.

48 Years later, the fascinating story of this community has been object of a of CIPCA publication: Francisco Pifarré and Xavier Albó (comp.) *El Espino, una semilla en el turbión* (El Espino, a seed in the squall), CIPCA, La Paz 1986.

49 It must be noted that before the definitive agreement with CIPCA was signed, people were already beginning to utilise the term Work Community, the same term that would later accompany CIPCA's daily affairs for many years.

50 Later converted into Intermon and then Oxfam-Intermon, a member of Oxfam International.

51 The colonies consisted of groups of nine "nuclei" (or communities), each one having its central group on the main road, and each nucleus containing 40 radial holding of 50 hectares each, so that each dwelling converged on a plaza or central point. At that time there were already more than 50 settled nuclei.

52 Her testimony was collected by Moema Viezzer in the well-known book "*Let me speak! Testimony of Domitila, A Woman of the Bolivian Mines.* Monthly Review Press, New York 1978 (Siglo XXI, Mexico 1977).

53 Paradoxically Carmen Alcoreza, co-author of the book and at that time a CIPCA sociologist, was the daughter of one of the principal members of the by then fallen military regime.

54 For example, from the instauration of universal suffrage in 1952, each party was entrusted with the task of printing and distributing its own blank ballots, with its distinctive colour (to facilitate voting for those unable to read). But a large part of the fraud lay in the pro-government people having distributed many more ballots and systematically destroyed those from other parties. However, there were many places in which the peasants kept the ballot of their choice hidden and well-folded whilst they displayed the military candidate's green paper. As one peasant leader said: "We are no longer the peasants of 1952".

55 In this respect, it should be mentioned that the contribution of CIPCA to the birth of the Single Union Federation of Peasant Workers of Bolivia (CSUTCB), the 26 of June 1979, was symbolised in the fact that the congress that created it was presided over by Víctor Hugo Cárdenas, who was then active in CIPCA outreach in Achacachi. Additionally, the

56 Shortly after his incorporation, Franz Barrios was detained by the Banzer government's intelligence services, during a party meeting in a neighbourhood of La Paz. He was put under house arrest in his home town of Ocurí. This was where the Tomás Katari Polytechnic Institute (IPTK), began to gestate, an institution that over the years became one of the principal NGOs in the southern Bolivian countryside. It should be mentioned that IPTK, just like CIPCA and INEDER, was financially supported by Novib, mainly because of personal intervention by Sjef Theunis, who was then director of that institution.

57 Ayllu is the indigenous word for community.

58 Gen. Juan Pereda (1978), Gen. David Padilla (1978-1979), Walter Guevara (1979), Col. Alberto Natusch (1979), Lidia Gueiler (1979-1980), Gen. Luís García Meza (1980-1981), Military Junta (1981), Gen. Celso Torrelio (1981-1982) and Gen. Guido Vildoso (1982).

59 See the 100 *first days of a long night* by the Permanent Assembly of Human Rights of Bolivia (APDHB), which contains the communiqués that circulated through a solidarity network.

60 Reference is made below to this incident.

61 It was Mario Sábato of the Order of Foucault, who was freed when it was discovered he was not Xavier Albó.

62 "La Mesa de García" is a play of words with the second family name of the soon-to-be dictator: "mesa" means also "table" in Spanish.

63 In Santa Cruz the conflict between *collas* and *cambas* is very intense, with ethnic-regionalist elements. These latter are, in this context, those born in the Oriente. The *collas* are the numerous immigrants from the Andean zones. Although their contribution as a workforce, qualified or otherwise, is fundamental for the development of the region, they have always been viewed with distrust by the Santa Cruz élite. This interethnic theme is still a matter of conflict in Santa Cruz today (see below).

64 Of undoubted importance in this case was the fact that the staff was made up mostly of men, who would not accept orders from a woman boss.

65 It is striking that the women regional directors during the years of dictatorship were replaced again by men when the country returned to a democratic political situation. In this sense it can be noted that CIPCA was not exempt from of a well-known general process: during the war, women have to occupy more public posts than in normal circumstances. When the men return after the war they again occupy the public posts that had temporally been in the hands of women.

66 In its institutional history, CIDOB has changed its name several times. The current name is Confederation of Indigenous Peoples of Bolivia.

67 Some CIPCA staff also participated in this process, by invitation of the CSUTCB.

68 The Bolivian System of Agricultural Technology (SIBTA) was later constituted. It consisted of four regional foundations for technological development: on the Altiplano, the Valleys, the Tropical Rainforests and the Chaco.

69 See the first chapter.

70 See, for example, Stavenhagen's analysis (1979).

71 There was also special support from the Jesuits Rafael García Mora, an agrobiologist who was present temporarily by permission of CIPCA Charagua, and Claudio Pou, an economist, who years later was definitively incorporated into CIPCA.

72 The first greenhouse projects failed mainly because of their modest size (2 x 8 m.). Only in 1990, when the water problem began to be attacked with the construction of elevated tanks and the greenhouses were widened to 6 x 24 m., was there much success.

73 The same occured in NGO's in e.g. Peru, where there was strong opposition against executing small irrigation works because they would benefit only half of the community. In Nicaragua, during the Sandinista regime, there were demands for change in the policy of agrarian cooperativism, because some members of the cooperatives had had so much success that they had used the profits to buy a house, and /or send their children to secondary school in the city. Those peasants were turning into people who were too rich, capitalists, bourgeois.

74 In November 1983, for example, the captain of the Eity peasant organisation formally requested the expulsion of CIPCA from the zone, because its people were "inculcating communist doctrines in the minds of the humble peasants, taking advantage of their cultural backwardness."

75 CIPCA and CORDECRUZ, *Cordillera rural development plan. Diagnostic-Strategy* (7 vols., 1986).

76 CIPCA and CORDECRUZ, *Cordillera Peasant Development Programme – PDCC* (9 vols., 1987).

77 65 Within CIPCA – as we will see in the following chapter – the other regional offices also began to make base-line studies and development plans, which were to be called micro-regional plans. This was greatly helped by the support of Claudio Pou, a Jesuit economist, who had been temporarily contracted to colaborate with the drawing up of the PDCC. He ended up being fully incorporated into

78   The San Julián colonisers had been very irritated for some time with the local headquarters of the National Institute of Colonisation, which did business lending its machinery for more lucrative activities, in stead of using them for the necessary water and road constructions in the new settlements. After fruitless negotiations, on the 24th of October they organised a massive and effective roadblock near the entrance to the Institute. On the third day a group of the blockaded hauliers, led by the *camba* brothers Tomelic (cattle-breeders and loggers), forced an employee of the Institute to hand them the keys to a tractor. Tomelic and a driver climbed up onto it and, with the cry of 'shitty *collas*', began to shoot at unarmed people, as they knocked down the barriers making up the roadblock. Most of the blockaders hid in the ditches, but some peasants counterattacked with sticks, stones and 'Molotov cocktails' (bottles filled with petrol). At the level of the last barrier, when Tomelic ran out of ammunition, they managed to grab him and they beat him to death along with his companion. The Santa Cruz press dedicated big headlines to the event, turning it into a 'savage assassination' due to the 'barbarism of individuals that had arrived from the Altiplano with the crude aim of colonising Santa Cruz'. They called a 'Santa Cruz Assembly', declaring a state of emergency. They then built a statue to the two martyrs.

  The previous paragraph continues: the national team of CIPCA, from which he went on to be the soul not only of the subsequent experiences of micro-regional plans, but also of the posterior systems of planning, follow-up and evaluation.

79   With the slash and burn system, after some 3 to 5 years comes the 'fallow crisis'; in other words, it is necessary to abandon the plot and migrate to another.

80   One of the most important reference documents for this chapter is a systematisation done by Xavier Albó, Rafael García Mora and Freddy Salazar. The document is entitled *An eight-year decennial,* 1988-1995. After a bridge year (1987), the decennial was to cover the years 1988-1997. However, having dictated the Law of Popular Participation in 1994, the political context underwent considerable modification when the new municipalisation was introduced. For this reason, it was decided to close the decennial after eight years of execution and enter a new sequence of strategic five-year plans starting in 1997.

81   In 1987 the APG only agglutinated the Guaraní of Cordillera Province. This was later extended to the whole Chaco region.

82   Agreement 169, on Indigenous and Tribal Peoples, recognises the aspirations and rights of those peoples to assume control of their own institutions, ways of life and economic development; likewise to maintain and strengthen their identities, languages and religions, within the framework of the States in which they live. It was ratified by the Bolivian State with Law 1257 on the 11th June 1991.

83   For example Villa Tunari, in the Chapare (tropical area of Cochabamba), which until 1993 did not receive even one peso from the national treasury, came to receive 1.2 million Bolivianos in 1994.

84   An example of the massive corruption in the distribution and entitling of lands is the case known as "Bolibras" in which the then Minister of Education helped himself to 100,000 hectares of the best land for the production of soya in Santa Cruz (Kay and Urioste, 2005).

85   Personal interview with Kees van Dongen, NOVIB's person responsible for Bolivia in those years.

86   It must not be forgotten that in 1970 there were not more than 25 NGOs in the whole country.

87   World Bank Operational *Directive* 14.70: *Involving Nongovernmental Organisations in Bank-Supported Activities*, Washington, 1989.

88   The name of the Charagua office, then Charagua-Camiri, was changed to 'Cordillera' in accordance with the name of the Cordillera province to which both Charagua and Camiri belong and which was then the area covered by this office.

89   The Decennial Plan began with the following directors: Marcos Recolons (national director), Hugo Rivas (La Paz), Carlos de la Riva (Cochabamba), Shigueru Matsuzaki (Santa Cruz), Oriol Gelpí (Cordillera). In 1989 Hugo Rivas was named director of FONDECO and Rafael García Mora replaced him as director in La Paz. In 1992 the first non-Jesuit national director was nominated: Hugo Fernández. In 1993, Shigueru Matsuzaki was named director of FONDECO, with headquarters in Santa Cruz; Eufronio Toro replaced him in CIPCA Santa Cruz. In 1994 Arno Loewenthal was named as adjunct to the national director; Armengol Caballero was the new director of La Paz and Rafael García Mora went to the regional office of Cochabamba. Finally, in 1995, Eduardo Mendoza was named director of Cordillera, replacing José Luis Córdova (1992-1995) and in 1996 María Eugenia Moscoso was named as director in Santa Cruz.

90   There have also been many articles written by sociologists and economists outside CIPCA, even to obtain a state doctorate (Van Niekerk, 1994). It may

91 be that the CDT proposal has not been adequate for the peasant families of Bolivia, but its impact on theoretical discussions about forms of economic organisation has been very important.

91 See CIPCA and CORDECRUZ, *Diagnóstico*, vol. II, p. 112-120.

92 It is opportune to record that criticisms of this model were developed in the years in which the socialist dream was not on the agenda of the professionals. It is also important to mention that many of those who have written articles, books and doctoral theses, critically analysing the CIPCA experience, themselves belonged to that era's group of dreamers.

93 This narration is an adaptation of the story that came out in the book *El Espino, una semilla en el turbión* (El Espino, a seed in the squall), CIPCA, La Paz 1986, pp. 144-147.

94 Only in Charagua was there a detailed plan, the PDCC. In the case of the Altiplano greenhouses and the Cochabamba fruit trees, studies had been made of the possibilities of having own experimental stations. Also studies made by other institutions were used.

95 In particular, the 1995 evaluation made a very preliminary estimate of the total in Dollars that each CIPCA regional spent, in relation to the Dollar increase achieved in the peasant economy. In LaPaz $11 were spent for every $1 generated, and $2 in Cochabamba. In contrast, only $1 was spent in Cordillera and in barely 20 cents in Santa Cruz (Mejía et al, 1995: 90). This was only a crude calculation that did not take other aspects into account, such as the non-productive activities of CIPCA, or the greater or lesser productive infrastructure that had previously existed. Neither was the most important variable factored in: the climatic conditions in each region.

96 Rather than improving income, the aim of this company was to concentrate efforts from the previous focus on the 'experimental station' on the lines which had produced good results and proved promising for the future. In this way it was possible to avoid expenses and concerns for CIPCA, conserving an activity necessary for the peasants, which is profitable in itself.

97 In other eras CIPCA had worked on projects for marketing coffee in Yungas or the recovery of potato in Cochabamba, but commercialisation was never a systematic part of a productive plan.

98 *Rescatistas* is the name given to those individuals who buy products in the place they are produced, frequently on the basis of links of friendship or kinship with the producer.

99 For example, prune liqueur in Khuluyu and smoked trout in Tiraque.

100 Openness from the East, after the fall of the Berlin wall, led some to believe that European counterparts would lose interest in Latin America. A hypothesis that was only half-true, because in the late 1990s there was a reduction in the amounts earmarked for Latin America, but these were not destined for Europe but for Africa.

101 In these latter two, CIPCA also participates as a member of the assembly of associates. In FADES, since its foundation, and in IDEPRO since 2004.

102 As an extreme example we could mention Switzerland, a country with geographical and demographic characteristics comparable with Bolivia. In Switzerland there is a subsidy to the countryside, because the State does not want to have unpopulated rural areas. The danger of empty zones is present in Switzerland because of the sparse population and the mountainous Alpine geography, which does not permit intensive, high-yield agriculture. Another example are the French and Spanish Pyrenees, which until this day receive subsidies from the European Community as zones difficult to cultivate for productive agriculture.

103 Until today the development cooperation has never had any self-critic, let only made its apologies to the rural communities.

104 In Cordillera, the diagnostic and the subsequent plan were the starting motor for the emergence of new specialised institutions, for example the office of land recuperation and a new educational project, for whose implementation the Workshop for Guaraní Education and Communication, (Teko Guaraní) was created.

105 Carrying out these studies involved investment, in some cases, of sums higher than 200,000 dollars.

106 The majority of cases have opted to group the municipalities, partly because in this way they could obtain some financial support. The new municipal scenario has brought many other NGOs and consultancy companies into being; these specialise in preparing plans and executing municipal projects (see also the following chapter).

107 This dilemma will also be examined in the next chapter.

108 The book *For a different Bolivia* had the audacity to keep indicating the ideal of a 'democratic and socialist society'. It justified maintaining this last term, so discredited today: "... because no better term exists with which to express this aspect of our social utopia. What would have lost credibility were

109 the 'real socialisms', that would perhaps be better defined as state capitalism" (CIPCA, 1991: 77, note 1).
109 Deforestation in the other ecological zones of Bolivia like Amazonia, the lowlands and the Chaco is rather a consequence of the intervention of big cattle-rearing and logging enterprises.
110 In turn, Mónica Crespo consulted two outstanding specialists in gender and development: Patricia Cottle and Carmen Beatriz Ruiz.
111 It should also be mentioned that in 2005 there were two women who occupied the posts of president and vice-president of the APG.
112 Generally known as the "mega-coalition".
113 NFR was created by the Mayor of Cochabamba, Manfred Reyes Villa.
114 At one point it was even declared officially that only 600 hectares of coca cultivation were left in the Chapare region. But months later came the admission that there had been an "error" in the zeros included in the satellite information and that the correct data was 6,000 hectares.
115 In the past he had participated, together with Alvaro García Linera – future vice-president of the Republic– in the Tupaj Katari Guerrilla Army (EGTK), a small urban-rural group that launched small-scale armed actions.
116 During these years, ideological and personal discrepancies provoked a split in the party created by Cochabamba peasants and coca-producers in 1994. On one side was the Assembly for the Sovereignty of the Peoples, led by Alejo Véliz (who latter became an ally of the NFR). On the other was MAS, Evo Morales' Political Instrument for the Sovereignty of the Peoples.
117 Brazil in 1988, Colombia in 1991, Ecuador in 1998 and Venezuela in 1999.
118 The members of the civic committees have given the name "half moon" to the territorial space of the departments of Santa Cruz, Beni, Pando and Tarija (see www.nacioncamba.org).
119 See Xavier Albó *Ojotas en el poder local, cuatro años después* (Sandals and local power, four years on), CIPCA and PADEM, the Paz, 2005; and Xavier Albó and Víctor Quispe *Quiénes son indígenas en los gobiernos municipales* (Who is indigenous in municipal government?) CIPCA, Ed. Plural, La Paz 2004 (on gender: pp. 75-78).
120 Luis Saucedo, who died in 2005, was a man of honesty, integrity and commitment. As a mayor he was responsible for many physical works and others that gave incentive to culture and education. Outstanding were the educational nuclei that were built in most of the Guaraní indigenous communities, the creation of health infrastructure, the construction of drinking-water systems for practically all the communities, irrigation systems for just as many others, several works in the urban centre of Charagua such as the refurbishment of the main square, expansion of the hospital, construction of a modern kindergarten, installation of a gas matrix, with a 13-kilometre pipeline to the barracks and the hospital, the acquisition of two new gas motors to provide electrical energy, a court for sports activitie, etc.. Another thing worthy of mention is the creation of the Chaco Ballet School, which has won various prizes in dance competitions.
121 In May 2006 the new government of Evo Morales announced various decrees designed to accelerate the application of the INRA Law.
122 New ideas on the peasant economy have already been developed in the 1980s in Peru, especially in the Catholic University of Peru and in research institutions like the Institute of Peruvian Studies (IEP).
123 At some point CIPCA accepted the new jargon – not without internal resistance – and even came to speak of three types of client: constitutive clients (peasants-indigenous families), operative clients (mayoralties) and functional clients (other development institutions). But this conceptual straitjacket was soon put aside once more.
124 The term 'strategic planning' comes originally from the US Defense Department and was introduced in private companies in the 1970s. Hopefully a term such as collateral effect or *collateral damage* (so closely associated with the war on terrorism) will not become part of the vocabulary of development cooperation. It should not be forgotten that the word *target* is already part of the vocabulary of agencies and NGOs.
125 Although these strategic plans are named 'quinquennial plan', in fact they cover only four years. After they have been running for three years, during the fourth year it is customary to carry out an external evaluation that at the same time serves as input to draw up the next strategic plan. Once the new plan approved without hold-ups – which was what always happened – it would begin to be executed during the fifth year of the previous plan. For this reason, each quinquennial plan ended up being, in truth, a quadrennial plan.
126 Indeed, only twice in 24 years, has the Company had to intervene directly. However the dependency existed, as vested in the person of the two jesuit

delegates. In the management committee, those two delegates had the right of veto. Again, although this right was never exercised, legally the other members of the management committee had less power.

127 The founder members of the CIPCA Assembly are: Xavier Albó, Marcos Recolons, Claudio Pou, Rafael García Mora, Francisco Pifarré, Javier Velasco, Mauricio Bacardit, Oriol Gelpí, Carlos Roca, Carmen Beatriz Ruiz, Fernando Aguirre, Gloria Querejazu, Miguel Urioste, Víctor Hugo Cárdenas, Carlos of the Riva, Shigueru Matzusaki, José Luís Córdova, Hugo Fernández, Eufronio Toro, Armengol Caballero, Leonor Arauco and Carmen Avila.

128 See the *Certificate of Foundation, Statutes and Rules of the* Centre of Research and Promotion of the Peasantry: CIPCA, La Paz, 1995, p. 2.

129 The results of the December 2005 presidential elections were a forceful confirmation of this analysis.

130 Hopefully, with the new government of president Evo Morales, a debate will be generated that permits the introduction of new concepts of economic development that are closer to the needs and interests of the peasant and indigenous population.

131 The library was transferred in 2007 to a new Foundation, the Xavier Albó Foundation.

132 PADA (Agricultural Products of the Altiplano) was the property of CIPCA until 1995. In 1995 it became the company PADA SRL, and in 2005 a trading company for rural products was created, called COMRURAL XXI, SRL.

133 It should be added that ACLO, a sister institution of the Jesuits, operates in another three departments (Chuquisaca, Tarija and Potosí). Finally, in 2007 CIPCA opened a regional office in the department of Pando, to cover the whole ecological spectrum of the Amazone region.

134 Unfortunately NOVIB decided in 2010 to withdraw from the entire Latin American continent, a decision that had a major impact on a lot of NGOs. For CIPCA it means that from 2011 onwards it will have to find other financiers to cover approximately € 300.000 per year.

135 As a cautionary note, it should be remembered that knowledge will never let itself be 'managed', only created and generated. What instead can be managed are the media through which knowledge is socialised. It is a pity that development cooperation agencies allow themselves to be carried along by these fashions, without fully understanding what they are recommending.

136 Hugo Fernández remembers that it was particularly difficult to have the withdrawal accepted from places such as Tiraque and Jesús of Machaqa, which at the same time were Jesuit parishes. Marcos Recolons and Xavier Albó (who were doing pastoral work in those places) argued for CIPCA not to withdraw. But ultimately they did not manage to convince the Assembly. With the new rules of the game, the Jesuits' votes carried the same weight as everyone else's.

137 Between 1996 and 2005 there have been three directors of CIPCA La Paz: Armengol Caballero (1996-1998), Roxana Liendo (1998-2002) and Carlos Hugo Laruta (since 2002). Along with institutional support from NOVIB and EED, the activities of CIPCA La Paz over this period have been aided by TROCAIRE, CAFOD, IPADE, Aid in Action (AA), Misereor and Intermón.

138 People on the Altiplano in those days drank powdered milk from New Zealand which reached Bolivia through the Leche Gloria company in Peru.

139 Over the years 1996-2005 CIPCA Cochabamba has had three directors: Rafael García Mora (1994-1998), Lorenzo Soliz (1998-2004) and Eduardo Acevedo (since 2004). Along with the institutional support of NOVIB and the EED, CIPCA Cochabamba's activities during this period has been aided by Veterinaries without Borders (VSF), the Swiss Development and Cooperation Agency's Programme of Support to Non-Governmental Organisations (NOGUB-COSUDE), the Bolivian Association for Rural Development (PRORURAL), the Water Land Peasant Programme (ATICA) and the "Las Segovias" Association for Cooperation with the South (ACSUR).

140 The Association of Municipalities of the Caine Basin was constituted legally on the 20th of October 1998. Its founding municipalities are Tarata, Arbieto, Sacabamba and Anzaldo of the Esteban Arze Province of the Department of Cochabamba; Torotoro, in Charcas Province, and Acasio and Arampampa, in Bernardino Bilbao Rioja Province, both in the Department of Potosí. CIPCA has concentrated on these last four, which are more abandoned and have a more homogenous problematic.

141 This integral focus corresponded to the setting-out of a sustainable rural development strategy, agreed upon by the NGOs belonging to the NOVIB Platform and made up of environmental, economic, technological, social, organisational and cultural elements. (see CIPCA-NOVIB *Desarrollo Sostenible desde los Andes* [Sustainable Development from the Andes], Clave Consultants, La Paz, 1998).

142 The conflict between regional leaders was also

143 partly due to the construction of the political instrument of the peasant organisations. On the one hand the Assembly for the Sovereignty of the Peoples (ASP) under the leadership of Alejo Véliz and on the other the Political Instrument for the Sovereignty of the Peoples (IPSP) under the leadership of Evo Morales, which then assumed the initials and legal status of the Movement to Socialism (MAS), which was joined by Román Loayza's sector.

143 Between 1996 and 2005 CIPCA Cordillera has had two directors: Eduardo Mendoza (1997-2000) and Marcelo Arandia (2001-2005). Together with the institutional support of NOVIB and EED, CIPCA Cordillera's activities over this period have been supported by the Fund for Development Cooperation of Belgium (FOS), Spain's Intermón and Manos Unidas, as well as MISEREOR and CRS.

144 The term comes from the common Spanish translation of *mburuvicha* (traditional authority) as "captain". The Guaraní people are currently structured in 24 captaincies and 340 communities with a population of approximately 75,000 inhabitants.

145 It should also be clarified that there were several discussions and some misunderstandings between CIPCA and one of the financing agencies concerning the agro-ecological proposal. The agency demanded an exaggerated and romantic emphasis on ecological matters.

146 Between 1996 and 2005 CIPCA Santa Cruz had two directors: María Eugenia Moscoso (1997-2001) and Eduardo Mendoza (2001-2006). As well as institutional support from NOVIB and EED, the activities of CIPCA Santa Cruz over this period was supported by Manos Unidas, FOS, MISEREOR and France's Secours Catholique (SC).

147 It should be mentioned that the traffic in land is nothing new. In many cases large companies and landlords, in complicity with State employees, have trafficked with land property. Sadly, there are also peasant and indigenous leaders who have committed the same crime, allowing themselves to be carried along by this desire for personal enrichment.

148 After several years of cultivating these export crops, and once the lands have become degraded, the big landowners sow pasture and over a longer period establish bovine cattle.

149 As an example, since 2002 an entity specialised in Geographical Information Systems (GIS) functions in CIPCA Santa Cruz and provides services to the other regional offices.

150 The Institute of Information and Communication for Development, IICD (Netherlands), and the Humanistic Institute for Development, HIVOS (Netherlands), finance a global project to introduce access to, and use of, information and communications technology (ICT).

151 Between 1997 and 2005 CIPCA Beni has had three directors: Oscar Bazoberry (1997-2000), Juan Carlos Rojas (2000-2003) and Carmiña García (since 2003). Along with institutional support from NOVIB and EED, CIPCA Beni in this period has also had help from Christian Aid and from the Swiss catholic agency *Fastenopfer*.

152 Between 1997 and 2005 the director of CIPCA North has been Eufronio Toro. Together with the institutional support of NOVIB and EED, CIPCA North has been aided by Secours Catholique, Intermón, Caritas, FOS and Misereor.

153 It should be clarified that the peasants (migrants) are much more numerous than the indigenous people in the Bolivian part of the Amazon.

154 Large land concessions for the exploitation of rubber and Brazil nut.

155 Collectors of latex from rubber trees.

156 Possessors of great swathes of land.

157 Prevalent here, for example, was the work regimen of the *habilito*, through which the rubber and Brazil nut collectors (just like the Guaraní cane-cutters or *zafreros* of Cordillera) initially received an advance in goods that is difficult to estimate financially. Thus the collectors contract a permanent debt that they never finally pay off, and are obliged to remaining working indefinitely for the *barraquero* boss.

158 The institutions that work in the Amazonian north are: Vicariate of Pando, Institute for Man, Agriculture and Ecology (IPHAE), Dutch Volunteers Service (SNV), Cáritas Pando, Centre for Legal Studies and Social Research (CEJIS), Association of Rural Cooperation in Africa and Latin America (ACRA), Herencia (Inheritance) and CIPCA.

159 For those interested in quantitative results, we can mention some figures from December 2003: 2935 families in 172 communities are in the process of implementing the economic-productive proposals in 124.845 hectares in different eco-regions of the country; irrigation infrastructures have been constructed for 283 hectares in the valleys and the Altiplano; in 2003, 594 tonnes of non-traditional products were commercialised through alternative channels; some 3.098 men and 2.485 women have been trained in agricultural production and product transformation; 361 men and 695 women were trained in the management and

160 administration of producers' associations (Soliz and Aguilar, 2005: 225-226).

160 It should be mentioned that political instability is a serious impediment to achieving concrete influence in rural development policies. Between 2000 and 2005, for example, Bolivia had five different ministers of rural development, each one with his/her own policy proposals.

161 There are agencies that think differently and that finance grassroots organisations, whilst explicitly asking them to supervise and keep an eye on the NGOs.

162 An example is Gerardo Blanco, mayor of Sacabamba, who has taken infinite numbers of CIPCA courses and whose municipality was proclaimed Bolivia's best in 2002.

163 It must be clarified that Evo Morales, in all his years of struggle, has never presented himself as indigenous person but as a union leader, independently of his ethnic origin. Only after being elected president did he put on the indigenous t-shirt.

164 According to the first results of the systematisation of greenhouses and of the trading company PADA. srl (now COMRURAL XXI, srl), in 2006 there were 120 families that worked with PADA and 12 associations, small companies and/or cooperatives that commercialised garden produce through other channels. Besides, the municipality of El Alto recommended and strongly promoted the use of greenhouses in small domestic urban vegetable gardens (see CIPCA, 2005).

165 Many soldiers have learned to read and write while doing their military service..

166 One might react cynically on reading that, a short time ago, the World Bank and the International Monetary Fund drew up a reference framework, stipulating when it is better to give subsidies instead of loans to poor countries (Internationale Samenwerking, July 2006: 25).

167 Travelling with Xavier Albó and walking with him in rural communities and villages involve stopping every five minutes, because there is always somebody who wants to greet him or who he wants to talk to. There is no corner of Bolivia that Xavier Albó does not know.

168 Besides, international NGOs have begun to execute development projects themselves, instead of providing the financial and/or human resources to national NGOs. Under the supposed argument that they are transferring their competence to the 'local', or that they are building capacities, they are executing development projects in open competition with national NGOs. Examples of this type of international NGO are CARE (USA) and the Foundation of Dutch Volunteers (SNV) of the Netherlands.

169 The journal of Holland's Ministry of International Cooperation relates the experience of a young Dutchman who in 2002 went to the Altiplano to help the Aymara. He tells how he introduced solar tents (greenhouses) and how, along with the local peasants, he constructed 17 sustainable greenhouses, simply without considering that Bolivian NGOs like CIPCA and SEMTA had already introduced these (greenhouses) in the 1980s. Now the young man has formed a new NGO in Holland to raise funds (Internationale Samenwerking No. 7, 2006: 50). The positive aspect of this experience is the great enthusiasm and social commitment of the young Dutchman. The negative side is that they want to construct totally new structures as if local organisations did not already exist that were trustworthy, consolidated and professionally experienced.

170 It should be clarified that consultancy companies have emerged which act alongside NGOs and which have the same objective of support for the most disadvantaged sectors in society. We might mention, in the case of Bolivia, the important contribution of the Centre for Studies and Projects (CEP) and Clave Consultants.

171 The most striking development was in 2010: NOVIB unilaterally took the decision to terminate the finance to all its counterparts in Latin America from 2011 onwards, without even having done an evaluation of their performance and results. One has to ask: why did the NGOs have to accept all the evaluations in the past for the financing agency to then go and make unilateral decisions on the basis of arguments that have nothing to do with the NGO. How can this same agency do such a thing having previously talked for so many years about horizontal relations?

172 Although the commission carried out a study on the workings of the ACF in Holland, its conclusions and recommendations are equally valid for NGOs in Bolivia or in any other country.